Festivals
of
Interpretation

SUNY Series in Contemporary Continental Philosophy
Dennis J. Schmidt, editor

Festivals
of
Interpretation

Essays on Hans-Georg Gadamer's Work

edited by

Kathleen Wright

State University of New York Press

Published by
State University of New York Press, Albany

©*1990 State University of New York*

All rights reserved

Printed in the United States of America

For information, address State University of New York Press,
State University Plaza, Albany, N.Y., 12246

Library of Congress Cataloging-in-Publication Data

Festivals of interpretation : essays on Hans-Georg Gadamer's work /
    edited by Kathleen Wright.
        p. cm. — (SUNY series in contemporary continental
    philosophy)
        ISBN 0-7914-0377-7. — ISBN 0-7914-0378-5 (pbk.)
        1. Gadamer, Hans-Georg, 1900- — Contributions in hermeneutics.
2. Hermeneutics.   I. Wright, Kathleen, 1944-   . II. Series.
B3248.G34F45   1990
121'.68'092—dc20   89-28925
                                                                          CIP

10 9 8 7 6 5 4 3 2 1

For Hans-Georg Gadamer

Contents

Contents

Part III: Hermeneutics and the Challenges of Poetry and Postmodern Thinking

Acknowledgments

I would like to thank the editors of:

Vandenhoeck & Ruprecht (Göttingen, West Germany)—for permission to translate and reprint part of Reiner Wiehl's article, "Schleiermachers Hermeneutik—Ihre Bedeutung für die Philologie in Theorie und Praxis" [originally published in *Philologie und Hermeneutik im 19. Jahrhundert*, eds. Hellmut Flashar, Karlfried Gründer, Axel Horstmann, 1979].

Communio (Paris, France, and Notre Dame, Ind.)—for permission to reprint in translation Jean Grondin's article, "Herméneutique et relativisme" [originally published in *Communio*, 5, no. 12 (Sept.–Oct. 1987)].

Kluwer Academic Publishers (Dordrecht, Holland)—for permission to reprint portions of David Couzens Hoy's article, "Dworkin's Constructive Optimism v. Deconstructive Legal Nihilism" [published originally in *Law and Philosophy* 6 (1987)].

Finally, I would like to thank Haverford College for supporting the translation of Jean Grondin's article, "Herméneutique et relativisme," and Mildred Mortimer for her excellent translation.

Introduction

Kathleen Wright

A "festival," Hans-Georg Gadamer reminds us, is an "experience of community. . . ."[1] Each of us who has contributed to this volume has been touched — unforgettably — by the "conversational civility" (Fred Dallmayr) of Gadamer and by the experience of community brought about by our conversations with him. In this volume, we take the occasion to communicate and to celebrate our initial and continuing experience with the work of Hans-Georg Gadamer on hermeneutics or interpretation.

Our essays explore three related dimensions of Gadamer's philosophical hermeneutics corresponding roughly to the true, the good, and the beautiful. Part I, "Situating Gadamer's Hermeneutics and Its Problems," focuses on the epistemological dimension of Gadamer's philosophical hermeneutics by discussing the problem of truth in interpretation. Part II, "The Practice of Hermeneutics," examines its moral and political dimension by considering the practice of interpretation in regard to questions of politics, justice, and law. Part III, "Hermeneutics and the Challenges of Poetry and Postmodern Thinking," opens up the dimension of the aesthetic and literary and explores how what we learn from language in the experience of poetry and postmodernism accords with Gadamer's account of language in his philosophical hermeneutics.

The scope of hermeneutics or interpretation emerges in the course of these essays. Hermeneutics is universal because, in Gadamer's words, "understanding belongs to the being of what is understood."[2] Gadamer's idea is that human understanding begins with what is always already interpreted and ends in interpretations that remain always open to further interpretation precisely because human understanding is historically affected and as such is and re-

1

mains finite. The inevitability of finitude requires abandoning hope for the certainty of an unmediated immediacy or for the perfection of a completely mediated immediacy such as we find in the projects of Descartes and Hegel respectively. Even though human understanding begins and ends with interpretations, what remains unending according to Gadamer is dialogue that replaces these and other projects that aim to overcome the finitude of human understanding.

Unending dialogue (*die Unendlichkeit des Gesprächs*)[3] remains marked by finitude inasmuch as it requires of one who would participate both integrity (*Redlichkeit*)[4] and conscientiousness (*Gewissenhaftigkeit*).[5] As Gadamer tells as well as shows us, integrity entails "acknowledging the commitment involved in all understanding"[6] and conscientiousness involves becoming historically conscious and critically aware of one's own hermeneutical situation. In response, the following essays explore the different dimensions and the universal scope of hermeneutics in the way most appropriate to Gadamer and his idea of finite human understanding. They seek to renew and to continue the unending dialogue, in short, to celebrate interpretation.

Upon reading Gadamer's *Truth and Method*, it often seems easier to grasp the *truth of method* that Gadamer is contesting rather than the *truth and method* that he is advocating. Reiner Wiehl's essay, "Schleiermacher's Hermeneutics," begins Part I by showing us why Gadamer's concept of truth can appear so elusive. Wiehl situates this concept within the effective-history of F. D. E. Schleiermacher's hermeneutics as it reaches into the twentieth century, a history that, Wiehl maintains, is "complex and intrinsically heterogeneous." This is so because there are two major developments of Schleiermacher's hermeneutics in this century—Wilhelm Dilthey's *methodical* hermeneutics of the human sciences and Martin Heidegger's *existential* hermeneutics. These two hermeneutics are different in kind and can be related to each other in different ways. What appears to be elusive about Gadamer's concept of truth comes, Wiehl argues, from the way he tries both to integrate these two kinds of hermeneutics and to retrieve a dimension of Schleiermacher's hermeneutics they have obscured.

Wiehl shows how Dilthey develops Schleiermacher's hermeneutics into a method for the human sciences by relying upon three distinct concepts of truth. These are, he notes, "truth as the complete agreement between an *inner* activity and its living *externalization* in the expression of human speech . . . truth as the intrinsic truthfulness of a significant literary work . . . [and] finally truth as a cognitive truth to be secured by method, as truth in the human sciences . . . ." When Heidegger develops his own existential hermeneutics, Wiehl argues that he does so indirectly out of Schleiermacher's hermeneutics by way of his criticism of Dilthey on truth and on method in the human sciences. Wiehl shows how Heidegger distinguishes his own existential hermeneutics from Dilthey's methodical hermeneutics by arguing that Dilthey's concept of truth is first of all "deficient" because of the residual Cartesianism in his first and third concepts of truth, and second, "derivative" compared to a more primordial "event of truth" where disclosure is always accompanied by concealment.

Gadamer's *philosophical* hermeneutics integrates existential and methodical hermeneutics by taking up Heidegger's concept of the event of truth and relating it to a concept of method. Gadamer joins truth and method, Wiehl explains, by "positing a circular relationship between the two kinds of hermeneutics." His apparently elusive concept of truth is, in fact, "ambiguous" in a positive and constructive way for it comprehends, in Wiehl's words, "on the one hand the refusal of absolute truth and the denial that this kind of certainty hits upon the essence of truth and on the other hand the postulate of a method according to which truth is to be based on uncontestable certainty, and is to be guaranteed and finally perfected in a methodical progress."

By joining truth and method, Gadamer is able, Wiehl shows, to reclaim a dimension of Schleiermacher's hermeneutics hitherto obscured. Schleiermacher's original insight was that hermeneutics was universal in that it had to do with the problem of understanding in general rather than with the particular problems of textual exegesis. According to Wiehl, Gadamer recognized in Schleiermacher's awareness of the temporal distance separating the moderns from the ancients the "insurmountable rupture in the continuum of the European historical tradition." Accordingly, Gadamer takes the *universality* of hermeneutics to have to do with the universal problem of (mis)understanding and not, as Dilthey thought, with a universal method in the human sciences that will lead to a perfect understanding. Consequently, Gadamer reclaims from Schleiermacher's hermeneutics a method of continuing to question the legitimacy of one's preunderstanding that is more appropriate to the event of truth because it is no longer modelled on the Cartesian ideal of a method that starts with absolute certainty.

Jean Grondin's essay, "Hermeneutics and Relativism," addresses the question of how this same universality of hermeneutics has enabled it to become today's *prima philosophia.* Grondin notes that to achieve this rank hermeneutics had to renounce the normative aim of classical hermeneutics defined as the science of the rules for interpreting texts. By abandoning normativity, however, hermeneutics abandoned the principle that there is only one correct meaning to a text. "The meaning of a written text," Grondin notes, "is reflected in the significance that it comes to have in a given historical context and for a well-defined community." Different historical contexts or interpretive communities, however, produce new meanings.

The appearance of multiple meanings creates the problems of relativism and of lack of objectivity. Grondin defends hermeneutics against the charge of relativism by rejecting the view that hermeneutics holds that "all opinions on a subject are equally good." "There are," he notes, "always *reasons*, be they contextual or pragmatic, that urge us to choose in favor of one opinion or another." Grondin goes on to unmask and undermine the metaphysics behind the absolutist standard of those who charge hermeneutics with relativism. Metaphysics, Grondin argues following Heidegger, "is essentially transcendence from the temporal toward the atemporal." Metaphysics, however, by seeking to deny finitude, remains inevitably linked to it. Hermeneutics simply acknowledges the inevitable fact of finitude. It is therefore beyond the problem of relativism precisely because it is self-consciously "postmetaphysical."

There is, Grondin explains, in hermeneutics a positive concept of the relativity of truth. Grondin points out that the Greek and Hebrew words for truth, *aletheia* and *'emet* respectively, which play a part in the hermeneutics of Heidegger and Paul Ricoeur, preserve a "memory of . . . the relativity of truth that is essential to human experience." Gadamer, Grondin notes, finds also at work in art and rhetoric a "concept of the truth that remains aware of its attachment to human finitude." Method on the Cartesian model is meant to ensure distance between the interpreter and the truth, and thus truth's neutrality. Truth in hermeneutics, however, is what matters. It matters in relation to one's own particular questions, and it matters in that it applies to one's own situation.

Grondin's essay ends with a discussion of the problem of objectivity. Objectivity in interpretation can no longer be absolutist, the kind of infallibility that goes together with a god's-eye view. "The naivete of such an objectivism," according to Grondin, "consists in leaping over the productive contribution of the interpreter, thereby misconstruing the preunderstanding that guides the work of interpretation." Not all preconceptions are, however, productive. Thus, Grondin argues, the "task par excellence of the interpreter must be to formulate his or her own hermeneutical situation, taking into account prejudices, expectations and questions that govern his or her research. To ignore the preconditioning structure of preunderstanding is to cut off oneself from the minimal condition of objectivity." There are two ways to accomplish this task. In cases where the interpreter treats texts from the past, becoming historically conscious may aid the interpreter in distinguishing productive from distorting prejudices. For there can be, Grondin claims quoting Gadamer, "a moment of truth in the fact that certain interpretations came to 'wield authority'." But if temporal distance is not available or if traditional interpretations have been systematically distorting, then dialogue alone is left to accomplish this task. Dialogue is ongoing and thus the objectivity of our interpretations is always provisional and can never be absolute. What guarantees the objective truthfulness of our interpretations, however, is just the very fact that they continue to prove true "within the forum of real communication . . . [where] we," Grondin concludes, "have to defend our opinions and to submit them to the judgment of another."

5

Robert J. Dostal's essay, "Philosophical Discourse and the Ethics of Hermeneutics," rounds out this discussion of hermeneutical truth in Part I by focussing on Gadamer's paradoxical claim that interpretation is both productive of new meanings and faithful to the text. Dostal explains how this paradox of interpretation engenders two, indeed opposite, criticisms of Gadamer's hermeneutical theory. Some critics think that his theory is "a creative one of interpretive fabrication that has little regard for the text interpreted." Others reject it as "too slavishly devoted to the interpreted text." Dostal corrects the one-sidedness of these two criticisms by analyzing the meaning of "productive" as well as the role of time. Dostal's ultimate aim, however, is to show that Gadamer's critics miss the mark. They fail to comprehend that "faithful productivity" is a way of capturing the virtues of humility and trust that, when taken together, constitute an ethics of interpretation.

Against the charge tht Gadamer's hermeneutics leads to "interpretive fabrication," Dostal points to Kant's productive imagination as the source behind Gadamer's use of the term *productive*. Kant's productive imagination, Dostal shows, admits of two developments. The first leads to "Nietzschean poetry . . . and creativity." The second leads to a Husserlian "phenomenological account of the constitution of things." Dostal argues that "it is just this phenomenological (and not Nietzschean) productivity that lies behind the Gadamerian attempt to retrieve the clasical notion of *mimesis* as productive rather than reproductive." Gadamer's concepts of the world and the matter at hand (*die Sache*) provide additional evidence that those who identify Gadamerian productivity with Nietzschean creativity are mistaken.

The fact that Gadamer allows "a certain authority [of the text] over the reader" has led some critics to believe that Gadamer's hermeneutics is "too slavishly devoted to the interpreted text." Dostal argues that such a conclusion comprehends "text" too monolithically. It does not take into consideration Gadamer's nuanced differentiation of kinds of texts in terms of their degree of authority where the "eminent," primarily literary, text has the greatest authority. The fact that not all texts have the same degree of authority over the reader speaks, Dostal argues, against understanding Gadamer's hermeneutics as requiring a "slavish devotion to the text."

Both forms of criticism fail to consider Gadamer's discussion of time. Dostal uses this discussion to show at length and in detail that Gadamer's hermeneutics is neither "nostalgic" because too bound to the past nor "historicist" and future-oriented because too cut off from the past. Rather, Gadamer holds, first, that "the past gives us our future," and "the future gives us our past," and second, that both past and future are united in their reciprocity (*Wechselwirkung*) as the present. This account of time in terms of reciprocity underlies, Dostal argues, Gadamer's concept of a "conversation with the text" where there is a "mutuality" of question and answer.

Dostal takes up Jürgen Habermas's objection to Gadamer's hermeneutics. According to Habermas, hermeneutics as Gadamer understands it fails to address the "difficulty in bringing together the mutuality of this conversation and the rehabilitation of the authority of tradition." Dostal does not dismiss this difficulty. Rather, he seeks to reformulate what is really behind it by introducing the idea of an ethics of interpretation implicit in Gadamer's understanding of hermeneutics. Dostal argues even though Gadamer holds that "although not all texts exhibit the same authority and the interpreter does not find himself belonging to all texts in the same way or degree," he also holds that "the virtues that should be characteristic of anyone as a partner in a conversation are those of trust and humility." These virtues, humility and trust, account for what Habermas finds objectionable about Gadamerian hermeneutics. And yet, as Dostal points out to Habermas, these very same virtues are akin to the Kantian virtue of respect "that Habermas [himself] would see prevailing in an undistorted speech situation."

Finally Dostal asks about the limits of this Gadamerian ethics of interpretation. Does this "charitable" reading of texts apply to texts other than those of poetry, or those texts of law and religion that have the same kind of standing as eminent literary texts? More specifically, does it apply to the interpretation of philosophical discourse? This second question reintroduces the matter of truth in

7

philosophy by calling attention to the difference between philosophical and poetic discourse.

There is, Dostal points out, a certain ambivalence on Gadamer's part as to whether philosophical discourses constitute eminent texts in the same way that literary texts do. Yet, "insofar as the distinguishing marks for philosophy are its truth-seeking character and its concern for the whole, these on Gadamer's account," Dostal states, "do not adequately distinguish philosophy, for it shares these features with poetry." Philosophical texts, as with literary, must therefore be read charitably. However, Gadamer maintains, Dostal argues, that these two kinds of texts possess different kinds of authority inasmuch as "literature, together with law and religion, calls for the subordination of the reader to the text in a way that philosophy does not." Dostal concludes that Gadamer's ethics of interpretation demands two different forms of charitable reading. In the case of philosophical texts, charitable reading "calls for philosophy, participation in the logic of question and answer." In the case of literary texts, it takes the form of bearing "witness and asks us to give ear to the tidings."

Gadamer's rehabilitation of tradition and authority has led some to criticize him for being insufficiently radical insofar as his hermeneutics neutralizes any basis for political critique. Although Gadamer has himself never claimed to be "radical," it is not always clear that he and his critics share the same understanding of what the terms *political* and *conservative* mean. The essays comprising Part II shed light in different ways on the meaning of these two terms by examining the significance of Gadamer's hermeneutics in regard to legal texts and questions of justice or politics.

Fred Dallmayr's essay, "Hermeneutics and Justice," begins Part II by setting Gadamer's discussion of justice against those contemporary liberal and radical political theorists who view justice "either as an abstract rule divorced from common practices or as a rhetorical ploy in the service of power." Dallmayr focuses his discussion on two early essays by Gadamer, "Plato and the Poets" (1934) and "Plato's Educational State" (1942). In these essays, Dallmayr argues, Gadamer suggests a different way to understand Plato's *Republic* and what it means to be *political* and to be *conservative*. They also show, Dallmayr concludes, how the politics of Gadamer's hermeneutics differs from the "shallow pragmatism and . . . *laisser-faire* liberalism devoid of normative yardsticks" with which they are sometimes associated.

It is significant for Dallmayr that both these essays were written and published during the period of Nazi Germany. Dallmayr reads both essays in light of Gadamer's statement in 1930 that classical "Greek philosophizing occurred in the midst of a pervasive crisis of culture. How in the dissolution of the old this philosophy seeks to preserve tradition, how in the midst of divisiveness and discord [*Entzweiung*] it attempts a reconciliation with an older way of life—this aspect is congenial and intelligible to us due to the divisiveness of our own moral condition." Dallmayr follows Gadamer in finding in Plato's *Republic* and other dialogues "eminent modes of political action or practice at a time when all other modes were blocked due to the corruption of public life." By exploring these eminent modes of political action, Dallmayr sheds light on the politics of Gadamer's philosophical hermeneutics.

Plato is clearly important for Gadamer inasmuch as philosophical reflection in Plato's *Republic* prevents one from "[b]eing . . . uncritically at home in the simple dictates of cult and custom . . ." and is therefore a safeguard against being dominated and manipulated both politically and otherwise. However, what interests Gadamer even more than this in Plato is how philosophical reflection can help one avoid the "modern individualist or subjectivist . . . withdrawal of the self from the state." Gadamer discovers in Plato that "doing one's own thing" (*idiopraxis*) as "being just" (*dikaiosyne*) is something more than simply a private virtue. It is also a public virtue that requires the "transcendence of narrow selfishness and the ability to perceive oneself in a larger communal context . . . ." As Dallmayr puts it, "*idiopraxis* is simultaneously an *allopraxis* . . . an opening to the 'otherness' of the *polis* (which turns out to be not simply an 'alien' otherness but constitutive for the own or self)." Gadamer finds in Plato, Dallmayr concludes, "a kind of self-guarding and self-regard," which combines "self-recognition" with that kind of recognition of others that makes up being politically just.

This understanding of "being political" as an opening to the others as another self is made possible by education (*paideia* or *Bildung*), the growth and preservation of reflectiveness brought about within a dialogue among friends. As Dallmayr notes citing Gadamer: "Political education in Plato's sense, we read, is 'anything but indoctrination in a finished or predetermined ideology. Precisely by inquiring behind or beneath traditional moral conceptions it offers a new experience of justice; thus, this education is not an authoritative manual based on an ideal structure but rather lives from questioning alone.' " For Gadamer, Plato's *Republic* as well as his other dialogues are "eminent" because they imitate and produce this understanding of political action or practice in the form of ongoing questioning of traditional moral conceptions. Especially but not only at the time of "the total destruction of public justice brought about by Nazi tyranny and ideological manipulation," the practice of philosophical dialogue is and remains for Gadamer "conservative" precisely because it *conserves* the practice of political questioning.

David Couzens Hoy's essay, "Legal Hermeneutics: Recent Debates," connects Gadamer's hermeneutics with two recent debates about the U. S. Supreme Court's powers in regard to interpreting the Constitution of the United States. The first debate is between conservative and liberal legal theorists; the second, between liberal and radical legal theorists. Hoy starts by noting the often overlooked fact that according to Gadamer "law provides us with the best example for thinking about how interpretation works." Hoy shows that U. S. Constitutional law and its interpretation can be related to Gadamer's hermeneutics in the following ways. First of all, legal interpretation in the United States clearly exemplifies Gadamer's claim that understanding is necessarily linked to application. Second, the way a law is applied to a current case is always influenced by precedent, that is, by the history of intervening interpretations of the law, and precedent, Hoy argues, is equivalent to Gadamer's concept of effective-history (*Wirkungsgeschichte*). The legal practice of *stare decisis*, of "maintaining consistency with precedent," illustrates, Hoy argues, "Gadamer's notion that a tradition of interpretation always conditions our understanding, whether we know it or not."

Hoy employs Gadamer's concept of "hermeneutical self-consciousness," that is, the taking into account of the intervening history of interpretation and of how this history conditions our understanding, to criticize the conservative legal theory called *originalism*. Originalism, recently associated with Attorney General Edward Meese and Robert Bork, holds "that judges should rule only in conformity to the original intentions and norms of the framers or ratifiers of the Constitutional provisions." This theory, Hoy explains, involves a "narrow intentionalism" that disregards the effect of the history of Constitutional law. Hoy criticizes originalism by arguing, following Gadamer, that it is impossible to rule out the effect of precedent and to return to the original understanding of the Constitution. Even if establishing the intentions of the framers and ratifiers of the Constitution were possible, each text still appears within a context that is constituted by the intervening history of the interpretation of the text. This means that "our reading [in this case, of the Constitution] is conditioned by the document's history of interpretation, even if we try to disregard it." Precedent, Hoy argues, again following Gadamer, "commends" without "commanding." It conditions our understanding of a law without at the same time being "a rule that determines its future applications." Hoy shows that Gadamer's hermeneutics provides compelling reasons to reject the conservative legal theory of originalism. And he suggests that Gadamer's hermeneutics is most closely allied with Justice William Brennan's "liberal understanding of interpretation."

The remainder of Hoy's essay examines how Gadamer's hermeneutics can help avoid both the critical monism of a liberal legal theory such as that of Ronald Dworkin and the nihilism of the radical legal theories associated with critical legal studies. The liberal legal theory of interpretation elaborated by Dworkin in *Law's Empire* holds that "law should be construed as having an ideal integrity, including conceptual coherence and moral purpose." Dworkin, Hoy shows, agrees with Gadamer that the actual authors and ratifiers of the Constitution cannot be the source of this integrity. Dworkin avoids "narrow intentionalism" by following Gadamer and shifting the responsibility for the law's integrity from the original authors and ratifiers to the subsequent interpreters of the law. For Dworkin, however, as opposed to Gadamer, the law's "integrity is achieved only by postulating that the law is written by a single author, the community personified." The "community personified" is, however, the construct of an ideal interpreter whom Dworkin calls Judge Hercules. Hoy shows that Dworkin's concept of an ideal interpreter introduces a form of "critical monism," which is "the view that all the questions about all the features of a text must be postulated as being resolvable, at least ideally."

Dworkin's optimistic construction of the law in its "pure integrity" by means of an ideal interpreter calls forth, Hoy shows, the objection from critical legal studies theorists that "the law is shot through with contradictions, and that those contradictions invalidate the entire legal process." Hoy turns to Gadamer's hermeneutics as a way to avoid both "optimistic construction" and "nihilistic deconstruction." Gadamer's hermeneutical pluralism would involve "constructive interpretation" insofar as it shows, in the words of Dworkin, "the object of interpretation *in its best light*." However, showing the object of interpretation in its best light could also involve criticizing "existing law as lacking 'inclusive integrity,' or complete coherence." Criticism would, therefore, be plural thereby making possible "disagreements [about the law's interpretation that] can be reasonable without necessarily being resolvable." Hoy's conclusion that "a more moderate, hermeneutical pluralism suffices" "to make sense of the adjudication of conflicts of legal interpretation" furthers our understanding of the actuality of Gadamer's hermeneutics. At the same time, it demonstrates that "[i]nterpretive *method* and substantive *politics* may not necessarily entail each other."

Georgia Warnke's essay, "Walzer, Rawls, and Gadamer: Hermeneutics and Political Theory," explores the concept of a "hermeneutic political philosophy," which she finds explicit in the "postmodernist bourgeois liberalism" espoused by Richard Rorty and implicit in the recent work of Michael Walzer and John Rawls ("Kantian Constructivism" and "Justice as Fairness: Political not Metaphysical"). This kind of hermeneutic theory differs from the political approaches taken by Habermas and Rawls (earlier in *A*

Theory of Justice), which involve universal structures of communication or an ahistoric "original position." A hermeneutic political theory attempts instead "to clarify for the democratic culture to which they [Walzer and Rawls] belong its own political norms and values and to resolve for it the apparent contradictions in its beliefs and practices." In her essay, Warnke exposes the problem of subjectivism in the hermeneutic political theories offered by Walzer and Rawls and concludes that "Gadamer's hermeneutics seems . . . to offer a more penetrating examination of these questions than 'hermeneutic political philosophy' has yet provided."

Warnke's discussion begins with Walzer's *Spheres of Justice* and his interpretation of our political norms and values in the case of the fair distribution of medical health care in the United States. Walzer, in reaction to the Kantian strategy pursued by Rawls in *A Theory of Justice*, argues that goods such as medical care are "socially and historically constituted" and that the "meaning of a particular good for a given community already includes principles for its just allocation." According to Walzer, care of the body, at one time a private affair, has come to be recognized to be a need supported by society. Furthermore, to "conceive of health care as a need is to presume that no other criterion enters into its distributive norms. There is no wealth- or achievement-requirement for receiving care; rather, it is to be distributed equally to all those who need it *because* they need it." Walzer argues that because of the new interpretation of health care as a need the U. S. health care system is unjust and must be reformed in order to eliminate the discrepancy between the health care affordable by the rich and that delivered to the poor.

Warnke uses Dworkin's criticism of Walzer and Walzer's response to bring out the subjective nature of Walzer's interpretation of the distributive norms internal to the interpretation of health care as a need. But Dworkin's own interpretation of the distributive norms for the delivery of health care still understood as a need seems equally subjective. For Dworkin, "justice requires leaving medicine to the market but insists on just the qualifications and exceptions that we have made." Warnke's point here is that neither Walzer nor Dworkin are able to justify their interpretations of shared social meanings and the norms of distributive justice they imply.

Warnke finds the same problem of subjectivism in the recent theory of distributive justice proposed by Rawls. Rawls, Warnke points out, has reconsidered his conception of "reflective equilibrium" and reinterpreted the point of his earlier theory of justice. Rawls's theory is now akin to that of Walzer insofar as its point is, in his words, "to articulate and to make explicit those shared notions and principles thought to be already latent in common sense . . . ." Rawls's new "hermeneutic" political theory gives rise to two principles of justice that, in turn, require "both political and economic reform . . . ." By contrasting Rawls's interpretation of "the meaning of the liberty and equality of democratic citizens" with that of Walzer, Warnke shows how the problem of justification and subjectivism recurs. The liberal and communitarian interpretations seem, therefore, to be both subjective and there appears to be no way to demonstrate the objective validity of one or the other of these competing interpretations of our shared notions and principles.

To solve this problem of subjectivism, Warnke turns to Gadamer's hermeneutics. She shows first how Gadamer's rehabilitation of the role of prejudice might seem rather to offer a dissolution of the problem of subjectivism by way of "endorsement" rather than its solution. But once Gadamer's rehabilitation of prejudice is taken together with his concept of effective-history, then a solution to the problem of subjectivism emerges. According to Warnke, "Walzer and Rawls may offer contrasting interpretations of our supposedly shared social meanings; still, their interpretations are not for that reason alone arbitrary. Rather, they represent the articulation of different traditions of interpretation and are justified by the authority of these traditions." Each of these two interpretations of justice, freedom, and equality solves the problem of an ungrounded subjectivism, Warnke concludes, insofar as each is historically grounded.

Recognizing that "our differing political views reflect differing strands of our sociopolitical heritage" is, however, only the first thing one can learn, according to Warnke, from Gadamer's hermeneutics. It also teaches us the continuing need for hermeneutic dialogue with the texts comprising this heritage. Such a dialogue, Warnke argues, constitutes in fact "the process of tradition." So, for example, Walzer and Rawls do more than reformulate the communitarian and liberal strands of our sociopolitical heritage. They each articulate "new perspectives on old traditions," thereby extending the "old traditions to deal with new problems." Moreover, they do so, Warnke concludes, "*because* of the dialogic encounter with the other." In closing her discussion of the problem of subjectivism in the political theories of Walzer and Rawls, Warnke suggests that what we can learn from Gadamer is to ask a different question: "In assessing the view of our political heritage offered by either Rawls or Walzer, then, the crucial question might not be which has captured the essence of our self-understanding; it might be, rather, whether either has exhausted it and how we might broaden our view of ourselves to include both the image of rational life-planners and that of citizens."

Dieter Misgeld ends this discussion of the politics or the political application of Gadamer's hermeneutics on a more cautious note about what we can learn from Gadamer. His essay, "Poetry, Dialogue, and Negotiation: Liberal Culture and Conservative Politics in Hans-Georg Gadamer's Thought," begins with Gadamer's claim that language realizes itself only in conversation. Misgeld asks of Gadamer and his hermeneutics "what resources there are for members of modern societies sufficiently sensitive to the problem [of the growing disappearance of the art of conversation] to maintain and develop their capacity for dialogue in the face of the massive onslaught of highly publicized, anonymously directed modes of communication." Misgeld argues that Gadamer offers a "deeply, even if prudently, conservative" assessment of the resources available to develop the capacity for dialogue.

Gadamer maintains that the most profound and enduring solidarity between people occurs within conversations and that, compared to conversation, the language of the mass media "communicates" but "can never convey or institute this sense of solidarity." Misgeld summarizes what is so significant about conversation for Gadamer: "When this dialogue takes the form of a cooperative search for a shared understanding, be it of a subject matter or of the right attitude to take with respect to an important decision, a growth of persons beyond their individual point of view or their singularity (*Einzelheit*) may occur." Dialogue, as Gadamer understands it, is constitutive of "friendship" because it builds "a form of commonality (*Gemeinsamkeit*)."

Misgeld argues that Gadamer's "skeptical attitude" toward our modern technological civilization follows from this concept of conversation as a resource that nourishes the growth of human solidarity. In Gadamer's own words, the gravest danger for our civilization with its "technically organized forms of life" is "the elevation of adaptation as a quality of privileged status." Such adaptation, he believes, is the result of "instrumental, technical thinking." For Misgeld, Gadamer's privileging of the growth of solidarity in conversation over adaptation accounts for his privileging of "a form of cultural learning [humanistic and literary studies] not widely available, withheld from large sections of the population in modern societies." As a result, Misgeld concludes, "his ideas are most directed to cultural and educational elites still firmly rooted in traditions of classical learning."

Misgeld holds that Gadamer is not "favorably disposed toward the development of modern democracies and of some mass movements carrying forward the claims of democratization and of the universalist emancipatory ideals of the Enlightenment," and that this is so because Gadamer "fails to perceive the difference between emancipatory and technocratic politics." For Gadamer, both forms of politics fail to recognize, to quote Misgeld, that "political decisions are finite and that they are based on limited knowledge gained in the interpretation of situational constraints and subject to a great variety of standards of measurement and evaluation." Misgeld claims that Gadamer holds on here to "an older conception of politics," which thinks of the politician as the "statesman" "who always must make decisions under conditions of uncertainty." For the statesman and, Misgeld argues, for Gadamer, the "*fundamental* condition of politics" is "opposition, conflict, possibly enmity, or the *lack* of friendship . . . ." Under this condition, dialogue can offer no resource for political solidarity and must give way to negotiation. For negotiation, "the formal process of weighing different interests and coming to an agreement about their respective legitimacy," does not require friendship — only civility.

Misgeld identifies Gadamer with other German conservatives of his generation. Although the culture he advocates is liberal, the politics of his hermeneutics remains conservative. Gadamer's *radicalism*, according to Misgeld, emerges, however, in his love of poetry. Within "the babble of electronifically magnified voices," poetry speaks, to use Gadamer's words, "in an almost imperceptible voice (*mit leiser Stimme*)." As Misgeld points out, it is for Gadamer "as if only the least intrusive words, words spoken with the greatest care, and with quiet insistence, can once again establish what you and I have in common or help us rediscover what we already have in common." This explains Gadamer's fascination for the poetry of Rainer Maria Rilke and Paul Celan. Their poetry teaches that the "concealment of meaning in contemporary poetry, far from being an artificial aesthetic or literary device, is demanded by a sociocultural situation, in which poetry can only survive by means of the most subtly and intransigently produced discretion." Poetry, according to Gadamer, has not yet "fallen silent" and continues to provide to any and all who listen a source of language wherein we "reach beyond ourselves and find a world beyond that of publically approved, conventional meaning."

Perhaps no theme recurs with such persistence in the works of Gadamer as that of the relation between philosophy and poetry, the subject of Part III of this volume. As with Heidegger, Gadamer finds in poetry a unique experience of language that provokes thought. This experience of language in the poem leads both Heidegger and Gadamer to question the language *of* thought. The poetry that provokes their reflections on the language of thought, however, is different even though it is in each case poetry written for and "in a destitute time." For Heidegger, it is the poetry of Friedrich Hölderlin. For Gadamer, it is the poetry of Paul Celan.

Véronique M. Fóti's essay, "Paul Celan's Challenges to Heidegger's Poetics," uses Gadamer's insistence on the significance of the poetry of Paul Celan to question the limitations of the poetics proposed by Heidegger based on his reading of Hölderlin. For Fóti, Heidegger's poetics is related to his politics. "An *Auseinandersetz-*

ung with totalitarianism and, most of all, with the totalitarian rhetoric that had enthralled him," Fóti claims, "inaugurates Heidegger's philosophical poetics and ushers in the analyses of art and technicity." It is therefore surprising, she notes, that Heidegger fails to deal with the poetry of Celan and his "agonized effort to articulate the possibilities of meaning and communion still open to a language that has been put into the service of totalitarianism and has passed through the Holocaust." It is just this probing of "the possibilities of meaning and communion still open to a language" that brings Gadamer to concentrate his attention on the poetry of Celan.

Fóti finds two aspects of Heidegger's poetics challenged by Celan's poetry. They are, in Fóti's words, that the "inmost site" of poetry is a "place of convergence," which "resolves ambiguity and reconciles the differential im/partment of poetic articulation," and that "duality and polarity, such as that of Celan's counterplay between 'I' and 'you' that has been richly explored by Gadamer . . . is collapsed . . . ." Fóti maintains, following Gadamer, that "Celan's poetry . . . resolutely resists these unifying moves."

Fóti begins with Celan's poem, "A la pointe acérée," in order to show how its poetic diction resists Heidegger's concept of *reading* as the gathering together by a "col-lecting (*Lese*), that remains [in Heidegger's words] 'drawn and, at the same time, sustained by the fundamental trait of sheltering (*des Bergens*).' " She finds in this poem "[i]rreconcilable fissionings and redoublings [which] have come about through the cataclysm and through the sclerosis of language." Fóti concludes that in this poem "reading and writing become a 'col-lecting' of traces, a multiple *auflesen* marked off from the *auslesen* (selecting, electing, singling out) that Heidegger emphasizes in his discussion of *legein* . . . ."

Fóti singles out Celan's poem, "Engführung," in order to show at length and in detail how Celan's understanding of poetic language reveals the limitations of Heidegger's poetics. The way rupture works in this poem shows two things. First, "the failure of any 'pure word' in the face of . . . the Holocaust" shows, Fóti argues, that "the disclosive power of the *logos* is not, as Heidegger took it to be, ahistorically secure." Second, the "disarticulating and fissioning" of poetic language shows, she claims, that "language or

18

'saying' cannot accomplish what Heidegger asks of it, namely, 'to show, to let [something] be seen and heard' . . . in the manner of *phainesthai* . . . . On this last point, Fóti follows Gadamer who finds Celan's poetry challenging precisely because, in his words, the "postulate of harmony which we have so far kept intact as an assured expectation of meaning (*Sinn*) in every encountered obscuration of Meaning, has withdrawn itself . . . ." Rupture, Fóti concludes, enacts silence but Celan's silence, unlike Heidegger's "resounding of silence (*das Geläut der Stille*)," reveals rather than conceals "the dispersive and ultimately undecidable character of writing and linguistic articulation and, together with it, the political dimensions of the *logos*."

Fóti ends her discussion by turning to Celan's "Der Meridian" and "Edgar Jené und der Traum vom Traum." Fóti finds here that even as the poet "raises questions concerning the interpretive resources still available to poetic language in the face of history," his poetics is "not ultimately one of rupture and disintegration, but one that insists on keeping itself 'in the mystery of encounter' . . . ." According to Fóti, the mystery that one encounters is the Other which means " 'every thing' as well as 'every human being.' " She concludes that "the most important challenge which Celan poses not only to Heidegger's poetics but to our time" is this "quest of a relation to the Other . . . , a quest for a poetics that can reinstate the possibility of human dwelling and community through an articulation of the temporality and topology of the Other . . . ." Although Fóti does not explicitly say so, this challenge is also what provoked Gadamer to think through the poetry of Celan.

Dennis J. Schmidt's essay, "Poetry and the Political: Gadamer, Plato, and Heidegger on the Politics of Language," turns to Gadamer's early essay on "Plato and the Poets" (1934). As with Dallmayr, Schmidt recognizes in the topic and the timing of this essay Gadamer's opposition to the Nazification of Germany. Schmidt's aim is to take up again Gadamer's question about "that which always only remains a lacuna in Heidegger's own work: namely, the real and effective power of language at work in culture and political practice." Schmidt follows Gadamer's reading of Plato and starts not with the liberal concept of "free and equal judiciary subjects born with rights" but with "action and speech themselves as the basic uncertainty of all political matters . . ." and with the "in-between" (Hannah Arendt) that they constitute.

Gadamer's concern in "Plato and the Poets" is, according to Schmidt, not "political poetry, not poetry about politics, nor the politics of poetry, certainly not what Walter Benjamin and Bertolt Brecht described as the 'aesthetization of the political,' but *the meaning of political life that is found at the site of poetry's own possibility*." Plato enters into the already "ancient quarrel between philosophy and poetry" in order to transform the point in dispute. The issue for Plato becomes not only who truly provides "the paradigms of ethical discourse" but also "the relation between the possibilities of language and political action." It is well-known that Plato holds that because the poet is an imitator, the poet, to use Schmidt's words, "taps into and plays with the dimension of language that relates to the irrational side of the soul . . . ." The problem of *mimesis*, Schmidt argues following Gadamer, is that it leads not to self-knowledge but to self-diremption. In Gadamer's words, "One who only really imitates an other, 'mimes' it, is no longer self-contained; he impresses himself with an alien form. But at the same time one only imitates the other, that is, one is no longer oneself and is also not the other. *Mimesis* thus refers to a self-diremption." In other words, the irrational soul, be it the soul of the poet or of his or her listeners, is unstable, and a threat to "political stability, to control and to the security of power." Plato's point, Schmidt argues again following Gadamer, is more than that poetry can be put to dangerous uses. Rather, poetry "in its very possibility is hostile to the ideals and security of any state."

Schmidt explores how this understanding of poetry and the political differs from the poetics of Aristotle, Friedrich Nietzsche, and Heidegger. His question is, "What does it mean for *praxis* that language, that by which we bear witness to our being and being-together, harbors this nondomesticable element?" Heidegger, in particular, Schmidt thinks, understood "the fundamentally *anarchic* potential of language." What Heidegger claims to learn from Hölderlin is however that "poetry . . . reminds us of this authentic hesitation [between memory and hope] that should accompany every relation to the *polis*." Plato stands between Heidegger and Gadamer, as Schmidt's title suggests, thereby distinguishing how they think the relation between poetry and the political. Gadamer, unlike Heidegger, learns from Plato and thus teaches something different. Language is a "primary constituent of community" and it "articulates and draws the line of every *polis*." At the same time, however, language discovers "the lability and mobility of the borders of the *polis*." In other words, language in a dialogue finally encounters the indomesticable. The *polis* both comes into being and is called into question "in words."

My own essay, "Literature and Philosophy at the Crossroads," ends this volume as well as the discussion of the relation between philosophy and poetry. I focus on two concepts, text and intepretation, which were to be the matter at issue (*die Sache*) in a 1981 conversation between Gadamer and Jacques Derrida in Paris. Although a colloquium occurred, a conversation—as Gadamer understands it—failed to take place. In my essay, I renew the conversation between Gadamer and Derrida on text and interpretation and link this to the question of the relation between philosophy and literature.

I first take up Derrida's claim that there is another way to think about text and interpretation than that of the "hermeneutical tradition [that extends] from Schleiermacher to Gadamer." Fundamental to this claim is the belief that philosophy (and philosophers such as Gadamer) forgets the text of philosophy. I explore the idea that Derrida's deconstructive interpretation of the text of philosophy is best understood as a form of literary criticism. Rejecting this idea, I turn next to Rodolphe Gasché's proposal that Derrida's deconstructive project be read in connection with the philosophy of reflection or transcendental philosophy. According to this reading, Derrida works with three concepts of text ("empirical," "idealistic," and "dialectical") in his deconstructive interpretation of the texts of philosophy.

I discuss next Derrida's concept of interpretation as a two-step process and examine three kinds of inconsistencies that are opened up in the text of philosophy by the second step. These inconsistencies pertain to the formation of philosophical concepts, to the privileging of speech over writing in philosophy, and finally to the purity of the texts of philosophy as a genre of writing distinct from literature. I end this first part of my essay by arguing that Derrida (and deconstruction) continues to maintain the *distinction* between philosophy and literature that he claims to question.

In the second part, I propose what might be Gadamer's response to Derrida's claim that the text of philosophy is forgotten and remains unthought by philosophy. I begin first with Gadamer's statement that interpretation is a "conversation with the text." I connect Gadamer's analysis in *Truth and Method* of the three ways the *I* of the interpreter can relate to the text as an *other* with Derrida's three concepts of text to show that none of Derrida's concepts capture Gadamer's "hermeneutical" concept of the text. I argue next that Gadamer does not forget but instead recollects the text of philosophy, specifically the text of Plato's dialogues, by means of his concept of interpretation as a conversation. This argument depends on recognizing that Gadamer reduces the text of the interpretation eidetically to the text of Plato's philosophy, which becomes the model for the text of interpretation no matter what kind of texts are being interpreted.

I turn next to Gadamer's claim that in the fusion of horizons that marks the event of understanding the text, the text of the interpretation disappears and only the text that has been interpreted stands written. I show first what Gadamer means by "stands written" by examining Gadamer's imaginative variation of eminent texts and his eidetic reduction of such texts to the poetic text. I explore why for Gadamer the text of lyric poetry becomes the standard for the eminent text and relate this to the productivity that characterizes all texts to be interpreted. I end my discussion of Gadamer's philosophical hermeneutics by focussing on the speculative structure of language and the relation between philosophy and literature. I conclude that the language and text of the interpretation modelled on Plato's philosophy *merges* with the language and text to be interpreted modelled on the lyric poem in the fusion of horizons that marks the event of understanding.

The essays in *all* three parts of this volume engage and clarify concepts crucial to Gadamer's philosophical hermeneutics. Among these are, for example, effective-history, hermeneutical truth, the paradoxical productivity of interpretation, the commitment to the Western tradition of philosophical questioning in the face of the continuing rupturing of traditions, and the role played by language in dialogue and in poetry in the emergence of a sense of community that remains open-minded and hermeneutically conscious. Thus, the three-part structure of this volume, the sequencing of the true, the good, followed by the beautiful, is meant to appear only to disappear as we gather in the end by means of these dialogues with the work of Hans-Georg Gadamer the full, three-dimensional actuality of finite human understanding and celebrate the relevance of interpretation.

Notes

1. Hans-Georg Gadamer, *Die Aktualität des Schönen* (Stuttgart: Reclam, 1977), 52; in English, "The relevance of the beautiful," in *The Relevance of the Beautiful and Other Essays*, trans. Nicholas Walker, ed. Robert Bernasconi (Cambridge: Cambridge University Press, 1986), 39.

2. Hans-Georg Gadamer, *Wahrheit und Methode* (Tübingen: J. C. B. Mohr, 1965), xvii; in English, *Truth and Method*, trans. Sheed and Ward Ltd. (New York: Seabury Press, 1975), xix.

3. Gadamer, *Wahrheit und Methode*, xx; *Truth and Method*, xxii (translation modified).

4. Gadamer, *Wahrheit und Methode*, xiv; *Truth and Method*, xvi.

5. Gadamer, *Wahrheit und Methode*, xxix; *Truth and Method*, xv.

6. Gadamer, *Wahrheit und Methode*, xiv; *Truth and Method*, xvi.

Part I

*Situating Gadamer's Hermeneutics
and Its Problems*

Schleiermacher's Hermeneutics*

Reiner Wiehl

*H*ermeneutics has become a key concept during this century in reflections about philosophy and the method of the sciences. An adequate analysis of the general importance of F. D. E. Schleiermacher's hermeneutics and in particular of its role in respect to the philological sciences presupposes this background of a general development of hermeneutics. Thus, in carrying out this analysis, one does well to remember the hermeneutical principle of effective-history (*Wirkungsgeschichte*) and its methodical function. If it is the case that any possible datum that is to be understood is given both with other data in a context of effective-history and with the understanding that they influence it, then this assumption constitutes one of the conditions that makes possible an access appropriate to that datum which is to be understood.[1] The effective-history which we have to attribute to Schleiermacher's hermeneutics is complex and intrinsically heterogeneous. If we limit it to its most recent development in this century, then two basic features of it in particular emerge in keeping with this simplification. These two features cannot be immediately harmonized with one another and ultimately can be related in more than one way. The first is a methodical hermeneutics of the human sciences linked to the name of Wilhelm Dilthey, and the second is an existential hermeneutics linked to the name of Martin Heidegger.

We have Dilthey to thank for establishing hermeneutics as the universal organon of "historical reason." He elevated hermeneutics to the level of a conclusive basic science and the universal technique

*Published originally under the title "Schleiermachers Hermeneutik — Ihre Bedeutung für die Philologie in Theorie und Praxis," in *Philologie und Hermeneutik im 19. Jahrhundert*, eds. Hellmut Flashar, Karlfried Gründer, and Axel Horstmann (Göttingen: Vandenhoeck & Ruprecht, 1979). What follows is Kathleen Wright's translation of "The philosophical effective-history of Schleiermacher's hermeneutics," which is the first of three sections.

(*Kunstlehre*) for the human sciences. These sciences — encompassing all of the philosophical-historical sciences — are no longer to be distinguished from the natural sciences with regard to their methodological tools (*Instrumentarium*). Rather, the decisive difference between them lies in the direction of their cognitive interest and, correspondingly in their objective (*gegenständlichen*) intention and its objective (*gegenständlicher*) fulfillment. According to Dilthey, it is the singularity and individuality of human life-expressions that in their historical diversity constitute the object of the human sciences. Hermeneutics as the universal technique of understanding in the human sciences becomes necessary everywhere where "the understanding of the singular" is to be raised up to "what is universally valid."[2] The question whether the technique of hermeneutics can be regarded as a scientific method poses itself here from a perspective according to which this technique cannot, by definition, belong to the methodological tools that allow the natural and the human sciences to qualify in like manner as sciences in respect to method.

There are, above all, three effective-historical components in Dilthey's conception of a universal hermeneutical science and technique that influence access to Schleiermacher's hermeneutics. First, certain concepts of understanding and interpretation are established as basic concepts of hermeneutics, and this in immediate connection with the concepts of life, of human life-expressions, and of the expression of what is internal to the psyche in the external world of appearances. Second, an essential, close connection between hermeneutics and the philological sciences is demonstrated by means of a historical and systematic sketch. Third and finally, there is the availment of different concepts of truth, or rather the absence of a concept of truth, which is defined in a uniform way with regard to hermeneutics as science and as technique.

Hermeneutics presupposes the possibility of understanding between human beings as a basic condition of social action and as a vital source of human happiness in human relations. Dilthey called on the universality of the existing use of language to justify the definition he gave of understanding. According to this usage, understanding should designate that kind of "event" "in which we know what is internal from signs which are given to sense from the

27

outside,"[3] that is, something psychical that externalizes itself in sense perceptible signs. These life-expressions constitute the data of understanding and of interpretation. Interpretation is an art that comes to the aid of understanding. It increases the possibilities of developing an understanding and contributes to a realization of understanding by overcoming the barriers that correspond to it. One can also say: interpretation is an artful form of understanding.

However, as with any art or science, this kind of art of understanding and of interpretation presupposes the reproducibility of its data and the possibility of turning repeatedly to one and the same object. Interpretation therefore requires as a condition for its possibility that the life-expressions of human beings can be fixed and, thanks to the media which fix them, reproduced. For Dilthey, the extraordinary affinity between hermeneutics and philology is based on the special character of human language, which as written language constitutes the most important instrument for fixing human life-expressions and at the same time is an excellent medium for truth. In language "alone what is internal to a human being finds its completely exhaustively and objectively understandable expression." For this reason, "the art of understanding centers on the interpretation of the remnants of human existence preserved in writing."[4]

Dilthey allows a broad conception of literature and philology with regard to hermeneutics. The former encompasses the entire variety of human life-expressions that remain handed down in writing, and philology comprehends the "whole of activities" "by means of which history comes to be understood."[5] Hermeneutics is, therefore, primarily and generally philological hermeneutics. It stands in a relation of extraordinary affinity to the "great" works of literature. Here greatness is merely another expression for acknowledged truth: "The work of a great poet or creator, of a religious genius or of a true philosopher can always only be the true expression of his [or her] spiritual life." Although untruth usually dominates in human society, we possess in these great works sources of truth and a guarantee of a possible "complete and objective interpretation."[6] This kind of work is, Dilthey emphasizes, always true. For this reason, it can also serve as a guide for understanding other

28

data whose affinity to the truth cannot be so straightforwardly presupposed.

Several concepts of truth can accordingly be distinguished within Dilthey's conception of a hermeneutical science and technique: (1) truth as the complete agreement between an *inner* activity and its living *externalization* in the expression of human speech; (2) truth as the intrinsic truthfulness of a significant literary work that, embedded in a historical tradition, is given as an object in the external, transsubjective world; and (3) finally truth as a cognitive truth to be secured by method, as truth in the human sciences, as the goal of philological, historical research, and as the possible result of the application of hermeneutical technique. These different concepts of truth are so closely connected that, on the one hand, the first two seem to be established for the sake of the third. The first two truths ought to obtain as conditions for the possibility of the third truth. On the other hand, however, access to the first two truths depends ultimately on the possibility of the last truth named. We do not find the problem of truth sufficiently explained in Dilthey's foundation of the hermeneutical human sciences. The conceptual tools (*Instrumentrium*) he develops are just as insufficient for this kind of foundation. This is what ultimately provoked Heidegger's criticism in his project of an existential hermeneutics of human existence.

When we consider this second decisive direction of hermeneutical reflection in our century, above all what it has in common with the hermeneutics of the human sciences urges itself upon us. Hermeneutics is here as there conceived to be *critique*, and in both cases first and foremost a critique of traditional metaphysics. However, the one critique speaks thereby of historical reason, the other of the forgetfulness of Being of the ontological difference. These completely different keywords announce fundamentally different forms and objective directions of critique. The one wants to transport back into history that reason which has developed out of history. The other wants to go back even to the presuppositions of this kind of transportation back into history.

The critique of Dilthey's foundation of the human sciences plays an important methodical role in Heidegger's existential hermeneutics.[7] Even as he finds fault with Dilthey's foundation for the superficiality (*Vordergründigkeit*) of its concept of truth as well as for the obscurity and ambiguity of its conceptual tools, this critique aims above all to make it clear that what is criticized as "deficient" is a necessary deficiency from the point of view of what is at issue. According to this demonstration, the modern human sciences in their Diltheyan form together with their conceptual tools belong in a far-reaching traditional context in which they, along with philosophy and metaphysics, and to that extent along with their own objective givennesses, are linked by general ontological presuppositions. Thus, it is not difficult to read from the basic concepts of these human sciences their connection with the effective-history of Cartesianism. One need only look at the role played in this foundation by the division between the inwardness of the subject and the externality of the world of objects. The real critical intention of this demonstration is to be found in its thesis: neither the human sciences nor any thinking oriented by traditional metaphysics can catch sight of the ontological presuppositions of their own effective-historical context; and because of this the truth one comes across within this closed region must always have something "derivative" about itself.

Heidegger's hermeneutical critique of the hermeneutical human sciences and especially of Dilthey's foundation of them has become an important model for a general type of critique of science. In relation to our concerns here, however, what is of interest is only the question of the effective-historical importance of Heidegger's critique for the reception of Schleiermacher's hermeneutics. Its importance is, however, already guaranteed in that Dilthey's hermeneutics of the human sciences represents the decisive medium of this reception. The critique of a mediating instance, however, necessarily influences its mediating function, and therefore also those kinds of reception that orient themselves by such a mediation. Not only is the critique of the obscurity and ambiguity of the concepts basic to the human sciences important here, especially the critique of their grounding in concepts of life and of the relation between the inner and outer world. What is especially important is first of all the critique of the human sciences's concept of truth and of the method based on it. The concern for a more original foundation of truth is what is most important and what primarily justifies the critique.

Heidegger even laid claim to a method that he characterized as "phenomenological" for existential hermeneutics. A preliminary analysis of the meaning of the term *phenomenology* serves as a first introduction into the complex of the conditions of phenomenological hermeneutics.[8] This analysis can be looked at also as the first step leading into the critique of the hermeneutical human sciences, because the theory and practice of these sciences presuppose the concept of a phenomenon. Phenomena of linguistic expression, be they of spoken language or of written signs that have been handed down, are what constitute the data for understanding and interpretation. But what do we mean by phenomena here? And to what extent must the human sciences allow themselves to be blamed for using the concept of phenomenon obscurely? According to Heidegger's analysis of the meaning of phenomenon, we speak of phenomenology at first always when something is openly manifest and of the logical in the broadest and most original sense of the word when something is to be made manifest. Thus, according to its proximate meaning, the term *phenomenology* refers to the multiplicity of what is evident and of what is to be made evident. It refers, however, beyond this to the essential connection between both: between that which is manifest and that which is to be made manifest.

Traditional epistemology, even before phenomenology, started with the relation between the mode of its evidence and the mode of specific access to whatever happened to be phenomenologically given. According to Heidegger, however, this well-known relation, regardless of how it was comprehended, conceals the real question of truth. This becomes clear with regard to the traditional use of the concept of phenomenon, especially with respect to the traditional distinction between two kinds of phenomena: the *illusion (Schein)* of something and the *appearance (Erscheinung)* of something. Both concepts of phenomenon extend into each other in ways that are not at first transparent. We ordinarily say something such as the following: something seems *(scheint)* to be in a certain way. Either we mean by this that it is not really so in truth, but instead something quite different; or, we mean that we are leaving it altogether open how it actually is and that we recognize both possibilities in regard to the given phenomenon: that it either is as it seems to be, or that it is also other than it seems to be.

Accordingly, illusion and appearance can be marked off provisionally from one another in the following way. In the case of an illusion of something, something shows up as something that it is not "in truth" and not as what it "in truth" is. However, when we speak of appearance, we generally mean the following. There is something in the appearance that precisely does not appear and that, either possibly or necessarily, can on the whole not appear, and it is this something that is "in truth" what matters. The something that is "true" does not accordingly appear "in truth" in the given appearance. These provisional concepts of illusion and appearance allow for many interpretations, many ways to conceive of the possible relation between them, as well as many ways to conceive of the modality of their validity either as illusion or as appearance.[9]

What is common to both phenomena, illusion and appearance, is their "phenomenological" character. In both cases, something is obviously manifest, and in both cases there is the concern to make something manifest. Common also to both is that, with regard to the search after truth, openness and concealment, presence and absence, accessibility and refusal are inextricably bound up with one another. Furthermore, what is above all common to both is that the connection of what is bound up with another remains in the dark. Heidegger spoke of that event that sheds light on the darkness surrounding the connection between openness and concealment as the event of truth, and he linked the phenomenological, hermeneutical method to the concept of such an event. The exposition of illusion and appearance each conceived of as a phenomenon is supposed to have at first only the function of preparing for this concept of truth. This concept is extremely important now with regard to three things: first, the hermeneutical concept of a sign; next, the determination of the relation between understanding and interpretation; and finally, the question of what can be the ideal of methodical, hermeneutical practice.

Initially, the problem of the understanding and interpretation of linguistic signs seems to be limited, especially in the domain of research in the human sciences, to the question of whether the interpreter's linguistic competence is sufficient.[10] One would argue at first in the following way. If one wants to understand adequately or to interpret the given complex of signs, one must master the grammatical and syntactical rules (*die Regeln der Zeichensetzung*), and in particular one must be acquainted with or be able to infer the meaning of the signs. And one would argue that this is all there is to say about the question of what the conditions are that make an appropriate understanding possible.

In his analysis of the sign, Heidegger made clear that this kind of limited perspective is based on an inadmissible abstraction that necessarily distorts the phenomenon "sign" and prevents its adequate description. It is not the case that signs are the primary givens in the process of understanding and interpretation. If they were to be so conceived, then not only would the essential presuppositions of this process be overlooked but also what the process really is would, as a consequence, be mistaken and at the same time its chances for success considerably diminished. Prior to any sign, what is truly given is a whole network of referrals in which various kinds of "tools" are to be found within reach of our ordinary everyday practice of living.[11] Human beings are very familiar in and through their practical involvements (*Umgang*) with the tool that is "ready-to-hand" for them. This holds true even for such a special kind of tool as the sign. However, it is not necessarily the case that this tool [the sign] is explicitly observed in general as an instrument or as that which is ready-to-hand in this familiar everyday way in which we are involved practically with such ready-to-hand tools. Instead, practical involvement with given signs occurs always at first within the realm of the possibility of being able to follow or not to follow what the sign refers to. It is under special circumstances that the tool as such and in particular the sign as sign first "strikes our attention." This occurs when the easy involvement with the tool with which we are accustomed meets with difficulties or breaks down, when a sign that we need is missing or a sign which is evident is unable to do its job. Under such circumstances, a sign can even present itself as something that is completely meaningless.

The hermeneutical concept of a sign is extremely important for locating how theory and practice belong together in relation to hermeneutics in general. The analysis of this concept shows on the one hand that a practical involvement with a so-called tool, especially an involvement with a sign whatever kind it might be, cannot be looked at as atheoretical or as pretheoretical, for example, because this kind of tool is generally not explicitly grasped in its instrumental character or as something present-to-hand as such. It is, rather, the case that practice has its own way of looking at things (*Sehweise*) that can be distinguished as circumspection (*Umsicht*), fore-sight (*Vorsicht*), and regard (*Rücksicht*). It shows on the other hand that it is not the case that the realm of practical involvement is abandoned and the realm of pure theory is attained when this or that tool, this or that sign, appears explicitly as tool, as sign. Rather, signs disclose themselves as signs primarily, just as the tool as such generally does, in practical involvement and, in fact, under the circumstances mentioned previously. These circumstances are responsible for the fact that art and method are required for the practice.

We can see how the hermeneutical analysis of the sign is significant for the concept of hermeneutics in general if we look at it in connection with an ambiguity basic to the relation between existential hermeneutics and the hermeneutics of the human sciences. This ambiguity is first laid out in Heidegger's critique of the self-grounding of the human sciences and is retained throughout Gadamer's attempt to integrate the one kind of hermeneutics with the other. In the framework of Gadamer's interpretation, this ambiguity acquires a productive effective-historical meaning with regard to the reception of Schleiermacher's hermeneutics. The ambiguity of this relation is ultimately a kind of ambiguity about the concept of truth and its methodical implications and consequences. If, on the one hand, disclosure and concealment are linked inseparably in each authentic event of truth, then everything humans say must remain fundamentally ambiguous and subject to misunderstanding. Each thing said must itself allow it to remain open to what extent its meaning is or is not truly and completely disclosed in this or that process of understanding and interpretation. Still more, an event of truth completely allows for the possibility that just where the truth seems to be possessed and absolutely certain there the extent of the distance from the truth is particularly questionable. Measured against this kind of event of truth, a truth that is unconditional and absolute is no more than a state of affairs that is particularly worthy of questioning. This "hermeneutical ambiguity" in all events of truth stands in express opposition to modern science's Cartesian ideal of method, an ideal that ultimately also supports modern human sciences. Thus, there is on the one hand the refusal of absolute truth and the denial that this kind of certainty hits upon the essence of truth and on the other hand the postulate of a method according to which truth is to be based on uncontestable certainty, and is to be guaranteed and finally perfected in a methodical progress.

In his interpretation of existential hermeneutics and the hermeneutics of the human sciences, Gadamer tried to bring these two heterogeneous concepts of truth into a constructive relation. However, positing a circular relationship between the two kinds of hermeneutics had to generate a specific ambiguity. On the one hand, the concept of truth of existential hermeneutics claims to be the really fundamental one as opposed to that of the hermeneutics of the human sciences, which it refers to a realm of special and conditioned validity. On the other hand, the concept of original truth makes two things possible: the possibility of a critique of the foundation and the claim to truth of the human sciences, and at the same time also the possibility of a better foundation of these sciences. It was, above all, the existential analysis of the everydayness of human being that allowed both ways of looking at this to be related. Following this analysis, everydayness designates not only the realm of human life-practice (*Lebenspraxis*) as far as it precedes and "grounds" all scientific theory and practice. Everydayness also designates — in relation to that region where science is valid — a certain mode of behavior within this region.[12]

The ambiguity the concept of truth assumes when existential hermeneutics is joined to the hermeneutics of the human sciences, however, also affects the way understanding is related to interpretation (*Auslegung*) and doubles this relation. For inasmuch as hermeneutical ambiguity lays claim to universal validity, understanding and interpretation (*Auslegung*) must be necessarily and inextricably fused. This holds for each everyday practice be it prescientific or scientific. However, to the extent that the Cartesian ideal of a method of knowledge is recognized as valid, interpretation

(*Auslegung*) as the art and method of interpretation (*Interpretation*) is to be distinguished from that understanding which does not require art just as immediate certainty is to be distinguished from methodical mediation. The picture of Schleiermacher's hermeneutics projected by Gadamer seems at first glance to agree completely with Dilthey's, especially in the essential points. The latter saw Schleiermacher's hermeneutics to be particularly important because it went behind the traditional rules of hermeneutical practice to "the analysis of understanding," "thus to the knowledge of this intentional act itself" in order to "deduce from this knowledge the possibility of universally valid interpretation [*Auslegung*], its resources, limits, and rules."[13] In the course of establishing this foundation, Schleiermacher preserved in favor of their unity the biblical and classical hermeneutics that modernity had handed down "alongside one another," and uncovered the principles common to them in their separate grammatical, historical, aesthetic-rhetorical, and substantive interpretation. Dilthey adds to this estimation the important comment that this kind of "powerfully effective hermeneutics could only take place in the mind of someone who combined the virtuosity of philosophical interpretation with true philosophical ability."[14] He held Schleiermacher's interpretation of Plato to be the best evidence of this kind of virtuosity.

Gadamer also takes as his point of departure that Schleiermacher's hermeneutics makes understanding for the first time a problem that is both basic and necessarily universal, and creates a universal theoretical foundation for hermeneutics. However, Gadamer also states in this regard that because of the universality of the problem "theoretical reflection acquires a new significance. It is no longer a technique guiding the practice of critic or theologian. Schleiermacher, it is true, calls his hermeneutics a technique, but in a quite different, systematic sense. He seeks the theoretical foundation for the procedure common to theologians and literary critics, by reaching back beyond the concerns of each and to the more fundamental relation of the understanding of meanings."[15] Dilthey and Gadamer seem to agree thus far on the importance of Schleiermacher's hermeneutics in establishing their own foundation.

But if we look more closely at what appears here to be complete agreement in their valuation we find substantial differences. These differences relate basically to the concept of a universal technique and especially to hermeneutics as such a technique. Gadamer certainly does not want to say that hermeneutics loses its importance for literary critics and theologians because of the universal turn Schleiermacher gave to it. And he also wants to maintain that with this turn it is not just that hermeneutics abandons its exclusively ancillary function for the practice of literary criticism and theology. But what does he mean here by speaking of the new significance of theoretical reflection and of a new technique, a technique with a systematic sense? For Dilthey, the function of working out a general foundation for hermeneutics was primarily methodical and practical. The philological, historical human sciences achieved in this manner both a general justification of their independence and [specifically] the independence of their method from that of the natural sciences. Beyond this, the universalization of hermeneutics can claim for itself that kind of cognitive value that is granted to any theory and the practice that is based on it when this theory achieves a higher degree of universality compared to the one that preceded it. An increase in the degree of universality is connected with an increase in the degree of objectivity. It signifies an expansion of the horizon and at the same time an extension of the region of application and validity. The value for cognitive practice lies beyond this in the way that certainty is increased in the appropriate application lowering the risk of false inferences.

Dilthey saw the importance of Schleiermacher's hermeneutics with regard to the philosophical-historical human sciences that he himself grounded and assigned it its outstanding position within the history of the development of these sciences. When Gadamer speaks of the new significance within this hermeneutics of theoretical reflection, he does so with regard to the universal character that it achieves. Theoretical reflection grows by means of this universalization beyond its traditional task of guiding what were always individual, concrete processes of interpretation. Above all, hermeneutics achieves a generally formal character in this universalization. With regard to this characteristic of formalization, however, Gadamer's analysis goes in a quite different direction than does Dilthey's. One cannot overlook the fact that Gadamer is guided by Heidegger's phenomenological-hermeneutical critique of

Dilthey's foundation of the human sciences and the "more original" concept of truth that is put forward there. Against this philosophical background, Gadamer demonstrated "Dilthey's entanglement in the aporias of historicism," and in particular the dependence common both to Dilthey and to Schleiermacher on the idealistic metaphysics of the Romantics. But it was, above all, his own distance from the Cartesian ideal of a method of the sciences that enabled Gadamer to discover a new access to the hermeneutics of Schleiermacher. To do this, he established a direct connection between Heidegger's thought of the European history of Being as the event of phenomenological, hermeneutical truth and the classical theory of estrangement in the continuum of the European tradition. Gadamer departed from Dilthey's access to Schleiermacher's hermeneutics and achieved his own access in no small part because of Hegel's *Phenomenology of Spirit*.[16]

Gadamer's (rather than Dilthey's) reception of Schleiermacher provides a quite different answer to our question here about the importance of Schleiermacher's hermeneutics for the theory and practice of philology. According to the former's reception, the importance we are asking about is ultimately to be found in the fact that a new consciousness arises along with the universalization and formalization of hermeneutics. In this new consciousness, the practice of literary critics and theologians is no longer to be taken as something self-evident or an activity that justifies itself immanently. In light of the insurmountable rupture in the continuum of the European historical tradition, the hermeneutical practice of literary critics and theologians can no longer view itself as naturally embedded in this occurrence of the tradition just as little as this occurrence can be held to be at once singular and natural in the way it is determined. This practice can no longer blindly believe in the validity of a definite canon of exemplary works handed down as unique and solely valid. Accordingly, Gadamer sees a connection, however it might be structured, between Schleiermacher's endeavor, which concerns a universal, formal hermeneutical technique, and the rising need within a consciousness of the temporal distance between the ancients and the moderns to legitimate explicitly the activity of hermeneutics as such and with regard to its relations to values.

Looked at this way, Schleiermacher's hermeneutics belongs to the circle of those responses that react to the loss of the foundation for a mimetic relation to the world.

This reflective and theoretical turn in Gadamer's analysis shows itself to be dialectical, especially in its discussion and criticism of Dilthey. Gadamer emphasizes the eminent role that the "stricter" hermeneutical practice plays in Schleiermacher compared to the "more lax" practice and, consequently, "misunderstanding arises on its own."[17] Gadamer concedes a greater significance in hermeneutics to misunderstanding than to understanding primarily in connection with Heidegger's concept of hermeneutical ambiguity. And this affects critically, above all, Dilthey's ideal of the method of the human sciences, which demands of hermeneutics that understanding approach perfection step by step through interpretaton. Conversely, Gadamer expressly links his comprehension of Schleiermacher to that of Dilthey on a very decisive point. This concerns the one-sided overemphasis of psychological interpretation compared to other forms of interpretation. Gadamer is led to this agreement with Dilthey by his interest in a critique of the hermeneutics of the human sciences and of existential hermeneutics, a critique that points out the foundations common to both forms of hermeneutics. But then Gadamer again played off Schleiermacher's concept of a divinatory understanding (according to which the process of understanding is the congenial reconstruction of the genial creative process) against Dilthey's attempt to secure for the comparative method a constructive, methodical meaning in the human sciences. On the one hand, the psychological interpretation takes on still more importance by Gadamer's emphasizing the divinatory in the process of understanding. On the other hand, Gadamer could not overlook the fact that the concept of congenial understanding is especially closely connected with Romantic aesthetics and "aesthetics of genius." But even though this concept of congenial understanding is problematic and worthy of criticism, it has in its favor that it is able to ensure the distance that was required both from the Cartesian ideal of method and from a rule based hermeneutics.

Notes

1. On the problem of effective-history, see Hans-Georg Gadamer, *Wahrheit und Methode* (Tübingen: J. C. B. Mohr, 1965), 324–60; in translation, see *Truth and Method*, trans. Sheed and Ward Ltd. (New York: Seabury Press, 1975), 305–41.

2. Wilhelm Dilthey, "Die Entstehung der Hermeneutik," in *Gesammelte Schriften*, vol. 5, 4th ed. (Stuttgart: Teubner, 1964), 317.

3. Dilthey, "Entstehung der Hermeneutik," 318.

4. Dilthey, "Entstehung der Hermeneutik," 319.

5. Dilthey, "Entstehung der Hermeneutik (Auxilliary Manuscripts)," 332.

6. Dilthey, "Entstehung der Hermeneutik," 320.

7. Martin Heidegger, *Being and Time*, trans. John Macquarrie and Edward Robinson (New York: Harper and Row, 1962), 62, 72–73.

8. Heidegger, *Being and Time*, 49.

9. On the relation between illusion and appearance in phenomenology, dialectics, and hermeneutics, see my "Begriffsbestimmung und Begriffsgeschichte," in vol. 1 of *Hermeneutik und Dialektik. Hans-Georg Gadamer zum 70. Geburtstag*, eds. Rüdiger Bubner, Konrad Cramer, and Reiner Wiehl (Tübingen: J. C. B. Mohr, 1970), 167ff.

10. See F. D. E. Schleiermacher, *Hermeneutik*, ed. H. Kimmerle, 2nd ed. (Heidelberg: Winter, 1974), especially the summary presentation of 1819 (73ff.), and on 78: "A successful execution of the art depends on linguistic talent and the talent for knowing the singularities of human nature." On the hermeneutical concept of a sign, see Emilio Betti, *Allgemeine Auslegungslehre als Methodik der Geisteswissenschaften* (Tübingen: J. C. B. Mohr, 1967), 42–88; see also Gadamer, *Wahrheit und Methode*, 144–45, 390ff.; *Truth and Method*, 135–36, 373ff.

11. Heidegger, *Being and Time*, 95–114.

12. Heidegger, *Being and Time*, 163–68.

13. Dilthey, "Entstehung der Hermeneutik (Auxilliary Manuscripts)," 327.

14. Dilthey, "Entstehung der Hermeneutik," 326.

15. Gadamer, *Wahrheit und Methode*, 167; *Truth and Method*, 157.

16. Gadamer, *Wahrheit und Methode*, 162, 324; *Truth and Method*, 153, 305.

17. Schleiermacher, *Hermeneutik*, 82-83; and Gadamer, *Wahrheit und Methode*, 167; *Truth and Method*, 157.

2

Hermeneutics and Relativism*

Jean Grondin

1. The Accession of Hermeneutics to the Rank of First Philosophy

*H*ermeneutics represents one of the dominant currents of contemporary philosophy. Hermeneutics is, however, a rather peculiar term to define a school of thought. Generally, philosophical schools are identified by -*isms*: neo-Kantianism, positivism, existentialism, structuralism, and so forth. As with other scientific terms ending in -*ics*, hermeneutics originally designated a discipline or a technique, not an orientation of thought. Logic, rhetoric, physics, metaphysics are not titles that characterize schools, but disciplines or domains of knowledge. In Greek, these terms were originally adjectives used to identify a *techne*,[1] occasionally an *episteme*. In the encyclopedia of knowledge, hermeneutics was conceived of as the science of rules governing the interpretation of texts, the *techne* of the *hermeneuein*. Now how did the discipline of interpretation become the name of a philosophical theory? In other words, how did hermeneutics become what we may call *contemporary hermeneuticism*?

The malicious will insinuate that, if hermeneutics compels recognition today as a privileged form of philosophical reflection, it is because philosophy has nothing else to do but interpret texts, having reduced itself to the exegesis of its own history. Somewhat disillusioned vis-à-vis its systematic or scientific possibilities, philosophy would have decided to be nothing more than a narcissistic return to its tradition; hence, its fundamentally hermeneutical vocation. However, this kind of caricature, even

*Published originally under the title "Herméneutique et relativisme" in *Communio*, vol. 5, no. 12 (Sept.-Oct. 1987). This essay was translated by Mildred Mortimer.

though partially true, does not reach the heart of the problem, which has to do with the promotion of hermeneutics to the rank of philosophical *theory*. For to practice the history of philosophy is not — because philosophers of all tendencies devote themselves to it — to identify ipso facto with a philosophical orientation.

If hermeneutics has been able to establish itself as a philosophical theory in our age, it is rather because we have become aware of the universality that the question of interpretation assumes today. Far from limiting itself to the strictly interpretative sciences, such as exegesis, philology, law, and history, the four disciplines that traditionally preoccupied hermeneutics or the *ars interpretandi* up to the nineteenth century, the problem of interpretation emerges today as one of the essential tenets of all knowledge. Epistemologists, such as Karl Popper, and historians of science, such as Thomas S. Kuhn, have taught us to what extent scientific theory is always interpretation, carving up and reading the real in terms of the more or less explicit demands of research and its historical, cultural context. Science is not limited, as positivists and common sense believe, to describing facts; it must organize them, conceptualize them, in two words, interpret them. Contemporary epistemology thus draws hermeneutical consequences from the Kantian distinction between phenomena and things-in-themselves. Science is not the simple reflection of the real such as it is in itself, but inevitably, schematization, interpretation, and translation motivated by phenomena.

Even more fundamental, we have also come to realize that interpretation plays a primary role in the realm of prescientific lived existence: in the orientation that we want to ascribe to our actions, the opinions that we embrace, and the value judgements that we have inherited from our education or from our milieu. One perceives the hint of this in Nietzsche's thundering words: "There are no moral phenomena at all, but only a moral interpretation of phenomena."[2] Nietzsche's perspectivism makes perceptible, for the first time in Western history, the virtual universality of the hermeneutical dimension. Behind all knowledge, attitudes, and actions lurks an interpretation of the real, of a real always already transformed in order to serve the interests of the will of power. This allows us to affirm that contemporary hermeneutics — represented in France by Paul Ricoeur, in Germany by Martin Heidegger, Hans-Georg

Gadamer, Jürgen Habermas, and several others, then in the United States by Richard Rorty—is the philosophy that seeks to measure this formidable universe of interpretation, discovered by Nietzsche, even if its theoretical expositions barely mention Nietzsche.[3] In taking into account the fundamental way interpretation enters into our relation to the world, hermeneutics does not renounce the universal claim of philosophy; it achieves it. Because every relation to the real, and therefore every theory, rests on an interpretation, hermeneutics has been able to acquire a universal importance. The universality of interpretation has just that authority to reorient contemporary philosophy to hermeneutics and to enable philosophy to maintain its fundamental claim to universality. Hermeneutics has become *prima philosophia.*

2. Normative Hermeneutics and Phenomenological Hermeneutics

By claiming the status of primary philosophy, twentieth-century hermeneutics no longer presents itself obviously as a hermeneutics in the traditional sense of the term, in other words as a science of the rules for interpreting texts. Classical hermeneutics tried to be essentially technical and normative. Its purpose was to show the rules or the method to follow when one seeks to interpret writings scientifically with a view to eliminating arbitrariness and subjectivism in the realm of interpretation.[4] Contemporary hermeneutics renounces this normative and technical project to place itself on a more elementary level. It will no longer teach how one must interpret (envisaged normatively) but how, in effect, one interprets; not what we should do, but "what happens to us over and above our wanting and doing"[5] when we interpret. What we have here is an approach that is resolutely phenomenological or descriptive, one that has become conscious of the fact that the hermeneutical order is prior to any attempt that aims to provide rules for or to discipline by a method the work of interpretation. Hermeneutics is able to aspire to the dignity of primary philosophy by renouncing its initially normative aim and by establishing itself as a phenomenology of interpretation.

The phenomenological transformation of hermeneutics seems to have to come with a turn toward pluralism. Whereas traditional hermeneutics, which was normative, had a tendency to think that a text could have only one meaning, hermeneutics, which has become philosophical, seems entirely disposed to accept the plurality of meanings that a single text can receive. A hermeneutics open to only one meaning seems to have changed into one that is open to pluralism.[6] Hermeneutical pluralism is carried to its extreme, for instance, in the words of Paul Valéry, "my verses have the meaning that one gives to them."[7] Even the medieval doctrine of the fourfold meaning of Scripture was not pluralist in the modern sense of the term. In his monumental history of medieval exegesis, Henri de Lubac speaks occasionally of the pluralism of this doctrine, but tradition has always recognized within this plurality "the unique privilege of inspired Scripture."[8] Plurality is desirable only in order to take into account the inexhaustible fecundity of the biblical text.[9] The multiple meanings (literal, allegorical, moral, and anagogical) Scripture can take on are not uncertain and dictated by pragmatic or utilitarian imperatives, but are willed by its author; therefore, they are willed by God. Each time it is a question of the "meaning granted by the spirit."[10] With regard to contemporary hermeneutics, on the other hand, there seems to be no limits that can be imposed on the multiplicity of meanings to which a text is susceptible. The meaning of a written text is reflected in the significance that it comes to have in a given historical context and for a well-defined community. One easily understands how hermeneutics was able, by the intermediary of Rorty,[11] to ally itself with pragmatism in the United States. Hermeneutics in Germany already suggests this tendency if we take into account the predominant role played by prejudices within interpretation. One reads in Gadamer: "Not occasionally only, but always, the meaning of a text goes beyond its author. That is why understanding is not merely reproductive but always a productive attitude as well."[12] A similar position seems to undermine the idea of progress in the order of understanding. This is a conclusion that Gadamer seems ready to endorse when he affirms in the same paragraph that it is not truly appropriate to speak of a "superior understanding" and that it suffices to say that one understands "in a different way." The pluralism of phenomenological hermeneutics, freed from its technical ambitions, will consequently display an almost unlimited tolerance in the face of the diversity of interpretation.

45

Tolerance can surely represent a hermeneutical virtue, but what are we to think of the relativism to which hermeneutical philosophy seems to lead? Must interpretations be declared of equal value because they are irremediably dependent on incommensurable contexts? Does the idea of objectivity preserve any meaning in the perspective of a radical hermeneutics? Unfortunately the great representatives of hermeneutics only rarely broach the question of relativism. The adversaries of hermeneutics are the ones who especially raise the specter of a relativism which leads to defeat or *anything goes*. Is hermeneutics in a position to dispel it? How is it possible to tolerate a certain pluralism while removing from it the suspicion of relativism? In the next section, I show that hermeneutics allows one to cast a new light on this question by asserting that the accusation of relativism does not have a true object and that relativism returns to an absolutist point of view, which is not immune to hermeneutical deconstruction. I will show later how, by distancing itself from relativism, hermeneutics restores a constraining meaning to the notion of objectivity.

3. The Hermeneutical Relativization of Relativism

In its defense against the charge of relativism, hermeneutics begins by recalling that, in fact, there has never been such a thing as absolute relativism. Relativism, understood ordinarily as the doctrine that all opinions on a subject are equally good, has never been advocated by anyone. For there are always *reasons*, be they contextual or pragmatic, that urge us to choose in favor of one opinion rather than another. As Rorty writes, the philosophers one terms *relativists* are simply those who estimate that these reasons are less algorithmic than many rationalists imagine.[13] The detractors of hermeneutical pragmatism describe as relativists those thinkers who take into account in their theories the interests and the situation of the interpreter. For pragmatism, it is *precisely* because these interests exert their will that relativism cannot be defended and that no one rallies under its banner. Therefore, according to hermeneutics, relativism is hardly more than a conceptual bugaboo constructed by those who possess a foundational conception of what truth or interpretation should be.

In the second stage of its defense, hermeneutics strives to show that the question of relativism only makes sense if one presupposes an absolutist point of view. Only one who claims an absolutist standard can speak of relativism. There is relativism only with respect to an absolute truth. But how is one to reconcile the claim to an absolute truth with the experience of human finitude, which is the point of departure for philosophical hermeneutics? According to hermeneutics, particularly that inspired by Heidegger, absolutism is left behind, linked as it is to metaphysics. What do we mean here by metaphysics? It is difficult to respond to this question, treated so superficially these days, but its adherents, its critics, and its etymology concur at least on one point: metaphysics is essentially transcendence from the temporal toward the atemporal. And what is the basis, one must ask, of this transcendence? Heideggerian hermeneutics answers: upon a refusal, if not a repression of the temporal, and thus of finitude. The claim to infinity remains the daughter of finitude. It is the exigency of finitude that seeks to deny itself. The truth termed absolute remains thus negatively defined with respect to finitude and temporality. Is it otherwise possible to determine positively this absolute, in other words, other than by the negation of the finite? According to hermeneutics, and many theologians declare this to be correct,[14] metaphysics has never been able to do this.

Hermeneutics wants to be a postmetaphysical philosophy, a *prima philosophia* without metaphysics (one knows that the two terms were usually synonymous traditionally). It seeks to conquer the metaphysical forgetfulness of time that, for Heidegger, signifies exactly the same thing as a forgetfulness of Being, by developing a rigorous discourse based on and beginning with finitude. Finitude becomes now the new universal of philosophy and the unacknowledged motivation behind all metaphysics. For hermeneutics, to go beyond metaphysical absolutism, is to leave wholly behind the problem of relativism.[15] The shadow of relativism ceases to be an obsession, or even pertinent once philosophy has set foot on the inescapable ground of finitude, where there is a new kind of rigor in thinking. The bugaboo of relativism would thus be the result of a double misunderstanding. Those who fear relativism take seriously an adversary that has never existed and that only makes sense from an absolutist point of view, the positive legitimacy of which has never been successfully demonstrated. One readily understands why hermeneutical thinkers themselves have set so little value on relativism. It is, in their minds, without object and the fruit of a preoccupation that is no longer valid because it is metaphysical.

4. *Toward a More Essential Relativity:* Aletheia *and* 'Emet

It remains nonetheless feasible, in a hermeneutical perspective, to ascribe to the idea of relativism a certain positive connotation. For it is always true to say that the truth is relative to whomever experiences it, although in a very precise sense: on the condition that one understands the truth as an experience of *meaning* that comes in response to the question of the one who seeks to understand. Hermeneutical truth always takes the form of a *response*, that is, to the question that perplexes the interpreter and that leads him or her to interpret a text. It goes without saying that the question is "relative" to its situation without being arbitrary. Relativity means here that the truth can be recognized as such only because it enlightens *us*, it illuminates *us*. The meaning dis-covered by interpretation is the one that comes to shed light on an obscurity, to respond to a question. The interpreter is constitutively invested in what is to be understood. There is no truth in itself if one means thereby a truth independent of the questions and expectations of human beings. The light that the truth brings takes form necessarily on the basis of obscurity, that of finitude in search of orientation.

The essential *relation* of truth to finitude is introduced in the Greek word for truth, *aletheia*. According to the highly probable etymology proposed by Heidegger, *aletheia* signifies, thanks to the privative *alpha*, the negation of the *lethe*, of the veiling. To think truth as *a-letheia* is to perceive in it the clearing up of obscurity, an experience of meaning that is more fundamental than the idea of an adequation of thought to the real suggested by the traditional concept of truth. The *lethe* that commands the dis-covering of a meaning remains constitutive of the appearance of the truth, as the expression of the finitude and the relativity essential to the truth. All *aletheia* is relative to *lethe*, every response to a question.

The comprehension of the truth as the experience of meaning for a finite being also speaks through the Hebrew term for truth, *'emet*. The first meaning of *'emet* is that of fidelity, of stability. The

Psalms often present the divine truth as a protection, a refuge, a rampart for the one who relies upon Yahweh. The truth signifies first "fidelity to someone who engages us in having confidence in him."[16] The truth understood as fidelity remains, of course, conceived in terms of man, in relation to his situation. When it is attributed to God, the truth is the promise of strength addressed to the human being (the Hebraic heritage that continues to determine the New Testament conception of the truth). It is decisive for the Judeo-Christian experience of truth that the human being engages himself or herself, by faith, in this offer of salvation. Is not this to think, hermeneutically, of the truth as *response* to an expectation? Without proposing a very specific exegesis of the Scriptures, which would go far beyond my theological competency, it seems to me that the biblical notion of *'emet*, on a merely linguistic basis, appeals to an experience of truth that indeed cannot be metaphysically demonstrated and which one attains only by means of faith. The believer is asked to rely upon a promise of truth, but without being able to hope for proofs or absolute assurances, and instead renouncing them. The truth would, therefore, be the contrary of a metaphysical certainty, absolutist or in-finite, in the sense of a withdrawal from finitude.

Greek language and Hebraic wisdom thus preserve the memory of a truth that one can call hermeneutical because it expresses the relativity of truth that is essential to human experience.

5. The Models of Art and Rhetoric

Hermeneutical philosophers, if one makes an exception of Heidegger for *aletheia* and Ricoeur for certain aspects of the Hebraic universe, quite rarely allude to these prefigurations of their understanding of the truth. Gadamer, for example, draws inspiration on the whole from art and rhetoric with a view to formulating a concept of truth that remains aware of its attachment to human finitude.

In discovering the meaning of truth, art enjoys a paradigmatic status[17] for at least two reasons. First of all, the artistic message is one that addresses itself directly to human sensibility. The senses, a mark of finitude, must be conquered so that aesthetic truth may be experienced. The message of the work of art does not enjoy an autonomous existence, as it were, identical for everyone and separable from the reaction it will arouse in the spectator. No, if art makes sense, it does so because of the commitment of the observer to what the work has to say and reveal to him or her. The exemplary function of art for the hermeneutical understanding of truth manifests itself, secondly, in the event character proper to the work of art. There is no work of art without presentation (*Darstellung*). The work is performed and achieves being through reading, contemplation, staging, and so forth. Artistic presentation in its uniqueness takes on the appearance of an *Ereignis*, of a *happening* that captivates us because it enlightens us, assails us, and surprises us. In other words, the human subject is not the master of the truth that transports him or her. The sudden occurrence of the truth illustrated by art precedes, by virtue of its immediacy, the methodical verification of truth. Gadamer uses the event character of aesthetic truth in his hermeneutics to demonstrate the derivative character of knowledge that must be controlled by method to be declared veridical. The idea of method introduces a *distance* between man and the truth, one that scorns the essential way understanding belongs together with what discloses itself as true. Aesthetic experience retains the proximity or the relativity basic to truth and understanding, which comes before all methodical putting at a distance.

This intuition is also found within rhetorical tradition. Gadamer detects there the trace of a truth felt like the enlightening experience of meaning and which cannot be wholly certain, because it is rooted in finitude. The rhetorical universe thus prefigures the hermeneutical one:

> This concept of clarity belongs to the tradition of rhetoric. The *eikos*, the *verisimile*, the probable [*das Wahr-Scheinliche*, literally, the true-shining], the clear [*das Einleuchtende*], all belong together and defend their own right over against the kind of truth and certainty which can be proven and known. . . . What is clear is always something that is said: a proposal, a plan, a conjecture, an argument, or something of the sort . . . . The beautiful charms us, without its being immediately integrated into the whole of our orientations and evaluations. Indeed just as the beautiful is a kind of experience that stands out like an enchantment and an adventure within the whole of our experience and

presents a special task of hermeneutical integration, what is clear is always something surprising as well, like the dawning of a new light which widens the domain of what is taken into account.

The hermeneutical experience belongs in this sphere because it is also the event of a genuine experience. That there is something clearly true about something that is said, without the implication that it is, in every detail, secured, judged and decided is, in fact, always the case when something speaks to us out of tradition . . . . The event of the beautiful and the hermeneutical process both presuppose the finiteness of human life.[18]

Hermeneutical truth, to the extent that it inscribes itself within the horizon of finitude, obviously fits into the domain of the plausible (*eikos, verisimile*), which is illuminating without being certain in all respects (the absolute certainty that would stem from metaphysics). For truth is always that which seems to us to be such, if we mean by this what successfully asserts itself as being within *our horizon*. The first (!) rule of Descartes's method complies with this demand of finitude; it urges "to accept nothing as true which I did not clearly recognize to be so." But is it possible to distinguish the truth that impresses itself upon me, the plausible, from what is true in itself? Ideally, perhaps. Nevertheless, what alleges to be true in itself must appear to us to be such; it must convince us of its objectivity. Thus, one does not escape the reign of plausibility. The history of science, that is to say, of scientific revolutions, can be read as the story of the way what an era or a community of scholars held to be truths in themselves came to be questioned. Convincing arguments, even though these are never exempt from rhetoric, can occasion us to abandon what we believed true. But the new knowledge that then impresses itself upon our mind is true only because it appears more plausible than the one it replaces and that we (now) judge to be erroneous or insufficient. Nothing would exclude a priori questioning in turn this new truth. Finitude remains principally open to possibilities of meaning and orientation that the future holds for it.

Gadamer is again inspired by the rhetorical tradition in stressing the role *application* plays in acquiring an understanding. To understand a text or a meaning is always to know how to apply it to our situation. The application, however, is not a process that begins *after* understanding. There is not first understanding and only later an application of what is understood to the present. To understand and to apply to one's own situation constitute, according to Gadamer, one and the same hermeneutical event. What is it to understand the meaning of a text of the past, if not to let it challenge us today? Negatively put, to understand nothing of a text means to be incapable of applying it to our situation, to find it impossible to connect it to our world, and to what we already know.

The valorization of the application secretly at work in all understanding draws attention to the eminently practical thrust of the hermeneutical experience. Understanding is invariably rooted in a *praxis* and always returns to nourish it. The practical horizon of the lived world (*Lebenswelt*) indicates the point of departure and the point of arrival of hermeneutical activity (a Gadamerian thesis whose sociological consequences have been developed by Habermas). Philosophical hermeneutics thus successfully dismisses the naive objectivism that would evaluate the truth of knowledge claims or a theory while bracketing the context of the *praxis* that makes them meaningful. Instead, for hermeneutical thought, the world of practical preunderstandings comprising our expectations, our prejudices, and our interests, makes possible the experience of truth, in other words, of meaning. Put still more simply: truth has meaning as truth only if it can be applied to our situation, to our experience of the world. Finitude demands it.

6. The Conditions of Objectivity

It is easy to grant to hermeneutics that there is a certain relativity to every authentic experience of truth. Undeniably, knowledge is nourished to a certain extent by the practical preunderstanding of individuals, in short, that an element of application exists in every act of understanding. Still, one can wonder if this relativity that has been purely descriptive until now, does not end up eliminating the concept of objectivity. Does phenomenological hermeneutics recommend, in a more normative perspective this time, the renunciation of the idea of an objective interpretation, which classical hermeneutics, let us not forget, was precisely destined to establish?

At first glance, it would seem so. It is not difficult to show, and Heidegger often tried to do this, that the concept of objectivity is no less imbued with metaphysics than is relativism. By transcending the realm of subjectivity, the claim to objectivity in its traditional form aspires indeed to some kind of atemporality or absolute truth. But perhaps in a postmetaphysical or hermeneutical universe it might be advisable to confer a less absolutist meaning on the concept of objectivity, especially in order to account for the fact that we already possess knowledge that can be considered objective without claiming to be absolute. To make room for objectivity within hermeneutics is not to commit oneself to an absolutist perspective, but only to recognize that some claims to knowledge and interpretations are more reliable than others. For example, we recognize that alchemy and chemistry, astrology and astronomy are not on the same level, and that a democratically elected government has a more legitimate mandate than a tyranny, and so on. If the problem of relativism always presupposes an absolute point of view, this does not necessarily also hold true for objectivity. For our knowledge can claim objectivity, but never infallibility. Hermeneutics' relativization of relativism cannot involve the forsaking of objectivity. The notion of objectivity must conserve its critical function. But what type of objectivity does it involve?

Certainly not an objectivity that wants to be the photographic reproduction of reality or of the sense of a text. The naivete of such an objectivism consists in leaping over the productive contribution of the interpreter, thereby misconstruing the preunderstanding that guides the work of interpretation. The understanding of a text, we have seen, is only articulated in response to the questions of the interpreter, which are conditioned by preconceptions or "prejudices." Of course, not all our prejudices are sanctioned in this manner. They are not all able to open the way to what the text has to say. It makes sense, therefore, to distinguish legitimate prejudices that allow the meaning of a text to be brought out, from illegitimate prejudices that make it less intelligible. What is *essential* to the work of hermeneutics, Gadamer insists, resides just in this distinction.[19] Whoever wants to disclose[20] the meaning of a text will succeed in contact with the text in abandoning those prejudices that proved to be illegitimate because they were incompatible with what was said. The most operative criterion here is coherency. It is hermeneutically indefensible to hold fast to a (pre)understanding that goes against what the text affirms. There is, therefore, an adequation of the text and intelligence but, for hermeneutics, it takes the form of an agreement between our preunderstanding and what the text says.[21] The hermeneutical conception of objectivity presupposes, therefore, that our preunderstanding can to a certain degree be made conscious. The task par excellence of the interpreter must be to formulate his or her own hermeneutical situation, taking into account prejudices, expectations, and questions that govern his or her research. To ignore the preconditioning structure of preunderstanding is to cut off oneself from the minimal condition of objectivity. For whomever pronounces himself or herself free of prejudices is all the more blindly exposed to their power. Prejudices will exercise their underground domination all the more strongly, and potentially distortingly, when denied or repressed.

Thus, the superiority of hermeneutics over naive realism in the matter of objectivity resides in the explicit awareness of the productive contribution of our preunderstanding to interpretation. Hermeneutical consciousness does not lead to the forsaking of objectivity but, on the contrary, to an exercise of rigor on the part of the interpreter in the name of objectivity. One can dissociate illegitimate prejudices from those that are fruitful and can pave the way to hermeneutical objectivity only by critically taking into account one's anticipations of the work. Making evident the prejudices that orient understanding is not destined to destroy objectivity, but to make it possible.[22]

The entire question now is to know what the basis can be for making the critical distinction between legitimate and illegitimate prejudices. Could one not lay claim to the hermeneutical radicalization of finitude and maintain that distorting prejudices will always end up imposing themselves and will, in spite of the openness exhibited by hermeneutical consciousness, block our access to the meaning of a text?[23] Is the interpreter continually able to sort out his or her own prejudices and to draw an adequate chart of his or her hermeneutical situation?

7. The Hermeneutical Productivity of Temporal Distance and Its Problems

According to Gadamer, the interpreter who deals with texts of the tradition has a distinct advantage when the moment comes to discern good from bad prejudices: *temporal distance.* In a text full of consequences, he writes, "It is only this temporal distance that can solve the really critical question of hermeneutics, namely of distinguishing the *true* prejudices, by which we *understand,* from the *false* ones by which we *misunderstand.* Hence the hermeneutically trained mind will also include historical consciousness."[24] A historical consciousness means here, in other words, a consciousness that will be able to take into account interpretations that have already been proposed concerning a work in the course of what German literary criticism calls its *Wirkungsgeschichte,* the history of the work's reception, of the interpretations that it produced in the course of history.[25] Thanks to temporal distance and to the interpretive work of one's predecessors, the interpreter can perceive that certain avenues of understanding have borne more fruit than others. And the avenues of interpretation or the prejudices that have, so to speak, strengthened in the course of tradition, appear to enjoy *eo ipso* a certain hermeneutical authority, susceptible of directing the current interpreter. They are not credible, of course, *because* tradition has declared them so. On the contrary, it is because they have been judged fruitful by tradition that they have succeeded in establishing themselves. Gadamer never teaches that it is necessary to accept all that has been bequeathed to us by tradition, only that there *can* be a moment of truth in the fact that certain interpretations came to "wield authority." The authority of the tradition must always rest, Gadamer quite rightly reminds us, on its being recognized by reason.

Gadamer illustrates the hermeneutical productivity of temporal distance by alluding to the almost insurmountable difficulty that the interpretation of contemporary art work represents: "In fact the important thing is to recognize that temporal distance [offers us] a positive and productive possibility of understanding . . . . Everyone knows the strange powerlessness of our judgment where temporal distance does not give us criteria that are certain. Thus the judgment of contemporary works of art is desperately uncertain for scientific consciousness."[26] This passage states that temporal distance grants us a positive and productive possibility of understanding. This is not in doubt. Temporal distance *can sometimes* serve us with a *clue* when the time comes to detect the most authoritative ways of interpretation. It is, however, only a clue, nothing more. Gadamer, therefore, goes much too far when he stipulates that "*only* this temporal distance can solve the really critical question of hermeneutics, namely of distinguishing the *true* prejudices by which we *understand* from the *false* ones by which we *misunderstand*" (emphasis added).

This too-general thesis contains at least two lacunae. On the one hand, it does not seem to take account of the cover-ups and distortions of which tradition can be guilty. Too often, tradition and temporal distance have contributed to affirm aberrant interpretations that obstructed access, say, to the original meaning of texts. History knows enough examples of texts that were touched up, eliminated, or interpreted in a direction favoring a well-determined reading and which, by lack of counterproofs, became canonical. How many times must the interpreter leap over the labor of the reception of works, a leap that is not easy, in order to discover their original meaning? Tradition can obviously play a very negative role in the transmission of meaning by prescribing a systematically distorted interpretation of a written work or even of a historical event. The legitimate prejudice risks (!) in this case being the one that dares to challenge tradition. On the other hand, the reference to the hermeneutical fruitfulness of temporal distance leaves intact the question of the interpretation of contemporary works. How is one to discern true prejudices where historical distance is lacking? There can be no doubt that the critical distinction between true and false prejudices certainly remains significant for present works.

On the occasion of the fifth edition of *Truth and Method* in 1986, Gadamer seems to have noticed the somewhat excessive character of his thesis concerning the legitimation of prejudices thanks to the way temporal distance sorts them out, because he modified the passage that declared that "only this temporal distance can solve the really critical question of hermeneutics . . . ." One now reads, "often temporal distance can . . . ."[27] As we can see, by this self-criticism, Gadamer offers a fine example of the demand for the critical revision of one's own opinions, defended by his hermeneutics!

Still, one does not find in his work a trenchant solution to the question about the foundation of the legitimacy of our prejudices and the interpretations that spring from it. But if one follows the postmetaphysical spirit of *Truth and Method*, it would be illusory to hope to discover something such as an absolute criterion that allows one to distinguish true from false prejudices. This kind of criterion would reiterate the absolutism of metaphysics and of methodical consciousness in its search for a universal key to truth. Hermeneutics has no difficulty in deciphering under this will for mastery and absolute certitude the same forgetfulness of finitude that it disclosed in the course of its relativizing relativism. Objectivity remains something to look to, and above all desirable, but in the realm of those means available to finitude. Otherwise, objectivity is condemned to being no more than a dream. On this path, the finitude that tries to test its prejudices benefits from a resource other than temporal distance. And this is *dialogue*.

8. The Openness of Communication

To renounce an absolutist or metaphysical point of view is equivalent to recognizing the fallibility of our opinions. But the fault, or the failure, of my conviction must often be pointed out to me by someone else. Knowing oneself to be finite and historically situated, hermeneutical consciousness is called upon to open itself to dialogue and criticism. Through the medium of communication, the testing of our preconceptions can be accomplished.

The advocates of contemporary hermeneutics are unanimous in emphasizing the virtues of dialogue in the search for objectivity.[28] Habermas even perceives there the only truly constraining source of truth, if not of salvation, in the midst of a desacralized world.[29] The understanding that is in language and *communicative* comes to substitute for the transcendent authority formerly assumed by myth, the sacred, or religion. No longer able to claim for ourselves metaphysical instances in order to objectively validate our opinions we would have no other choice, if we seek truth, than to attempt support our opinions within the framework of a consensus based on communication, in other words, of an understanding that results from communication itself and not from a constraint beyond communication.

It is evidently somewhat perilous to make a new absolute of communication. For we all know that communication does not always happen in a perfectly "democratic" manner. The context of communicative interaction, such as we live it concretely, frequently gives the impression of being none other than a perpetual conflict of wills for power, where the search for truth, even less for consensus, seems to be the last of motivations. This context is what compels Habermas to postulate an *ideal* situation of communication, therefore counterfactual, in other words, contrary to the lived reality of communication. He claims that this situation, to be ideal, is nonetheless the anticipation that is constitutive of all real communication, and which amounts to its raison d'être.

The conclusion that one can draw from this concept, granting that it is an idealization, is first of a critical order. It allows one to denounce, precisely in the name of a context of ideal communication, situations in which communication is systematically evaded or transfigured by the intervention of ideology, power, money, force, and so forth. One can surely question, in another connection, the concrete implications of this idealized communication, especially because Habermas has never really succeeded in showing that it is truly anticipated in every effort of communication. But this kind of question would take us beyond the limited scope of this essay.

The persistent valorization of communication allows us, nevertheless, to appreciate the philosophical originality of hermeneutics today. It tends to prove abandoning metaphysical absolutism without falling into a limitless relativism is possible. Dialogue serves well as a marker or rampart for the work of the hermeneutician. It is, therefore, within the forum of real communication that we have to defend our opinions and submit them to the judgment of another. The communicative rationality that unfolds here is that of the force of conviction that arises from the best argument. No other force is superior to it. In other words, all other imaginable force — and it is even permissible to think here of passions labelled irrational — must be able to take the form of an argument to carry approval. And, indeed, it does happen that we reject certain of our convictions if someone succeeds in revealing to us their incoherence or insufficiency (even if, *humanum humanum est*, the experience of dialogue teaches that the interlocutors often persist in defending manifestly untenable theses). But it does not follow that the truths that come to replace them are assured in a definite way. We adopt these new perspectives because they appear more enlightening to us, but nothing excludes them from becoming, in turn, indefensible later on. Communication constitutes a vital ally in the search for truth, but it does not provide an absolute Archimedean point, allowing us to escape our finitude. Intersubjectivity is only an enlarged subjectivity. This is already a great deal for this increase of the individual subjectivity enables communication to function as the critical arena where arguments can be advanced in favor of certain convictions of ours. These arguments, however, are never exempt from rhetoric and detached from human interests. What an individual is disposed to accept as a valid argument within the framework of communication remains profoundly, but also productively anchored in the hermeneutical universe of the social practices of a linguistic and historical community. That is why hermeneutics, which thinks this essential relativity, can lay claim to universality.

Notes

1. See the study of Pierre Chantraine, "Le suffixe grec *ikós*," in *Etudes sur le vocabulaire grec* (Paris: Klincksieck, 1956), 142.

2. Friedrich Nietzsche, *Beyond Good and Evil*, in *Basic Writings of Nietzsche*, trans. and ed. Walter Kaufmann (New York: Modern Library, 1968), 275. See also the more universal formulation: "[F]acts is precisely what there is not, only interpretations" in *The Will to Power*, trans. Walter Kaufmann and R. J. Hollingdale (New York: Vintage, 1968), 267.

3. Paul Ricoeur names Nietzsche among the masters of suspicion, but he concentrates particularly on Freud. The hermeneutics of *Being and Time* is constituted without decisive reference to Nietzsche. The debate that Martin Heidegger has with Nietzsche beginning in the 1930s is dependent on passing beyond the hermeneutical problematic. And Hans-Georg Gadamer's masterpiece, *Truth and Method*, reconstructs the history of hermeneutics and its accession to universality without acknowledging the privileged function of hermeneutics for Nietzsche.

In the course of recent years, however, Gadamer has emphasized more and more Nietzsche's pertinence to hermeneutics. See his recent studies, "Text und Interpretation," in *Text und Interpretation*, ed. Philippe Forget (Munich: Fink, 1984), 24–25 and "Das Drama Zarathustras," in *Nietzsche-Studien* 15 (1986): 1–15. In the meantime, specialists of Nietzsche had already drawn attention to the hermeneutical actuality of Nietzsche's work, particularly, Johann Figl, "Nietzsche und die philosophische Hermeneutik des 20. Jahrhunderts," in *Nietzsche-Studien* 10/11 (1981/82): 408–30.

4. See Wilhelm Dilthey, "Origines et développement de l'herméneutique," in *Le monde de l'esprit*, vol. 1 (Paris: Aubier, 1947), 319–40.

5. Hans-Georg Gadamer, *Wahrheit und Methode* (Tübingen: J. C. B. Mohr, 1975), xvi; in English, *Truth and Method*, trans. Sheed and Ward Ltd. (New York: Seabury Press, 1975), xvi. *Wahrheit und Methode* and *Truth and Method* will be abbreviated hereafter as *WM* and *TM* respectively. See Jean Greisch, "La raison herméneutique," in *Recherches de sciences religieuses* 64 (1976): 20: "The question is no longer: what to do to understand? but what happens when we understand?" See also Jean-Claude Petit, "Herméneutique philosophique et théologie," in *Laval théologique et philosophique* 41 (1985): 163.

6. Expressions introduced by Odo Marquard, *Abschied vom Prinzipiellen* (Stuttgart: Reclam, 1981), 129.

7. Paul Valéry, *Oeuvres*, vol. 1 (Paris: La Pléiade, 1960): 1509; cited by Gadamer in *WM*, 90 and *TM*, 85 as the expression of an "untenable hermeneutic nihilism."

8. Henri de Lubac, *Exégèse médiévale*, vol. 1 (Paris: Aubier, 1959), 33.

9. de Lubac, *Exégèse médiévale*, 61–62.

10. de Lubac, *Exégèse médiévale*, 355.

11. Richard Rorty, *Philosophy and the Mirror of Nature* (Princeton, N. J.: Princeton University Press, 1979), 357–94.

12. Gadamer, *WM*, 280; *TM*, 264.

13. Richard Rorty, *Consequences of Pragmatism* (Minneapolis, Minn.: University of Minnesota Press, 1982), 166. On this debunking of the accusation of relativism, see also Richard J. Bernstein, "Philosophy in the Conversation of Mankind," in *Hermeneutics and Praxis*, ed.

Robert Hollinger (Notre Dame, Ind.: University of Notre Dame Press, 1982), 72.

14. One thinks here of the theologies that try to work out a theological meditation without metaphysics, thus since the literally crucial experience of the death of God, proclaimed by Nietzsche, then confirmed by Heidegger as the consequence of metaphysical thought. See particularly Jean-Luc Marion, *L'idole et la distance* (Paris: Grasset, 1977); *Dieu sans l'être* (Paris: Fayard, 1982); Jürgen Moltmann, *Theologie der Hoffnung* (Munich: Kaiser, 1977); *Der gekreuzigte Gott* (Munich: Kaiser, 1981); Eberhard Jüngel, *Gott als Geheimnis der Welt* (Tübingen: J. C. B. Mohr, 1982).

15. Gadamer defends this point of view during an interview that we had with him in Heidelberg on March 5, 1985. It was the discovery of the hermeneutic of facticity developed by Heidegger in his course at Marburg during the 1920s that allowed him to go beyond the problematic of relativism at the same time as that of metaphysical absolutism. Indeed, one finds traces of a hermeneutics that surpasses relativism in a course of Heidegger from 1921 to 1922, given at Freiburg, that has just been published; see Martin Heidegger, *Gesamtausgabe*, vol. 61 (Frankfurt: Klostermann, 1985), 162-67. Later, there is hardly any question for Heidegger or Gadamer of relativism which is once and for all left behind.

16. "Vérité," in *Vocabulaire de théologie biblique* (Paris: Cerf, 1970), 1328-35.

17. The inaugural section of *Truth and Method* is appropriately entitled "The question of truth as it emerges in the experience of art."

18. Gadamer, *WM*, 460; *TM*, 441-42; translation modified.

19. Gadamer, *WM*, 252, 282; *TM*, 237, 266.

20. Gadamer specified that this openness is the only thing that should be required in hermeneutics; see *WM*, 253; *TM*, 238.

21. See *WM*, 252; *TM*, 237: "The only objectivity here is the confirmation of a preconception in its being worked out" (translation modified).

22. That is what Heidegger meant when he wrote that it is important not to get outside of the hermeneutical circle, of interpretation and preunderstanding, but "to come into it in the right way," in other words, in a critical manner by developing an explicit consciousness of the anticipations which determine understanding. See Martin Heideg-

ger, *Being and Time,* trans. John Macquarrie and Edward Robinson (New York: Harper and Row, 1962), 195.

23. An objection formulated by Claus von Bormann, "Die Zweideutigkeit der hermeneutischen Erfahrung," in *Hermeneutik und Ideologiekritik* (Frankfurt: Suhrkamp, 1971), 83-84.

24. Gadamer, *WM,* 282; *TM,* 266; translation modified.

25. On this problem, see my "La conscience du travail de l'histoire et le problème de la vérité en herméneutique," in *Archives de philosophie* 44 (1981): 435-53.

26. Gadamer, *WM,* 281; *TM,* 264-65; translation modified.

27. Gadamer, *Wahrheit und Methode,* 5th ed. in vol. 1 of *Gesammelte Werke* (Tübingen: J. C. B. Mohr, 1986), 304. See also 9.

28. Although with some nuances here and there that we should let pass in silence. Let us indicate only that Gadamer speaks particularly of dialogue, Rorty of conversation, and Habermas of communication. A more differentiated analysis of contemporary hermeneutics would mark here the bifurcation that determines its diverse ramifications. Whereas the idea of dialogue goes back to Platonic origins and the idea of conversation to a more unrestrained, a more "casual" framework, communication is connected more closely to scientific practice.

29. See Jürgen Habermas, *Theorie des kommunikativen Handelns,* vol. 2, (Frankfurt: Suhrkamp, 1981). 118-19. See in this regard my "Rationalité et agir communicationnel chez Habermas," in *Critique* 464-465 (1986): 40-59 and "De Heidegger à Habermas," in *Les Etudes philosophiques* (1986): 15-31.

3

Philosophical Discourse and the Ethics of Hermeneutics

Robert J. Dostal

It is the task of philosophy to discover what is common even in what is different.

— Hans-Georg Gadamer

I

Throughout his work Hans-Georg Gadamer delineates for us again and again what he takes to be three distinctive and particularly significant uses of language in law, religion, and poetry. Each of these brings with it the problem of interpretation, and in each of them in its own way the questions of practice are closely tied to the interpretive task. This tie between theory and practice is more immediate and obvious in the cases of law and religion than in that of poetry. But here, too, Gadamer shows us that the contemplative tarrying evoked by poetry is an act of human practice. Gadamer shows us the centrality of the interpretive act to these significant dimensions of linguistic practice through philosophical discourse. But of philosophy itself Gadamer has written only a little.[1] For him, philosophy also is a human practice for which interpretation is central. He has provided us with a philosophical account of interpretation in *Truth and Method* as well as numerous interpretations, not of law or of Scripture, but of poetry (especially Paul Celan) and of philosophy (especially Plato, Hegel, and Martin Heidegger). Rather than discuss philosophy directly, Gadamer has chosen, for the most part, to let the reader see a philosopher at work, that is, to let philosophy show itself through his work. The reception of Gadamer's work in this regard has not been univocal. Some have argued that, although Gadamer's own interpretive work is brilliant and insightful, his theory of interpretation is wrongheaded and cannot defend or give an account of Gadamer's own interpretive practice.[2] Such a view, of course, renders the Gadamerian oeuvre deeply inconsistent. It sees the philosopher of the interpretive process as not following his own interpretive dicta in his own interpretive practice. There is also quite another view of Gadamer's contribution — a view that finds no such inconsistency between Gadamer's interpretive work and his work on interpretation but claims that Gadamer's view of interpretation and his interpretive work, for example, his reading of Plato, is too traditional and oriented toward the past.

Put succinctly, those who make the former charge understand Gadamer's hermeneutical theory to be a creative one of interpretive fabrication that has little regard for the text interpreted. Those who make the latter charge present us with quite a different hermeneutics, for they find Gadamerian hermeneutics to be too slavishly devoted to the interpreted text. In our assessment of these charges we will see that each side gives priority to one of the two main aspects of what Gadamer has delineated as the paradox of interpretation. Both readings of Gadamer resolve the paradox one-sidedly — in favor of creativity or of fidelity. Gadamer calls for faithful productivity in his philosophical treatment of hermeneutics, and he exemplifies it in his work. It is not so much a matter of consistently applying a theory as of carrying out an ethics of interpretation that prizes the virtue of humility. Our look at the controversy around Gadamer's hermeneutical philosophy will give us a firmer grasp of his notion of philosophy and philosophical discourse that is, at the same time, grand in continuity with the self-proclamations of a proud tradition and humble before the truths that show themselves. A theme that will assist us in understanding Gadamer's treatment of the paradox and of philosophical discourse is the theme of time. Those who make the first charge object to what they take to be Gadamer's acceptance of the Heideggerian assignment of priority to the future, while those who make the countervailing charge object to a presumed Gadamerian assignment of priority to the past. I suggest here that Gadamer's own treatment of time is rather one that finds reciprocity between past and future and one that finds in the disclosure of truth an almost timeless unity.

II

The paradoxical task of interpretation according to Gadamer can be expressed, as I have above, as the task of faithful productivity. Gadamer does not use the term *faithful*, but, as I point out below, a requirement of his hermeneutics is the interpreter's trust in the text and the interpreter's modesty before the text. Humility and trust are the leading notions of what could be called, with some caution, the ethics of Gadamerian hermeneutics. Yet in *Truth and Method* and elsewhere, Gadamer insists that interpretation is to be productive and not reproductive.[3] Gadamer avoids the words *creativity* and *creative* because they exaggerate the power and authority of the interpreting subject over the text interpreted and the interpretation provided. Recall his critique of the Romantic notion of genius as well as his critique of Paul Valéry's "hermeneutical nihilism."[4]

Let us look more closely at the "productive" side of hermeneutics according to Gadamer. For the first group of critics, among them Leo Strauss, Stanley Rosen, and E. D. Hirsch, there is no significant distinction between *creative* and *productive*.[5] They make the mistake, it seems to me, which in another context Heidegger makes when he collapses the Judeo-Christian notion of creation with that of production or human making (*Herstellung*).[6] For these critics, the suggestion that the interpretive process is to be understood as a productive one is merely to say that the interpreter's creative imagination fashions what it wills from a text when it interprets it. To paraphrase Nietzsche in this regard, there are only interpretations.[7] This can only mean the denial of any fundamental distinction between text and interpretation, between author and critic, between text and world. As Harold Bloom would have it, any "strong" interpretation means simply to replace the text interpreted.[8]

In a now well-known letter to Gadamer, Strauss points out that Gadamer in *Truth and Method* is silent concerning Nietzsche and that Nietzsche is the decisive figure in the contemporary discussion of hermeneutics.[9] In his essay "Text and Interpretation," Gadamer acknowledges Strauss's point. Gadamer, of course, would not accept the mantle of Nietzsche. He finds Nietzsche in the alternative hermeneutics of suspicion and deconstruction.[10] Gadamer consistently maintains the distinction between text and interpretation, and he rejects the subjectivism and willfulness of Nietzschean creativity. When Gadamer takes up the term *productive*, he is thinking of Kantian science, not Nietzschean poetry. He is taking up the Kantian notion of the productive imagination, which synthesizes the disparate aspects of an experience into *an* experience. For this group of critics there is no important distinction between Kantian productivity and Nietzschean creativity. They accept Nietzsche's own claim to have revealed the secret of Kantian reason, that is, that Kantian reason is only a mask of the will to power.

There is undeniably a line of development from Kant to Nietzsche. There are good reasons for Nietzsche's claim. Because, for Kant, we do not know things as they are in themselves but only know things insofar as they can be appropriated by the human rational faculty, that is, through the schematized categories whose primary characteristic is spontaneity, it is indeed a short step to (1) abandon the notion of things-in-themselves that seems to make so little difference as to how experience is structured, (2) abandon the Kantian claim to a universal and ahistorical table of categories, and (3) turn Kantian spontaneity into the will to power. In this line of development the Kantian productive imagination of reason becomes Nietzschean poetry (*Dichtung*).[11] And the appeal to Kantian productivity seems to align any such view with Nietzschean creativity. On this view there is no thing-in-itself behind appearances, there are only appearances, that is, there are only masks and no persons masked, there is only interpretation and no texts interpreted: there are only interpretations.

But there is another line of development from Kant that also sees the importance of the synthetic activity of the imagination. And this is the development of Kantian transcendental philosophy into Husserlian transcendental phenomenology. As is well-known. Edmund Husserl too could not abide the split between the thing-in-itself and appearances. He asked that we realistically take appearances to be of things as they are in themselves. Things may be presented to us in many ways and thus take on many appearances, but this does not count against the claim that these appearances are just appearances of things as they are in themselves.

Phenomenological phenomenalism is neither Kantian phenomenalism nor empiricist representationalism. Furthermore, Husserlian phenomenology asks not only after the truth of things-in-themselves but is likewise concerned with how things present themselves to us in their various appearances, that is, a central theme of phenomenology concerns the modes of presentation of things. Gadamer, as Heidegger before him, is dependent on this development of the Kantian notion of productivity—the phenomenological account of the constitution of things. It is just this dialectic of appearance and thing, of phenomena and world, which Husserl carried out in opposition to neo-Kantianism, which is played out once again in Gadamer's paradoxical treatment of hermeneutics.[12] And it is just this phenomenological (and not Nietzschean) productivity that lies behind the Gadamerian attempt to revive the classical notion of *mimesis* as productive rather than reproductive.[13]

The simplest way to make clear Gadamer's commitment to this phenomenological thesis and his opposition to Nietzschean relativism is through the concept of world in *Truth and Method*. "The world," in Gadamer's formulation here, "is the common ground, trodden by none and recognized by all, uniting all who speak with one another."[14] He appeals explicitly to Husserl's treatment of perception and perceptual knowledge of things in which Husserl argued against Kantian phenomenalism and empiricist representationalism. In brief, the fact that any perception of an object is necessarily only of one side of the object is no argument against the perception being a perception of the thing. Gadamer writes similarly of the world:

> The variety of these views of the world does not involve any relativisation of the "world." Rather what the world is is not different from the views in which it presents itself. The relationship is the same in the perception of things. Seen phenomenologically, the "thing-in-itself" is, as Husserl has shown, nothing other than the continuity with which the shades of the various perspectives of the perception of objects pass into one another.[15]

On this phenomenological account we can dismiss any relativism of multiple worldviews as well as any strong commitment to an indefinite plurality of "worlds." We can also remove any reason to attach to things or the world the expression "in-itself," because this expression makes sense only in the Kantian (or alternatively, empiricist) contrast with subjective impressions that are not rooted in the thing. On Gadamer's account there is only the world and our varying views of it—views that may indeed have their own truth. He does allow the plural of world in quotation marks, for example, various historical "worlds." To this usage he comments: "Every such world, as linguistically constituted, is always open of itself, to every possible insight and hence for every expansion of its own world-picture, and accordingly available to others."[16]

It is precisely this openness and availability that is called into question by those who propose a more radical and Nietzschean hermeneutics. Insofar as the views expand to reach one another and connect, there comes to be a continuity of views in what Gadamer sometimes calls the *fusion of horizons.* This notion of continuity and fusion is most often singled out for critique by the deconstructionists and the Nietzscheans.[17]

It is indeed difficult to see how there might be such a fusion. If we think of it simply as a meeting of minds (or of wills), the obstacles seem overwhelming. Accordingly, Gadamerian hermeneutics has been depicted as naive or Romantic or even culturally chauvinist. Not only is the mind of the other inscrutable, one's own mind is not transparent to oneself. If we cannot know ourselves, how can we take up the pretense of knowing others? This difficulty, however, fundamentally misconstrues what Gadamer takes the interpretive process and its constitutive fusion to be about. What is at stake in the hermeneutical situation is not primarily the mind, meaning, or opinion of the other but the truth about the matter at hand, the notorious *Sache selbst.* As Gadamer writes:

> We see here again that understanding means, primarily, to understand the content of what is said, and only secondarily to isolate and understand another's meaning as such. Hence the first of the hermeneutic conditions remains the fore-understanding which proceeds from being concerned with the same matter [*Sache*]. It is this that determines what unified meaning can be realized and hence the application of the anticipation of completion.[18]

A basic presupposition of Gadamerian hermeneutics is that we have a common world as well as the things of the world in common. The concept of *die Sache*, the matter at hand, is correlative to that of world. Conversation or the interpretive task is not merely with another but about something. This "aboutness" aspect of understanding and conversation that phenomenologists have called *intentionality* provides the common ground. What makes this treatment of the hermeneutical situation unpalatable to many of its critics is their ignoring the significance of this "aboutness" relation. Their ignorance, it would seem, follows from their starting point — in subjectivity and subjectivism. To begin with the subject is to end there. Or, in the version of linguistic idealism, to begin merely with language is to end there — banging against the walls of one's own mode of discourse, of one's own *episteme*, within the prison house of language. Gadamer comments in this regard: "The focus of subjectivity is a distorting mirror."[19] Elsewhere he makes the remark that "language never stands for itself."[20] Any subjectivism or lingualism ignores the transcendence of language and human experience.

But if the Gordian knot of subjectivity and language can be so easily cut by the appeal to the truth of things of our world and the matters of our experience, why should a seemingly naive realism of this sort be at all concerned with interpretation and the meaning of the other or of texts at all? Why not simply attend straightforwardly to the matters at hand? The relevant philosophical discipline would seem in this case not to be hermeneutics but ontology. The answer, in short, is that, as Aristotle points out, we are talking animals. Though the "aboutness" relation need not be spoken or propositional, it very often is. We not only talk about things; we talk to or with someone about them, even if it is only to ourselves. We speak *with* someone *about* something. In conversation, we come to attend to our place in the world and the matters at hand.

In this as in other of Gadamer's philosophical commitments, Gadamer is a Platonist. For Gadamer, as for Plato, speech is never adequate to the truth of the matter but speech is necessary for us to attend to the matters at hand. All speech, oral and written, can serve as a reminder of truth, as a provoker of *anamnesis*. In a recent essay, Gadamer characterizes historically and philosophically his turn to conversation as a paradigm for hermeneutics in the following way:

> The hermeneutical turn to conversation, which I attempted, goes not only . . . back behind the dialectic of German Idealism to Platonic dialectic but also aims behind even this Socratic dialogical turn at its presupposition which is *anamnesis* sought for and awakened in *logoi.* This recollection, fashioned out of myth but quite rationally intended, is not merely the recollection of a single soul but rather always the recollection of a "spirit that may bind us" — we, who are a conversation.[21]

Anamnesis here for Gadamer is both emphatically social and historical in a way that the mythical face of the Platonic text often is not. Gadamerian recollection is not an identification of the self with the timeless and worldless divine thought thinking itself noetically. It is rather that which we come to recognize in conversation with human companions, that is, with friends. Such a memory is not mine or anyone's. It is ours. It can be called the tradition. Just as the relation to the other is one of sameness and otherness, so too is the relation to the past and to the tradition. Borrowing a commonplace term made philosophically significant by Heidegger. Gadamer writes that this "between" (*Zwischen*) is the hermeneutical situation in which we all find ourselves: "The place between strangeness and familiarity, that what has been handed down [*die Überlieferung*] has for us, is that 'between' [*das Zwischen*] between the historically intended distant objectivity and the belongingness to a tradition [*Tradition*]. The true home of hermeneutics is in this 'between.' "[22]

III

To be able to make some sense of this *Zwischen* and to be able to address the charges that Gadamer's hermeneutics is, from the one side, historicist and futuristic and, from the other side, nostalgic, we must come to terms with Gadamer's understanding of time and the human experience of temporality.[23] In his published work, Gadamer has not taken up the theme of time extensively, but the temporality of human experience and the hermeneutical situation is central to Gadamer's phenomenology of understanding and human being. Fundamental to this account of human temporality is the re-

70

jection of any linear or merely cumulative account of time that might accept the number line as a model for temporality. In *Being and Time* Heidegger calls this *clock-time*.[24] The understanding of time put to work in Gadamer's hermeneutics is rather "three-dimensional" and unified, just as it is in the phenomenological accounts of Husserl and Heidegger. The "dimensions" are, of course, the past, the present, and the future. Their unity and their symmetry can be expressed in the following two propositions, both of which this account would endorse: (1) the past gives us our future, and (2) the future gives us our past. In other words, Gadamer embraces and develops the phenomenological insight of the extended "now," whereby the past and the future are constitutive of the present. The present is just the meeting of the past and the future which are aspects of the present moment. A simple formulation of this is the following: "In our daily life we proceed constantly through the coexistence of past and future."[25]

It is important to recognize the endorsement of both of the above propositions whereby the past gives us our future and the future gives us our past. To endorse the former at the cost of the latter would be precisely the position of nostalgia for which Gadamer has sometimes been criticized. To endorse the latter at the cost of the former, would deny the obvious fixity of the past as it has been given to us. Insofar as the future is what we look to and will in our present engagements, such a simple assignment of priority to the future would make the past a mere function of our subjective will—individual or collective. Such a view seems implicit in many of those who would be free of the presumed bonds of the past by an act of the will.

This question of the possible priority of one of the "dimensions" of time is critical to the controversies around Gadamerian hermeneutics and the paradox of interpretation. Not only is it difficult to see how both propositions require endorsement, it may seem that Gadamer must be endorsing the primacy of the future because he is so deeply indebted, as he himself acknowledges in countless places, to the work of Heidegger, who in *Being and Time* granted phenomenological primacy to the future. In line with this we can find in Gadamer's work various versions of the thesis that the future gives us our past. For example, "history is only present to us in light of our futurity."²⁶ Or, "a sense for time is primarily a sense for what is future, not for what is present. This sense is present in prolepsis and refers what is present to what is not present."²⁷ It is on this account that critics such as Strauss and Rosen, critics who are most concerned about Gadamer's Heideggerianism, find a primacy of the future in Gadamerian hermeneutics.

If this is so, how can an astute reader of Gadamer, such as Jürgen Habermas, accuse Gadamer of being a traditionalist for whom the past has clear priority? Recall Habermas's review of *Truth and Method*: "Gadamer's prejudice for the rights of prejudices certified by tradition denies the power of reflection." Further, in the same review: "Hermeneutics comes up against walls of traditional framework from the inside, as it were."²⁸ Habermas is clearly right that one of the principal objectives of the argument of *Truth and Method* is the rehabilitation of tradition and authority. This rehabilitation refuses any such assignment of primacy to the future. Although history is rewritten in light of present concerns and future tasks, it is also correct to say on Gadamer's account, that the past gives us the future. In *Truth and Method*, Gadamer explicitly counters the Enlightenment opposition between tradition and reason, between *Überlieferung* and *Vernunft*: "It seems to me, however, that there is no such unconditioned antithesis between tradition and reason."²⁹ There is rather reciprocity (*Wechselwirkung*). In its more radical version, the Enlightenment opposition between tradition and reason becomes the Nietzschean opposition between traditional authority and will. Gadamerian hermeneutics cannot accept Nietzsche's claim that "the sea lies open. Never before has such an open sea lain before us."³⁰ The metaphor of the open sea is chosen precisely because of its indeterminate and indefinite character. Of course, Nietzsche is referring here primarily to the demise of the authority of the Christian tradition. He thinks of its demise as a loss of will, and he calls for the myths of the future as acts of will—of the will to power. For Gadamer, insofar as the past grants us our future, the future should not be taken as a function of the will. The directedness and determinacy of the future are not to be taken as strictures or constraints but, on Gadamer's account, as that which allows us to become ourselves.

This is not to say that Gadamer does not think of the future as open. He does. For example, in his essay, "The relevance of the beautiful," Gadamer writes: "The essence of what is called spirit lies in the ability to move within the horizon of the open future and the unrepeatable past."[31] The future is indeed open. It becomes determinate in the present in part because of the fixed past and not solely through the agency of subjectivity or the will to power. In the above essay, we see Gadamer again endorsing the "both . . . and" as opposed to the "either . . . or." After the above definition of spirit (*Geist*) Gadamer adds: "Mnemosyne, the muse of memory and recollective appropriation, rules here as the muse of spiritual freedom."[32] The freedom of the will is guided by the rule of memory. Such rule does not, on this account, contradict freedom. Although Gadamer is happy to talk about freedom, he again avoids the theme of will, which is inevitably bound up with a philosophy of subjectivity. Another statement rejecting such a philosophy, to be found in *Truth and Method*, reads as follows: "Understanding is not to be thought of so much as an action of one's subjectivity, but as the placing of oneself within a process of tradition, in which past and present are constantly fused."[33] Or in another formulation: "It is not so much our judgments as it is our prejudices that constitute our being."[34]

To take understanding as an event or happening of tradition or to say that our prejudices, not our judgments, constitute our being is not to assign primacy to the future. There is rather, as I have tried to show, a mutual reciprocity of past and future in the present—which reciprocity constitutes the unity of the three "dimensions" of time in the present. This reciprocity and symmetry is not a structural isomorphism, however. The past and the future are not, on this account, similar weights balanced on the fulcrum of the present. The future is open; it is the realm of possibility. The past is gone and irretrievable. Any repetition (*Wiederholung*) of the past cannot be the return of the same (*Wiederkehr des Gleichen*). Although the past and the future "coexist" with the present, neither the past nor the future can ever become present.

For the experience of time, Gadamer accepts and makes use of the metaphor of a flowing stream, which was the central metaphor of Husserl's phenomenology of time. In the essay "On Empty and

73

Filled Time," Gadamer calls "transition" (or "passing over," *Übergang*) the true being of time: "Transition appears as the true being of time, insofar as everything is at the same time [*zugleich*] in it and thereby past and future are together."[35] In attending to the passage of time, we attend to its ephemeral flux as well as to the connection between past and future in the present. This connection presents us with the unity of the different dimensions of time. Certain experiences bring this unity to the fore such that time seems almost to come to a halt. Gadamer is very concerned (particularly in some of his later essays) to show us how we often have such an experience of timelessness in play, in celebration, in art, or in the festival, for example.[36] Although we do not find eternity here, there is a kind of tarrying and lingering that gives us a sense of the unity of time and the contemporaneity of present and past. This unity and contemporaneity are essential to the hermeneutical situation within which we take up a text and converse with it. Only through such an understanding of human temporality does conversation and the possible fusion of horizons become a possible model of hermeneutics. And only through this notion of human temporality can Gadamer sustain his notion of the "classical" as that which withstands time and exhibits permanence.

IV

Understanding how time is considered in Gadamer's hermeneutics should help us see how his account cannot accept and should not be confused with the sort of historicism that insists on the irretrievability of the thought and work, the culture, of other historical periods. In conjunction with such a presumed irretrievability, our task vis-à-vis the remnants of these earlier periods would be merely to put them to work as best we can and as creatively as we can for our own purposes. The Nietzschean call to creativity is motivated not so much by the irretrievability of the past as by its burdensome character. Accordingly, Nietzsche calls upon us to forget the past, for forgetfulness is liberating.[37] We saw above, in contrast, how Gadamer entitles Mnemosyne, memory, the "muse of freedom."

Instead of asking us to forget the past or to note its irretrievability, Gadamer calls us to engage in a conversation with the past. The tenor of this conversation with past texts bears two seemingly incompatible characteristics. On the one hand, the conversation exhibits a mutuality of question and answer, and, on the other hand, the text exhibits a certain authority over the reader. We must allow the text to make claims on us, but in light of our common experience of the matter in question we can revise earlier readings of the text or pursue a new line of questioning with respect to the text, or criticize and reject the text. Habermas, who has been a careful reader and appropriator of Gadamer's hermeneutics, made such a mutual conversation the model for critical thinking and attempted to transform Gadamerian hermeneutics into a methodology for the historical sciences. Perhaps more than anyone else, Habermas helped us recognize a difficulty in bringing together the mutuality of this conversation and the rehabilitation of the authority of tradition. Both of these themes are fundamental to Gadamerian hermeneutics. Habermas separated the themes onto different levels of his enterprise — the historical-hermeneutical sciences and the critical.[38]

Gadamer concedes something to this criticism when in his writing on the theme of hermeneutics after the publication of *Truth and Method* he provides us with a more nuanced account of the sorts of texts we might encounter. In "Text and Interpretation," he distinguishes, for example, between genuine texts, pseudotexts, antitexts, and pretexts. On several other occasions he distinguishes within "genuine" texts between those that are "eminent" and those that are not. Simply because we are provided with some written objectification from the past, does not mean that the conditions for conversation are met. Not all such written objectifications are texts, and not all texts are eminent ones: "Through the mere fact of its being written down and read, a text does not yet belong to literature."[39]

It is the "eminent," that is, literary, text that most markedly bears authority for Gadamer. Perhaps it goes without saying that religious and legal texts bear such authority. While most philological hermeneutics is concerned primarily with written artifacts or objectifications in general and finds literature to be a subset of these, Gadamer's approach has been to look to significant religious, legal, and literary texts for insight into interpretation: "The explication [*Auslegung*] of literary constructs is, in the eminent sense, 'explication' or interpretation."[40] In reading, which is an "explication," we give voice to the literary text for the inner ear. The reason Gadamer calls the interpretive act *productive* in *Truth and Method* is, first, because the text requires this active reading for it to have life, and second, because the literary text is inexhaustible. As we saw above, for one reader to find something in a work and for another to find something quite different does not militate against the authenticity and truthfulness of such readings.

At the same time, throughout his work on the matter of interpretation Gadamer has delineated for us a hermeneutics of trust and not of suspicion.[41] A defining condition or presupposition of interpretation is the meaningfulness of the text, just as a defining condition of genuine conversation is such a presumption. Thus, in *Truth and Method*, Gadamer tells us how the reader listens to the text and belongs to it. In his introduction to his early essay on historical consciousness, Gadamer writes of his hermeneutics: "There is no intention to place the realization of the text aside from the text itself. On the contrary, the ultimate ideal of appropriateness seems to be total self-effacement because the understanding [*Verständnis*] of the text has become self-evident."[42] In "Texts and Interpretation," Gadamer insists against Nietzsche that interpretation is not an insertion of meaning but a discovery.[43] The successful interpretation actually finds what is there and gives it voice such that the interpreter and the interpretation are forgotten. The mediator disappears in the face of the mediated. "Unobtrusiveness" is a praiseworthy characteristic for any interpretation and any interpreter.[44]

All this constitutes a clear subordination of the interpreter to the eminent text.[45] We can call this not only a hermeneutics of trust but a hermeneutics of humility. The reader/interpreter does not arrogate to himself or herself the authority to make use of a text but freely grants authority to the text over the interpretation. The experience of self-understanding concomitant with an excellent interpretation that brings an understanding of a text is, at the same time, according to Gadamer, an experience of the loss of self.[46]

Although Gadamer never uses the word himself to describe the hermeneutical situation, we could extensively document humility as a hermeneutical virtue. But Habermas and those who share his critical concern must wonder how this is relevant to the less than eminent texts that are not classics. We will have to ignore here the question that concerns how texts become recognized as literature and as classics, that is, how they become canonical. But we cannot, in this context, ignore the question of the fit between this notion of the role of the interpreter vis-à-vis the classic text and the model of interpretation as a conversation. The Gadamerian answer, in short, is that, although not all texts exhibit the same authority and the interpreter does not find himself belonging to all texts in the same way or degree, nonetheless the virtues that should be characteristic of anyone as a partner in a conversation are those of trust and humility. This is not so unlike the Kantian virtue that Habermas would see prevailing in an undistorted speech situation, that is, the virtue of mutual respect. Kant's own phenomenology of the experience of respect makes paramount the feeling of humility and the loss of the self. This virtue of respect in the Kantian, and presumably Habermasian context, is not limited to conversation or relations with those of special authority. Rather, it is the virtue that best characterizes our relation to any other person. Similarly, this trust and humility are characteristic of the hermeneutical situation as such for Gadamer. A difference that is not insignificant between the Gadamerian and Kantian treatment of the relation to the other in this regard follows from the fact that the Kantian respect for the other is derived from respect for the law and the fact that the other bears the law within himself or herself. The virtues of the Gadamerian interpreter in conversation are not merely that of humility and respect but of trust as well; furthermore, these virtues of trust and humility are offered to the other not merely in virtue of the law but simply in virtue of the other as other, as partner in conversation. These virtues of trust and humility, which constitute the ethics of hermeneutics, might best be captured neither by Kantian respect, for the reason just suggested, nor by Aristotelian friendship, because humility is here important, but rather by *caritas*.

V

Together with law, religion, and poetry, philosophy is for Gadamer a preeminent mode of addressing and responding to our common hermeneutical situation. Philosophy, as the others, subscribes, in its own way, to the ethics of interpretation just outlined. Philosophy's primary concern, however, is not the right, nor the holy, nor the beautiful. Although philosophy is inevitably concerned with all three of these dimensions of human experience, it gives none of them primacy in the way these other modes of discourse do. Rather, philosophy's primary concern is the truth. As truth-seeking, philosophical discourse can be distinguished from what we have come to call *science* insofar as external matters are not the measure for philosophy in the way that they are for science. This is not to say that the relevant criteria for philosophical discourse are solely immanent. The measure of philosophical discourse is not this or that but the whole. From Plato and Hegel, Gadamer accepts this as a mark of philosophical discourse. This is why, in part, Gadamer tells us repeatedly that philosophical discourse is speculative.

Yet, insofar as the distinguishing marks for philosophy are its truth-seeking character and its concern for the whole, these on Gadamer's account do not adequately distinguish philosophy, for it shares these features with poetry. Gadamer follows Heidegger in calling poetry and philosophy the closest of neighbors. The question remains concerning that which distinguishes, for Gadamer, philosophy from poetry.

We find in Gadamer's work not only remarks about the neighborliness of philosophy and poetry—a neighborliness that distinguishes them as well as binds them—but also a common grouping of poetry with law and religion in contexts that seem to exclude philosophy. Gadamer often presents these three as exemplifying an aspect of the hermeneutical situation that is the "standing" quality of the texts of these modes of discourse. These texts, each in its own way, are given as completed and, in a certain way, self-fulfilling. They exhibit a certain "automony." Their almost self-sufficient and autonomous character together with their significance as legal or religious or poetic texts provide these standing texts with a high degree of authority for the reader. Presumably, because the poetic text can yield this kind of authority without religious and legal sanctions, the poetic or literary text is for Gadamer the eminent text of interpretation.

By implication the neglect of philosophy in the discussion of the standing text suggests that philosophical texts do not share this "standing" quality and the authority that comes with it. This would

78

seem to mark a major difference between poetic and philosophical discourse. Yet, in the 1977 essay "Philosophy and poetry," Gadamer accords the "standing" designation to philosophy as well: "The language of poetry and philosophy on the other hand can stand by itself bearing its own authority in the detached text that articulates it."[47] In this essay, Gadamer explains the proximity of poetry and philosophy. Both "stand written" in this important sense. In the 1981 essay "Philosophie und Literatur," Gadamer seems to have withdrawn this characteristic from philosophy. Here he is concerned again with the proximity of philosophy and poetry. After a discussion of the written and eminent character of literature, he asks what a philosophical text is. He then withdraws the question on behalf of another: "Or must one say that there is no philosophical text at all?"[48] Clearly, in context, this means in the eminent sense of literature. And the answer is that there is no philosophical text. Similarly, in the 1978 essay, "The Eminent Text and its Truth," Gadamer confines the notion of "eminence" to literature while explicitly excluding religious and legal discourse and never mentioning philosophical discourse.

Throughout Gadamer's writings what most obviously distinguishes philosophy from its neighbor poetry is the conceptuality (*Begrifflichkeit*) of philosophical discourse. "Philosophy moves exclusively in the medium of the concept," writes Gadamer in "Philosophy and poetry."[49] In this same essay, in just this context, Gadamer cites Husserl, Plato, and Hegel concerning the peculiarly conceptual character of philosophical discourse. Gadamer acknowledges that Husserl was right to insist that the eidetic reduction "is something that occurs de facto in all true philosophizing. For it is only the a priori essential structures of all reality that have always and without exception formed the realm of the concept or the realm of ideas."[50] Gadamer's own way of writing about that which is distinctive of philosophy, that is, its conceptual and speculative character, bears more clearly the mark of Hegelian and not Husserlian phenomenology. It is Hegel's treatment of the dialectically speculative character of philosophical discourse that is decisive for Gadamer's own language concerning the internal yet not solely immanent measure for philosophy because philosophy must attend to the whole.

The question that comes to the fore in this regard concerns this Hegelian imprint of Gadamer's hermeneutics. Does not speculative philosophy on the Hegelian model require completeness and finality? Gadamer finds, as does Hegel, the Absolute to be the concern of philosophy. Is the Gadamerian Absolute the Hegelian one? What of human finitude, a theme central to Gadamer's hermeneutics for which he acknowledges his deep debt to Heidegger?

It is just in this regard that Gadamer's treatment of philosophical discourse turns to Plato and the Platonic-Aristotelian notion of *nous*. Gadamer may stay by the claim that "Being that can be understood is language,"[51] but he also means to say that Being is not transparent and that we never find our language adequate. Hegelian dialectic and speculation must give way ultimately to the speculation and dialectic of Plato, for whom, as Gadamer cites him, philosophy is "in ideas, through ideas, toward ideas."[52] Yet, at the same time, the Platonic dialogue provides us with a model of the logic of question and answer that remains a model of philosophical discourse. This logic and the ignorance of Socrates are not merely exoteric for Gadamer's Plato but essential to philosophy—a clear corrective of Hegelian logic.

It is not surprising then that Gadamer singles out the *Phaedrus* as the text within the philosophical tradition that best deals with the question with which we are here concerned: the character of philosophical discourse and the philosophical text. It is in the *Phaedrus*, of course, that Plato delivers the Socratic attack on the writing of philosophy. Gadamer directs us to the truth of this obvious Platonic irony when he comments in "Philosophie und Literatur" that perhaps Plato was right in the *Phaedrus* concerning philosophy, that is, that philosophical texts are not properly texts at all but rather an intervention in an infinite ongoing dialogue.[53] Following this suggestion, the difference between poetry and philosophy would be the following. Poetic or literary texts, as eminent and "standing" texts, call us to recognize their singularity or individual distinctiveness and their unsurpassability, while so-called texts of philosophy invite us to conversation, argument, and revision.

It is difficult to develop this distinction on the basis of Gadamer's writings because both poetry and philosophy invite us to "the conversation that we are" and both invite us to participation. What is true of the hermeneutical situation must be especially true of eminent texts. And conversation and participation are essential to Gadamer's consistent description of hermeneutical experience. Yet in this fairly recent essay philosophy, which explicitly does *not* provide us with eminent texts, is singled out as conversational. It is this same essay that concludes by noting a common feature of poetic and philosophical discourse—the summons to participation. If we are to make some sense of this distinction and develop it in a way consistent with Gadamer's writings, we can recognize a difference in the sort of authority that literary and philosophical writings exert. Literature, together with law and religion, calls for the subordination of the reader to the text in a way that philosophy does not.[54] While the reading of both requires the charity discussed above, philosophy calls the reader to a more active participation, a participation in the same mode of discourse. Philosophy calls for philosophy, participation in the logic of question and answer. Literature, rather, bears witness and asks us to give an ear to the tidings. The critical response to literature is not to be confused with literature, while philosophy calls us to engage philosophically. The critical response to poetry is not poetry. The critical response to philosophy is philosophy.

Our opening citation may help us understand this distinction: "It is the task of philosophy to discover what is common even in what is different."[55] Here Gadamer paraphrases once again Plato's *Republic*. Poetic discourse, which is not primarily marked by the concept but rather by figures of speech and the interplay of sound and meaning, is, as suggested above, radically singular. It asks us to attend to the rich differentiation of human experience. Literature asks us to subordinate ourselves to the otherness of the other. Philosophy, through its concepts and categories, asks us to find what is common in the variousness of human experience. A presupposition both of philosophy and of literature is the possibility of attending to otherness and difference. Philosophy seeks to give voice conceptually to that which binds the self to the other in our common human experience. For Gadamer, unlike Hegel, literature is not subordinated to philosophy; literature is not the image of the concept. Nor can we state the identity of identity and difference. But we can seek to speak to one another about what we have in common, to ask about that which is not, and to listen to the voice of the other with charity.

Notes

1. Gadamer is concerned with relating philosophy to and distinguishing it from the modern natural sciences in the essays published in *Vernunft im Zeitalter der Wissenschaft* (Frankfurt: Suhrkamp, 1976); in English, *Reason in the Age of Science*, trans. Frederick G. Lawrence (Cambridge, Mass.: MIT Press, 1981). He takes up the relation of philosophy to literature in "Philosophie und Literatur," *Phänomenologische Forschung* 11 (1981): 18–45; and in "Philosophie und Poesie," in vol. 4 of his *Kleine Schriften* (Tübingen: J. C. B. Mohr, 1977), 241–48. On the relation between philosophy and literature, see also his "Philosophie und Hermeneutik," vol. 4 *Kleine Schriften*, 256–61; "Über die Ursprünglichkeit der Philosophie," vol. 1 *Kleine Schriften* (Tübingen: J. C. B. Mohr, 1967), 11–38; and "Beriffsgeschichte als Philosophie," vol. 2 *Gesammelte Werke* (Tübingen: J. C. B. Mohr, 1986), 77–91. Gadamer's *Gesammelte Werke* and *Kleine Schriften* will be abbreviated hereafter as *GW* and *KS* respectively followed by volume and page number.

2. See especially Stanley Rosen, *Hermeneutics as Politics* (Oxford: Oxford University Press, 1987), 164–66. Rosen's charge against Gadamer inverts Gadamer's defense of Heidegger against Karl Löwith. Gadamer claims that Heidegger's violent interpretations (by implication indefensible) do not follow from his theory of understanding (*Verstehen*). See Hans-Georg Gadamer, *Wahrheit und Methode* (Tübingen: J. C. B. Mohr, 1965), 473; in English, *Truth and Method*, trans. Sheed and Ward Ltd. (New York: Seabury Press, 1975), 456–57. *Wahrheit und Methode* and *Truth and Method* will be abbreviated hereafter as *WM* and *TM* respectively.

3. Gadamer, *WM*, 280; *TM*, 264.

4. Gadamer, *WM*, 90; *TM*, 85.

5. Rosen, *Hermeneutics as Politics*, 164–66. For Leo Strauss's letter to Gadamer, see "Correspondence Concerning *Wahrheit und Methode*," in *Independent Journal of Philosophy* 2 (1978): 5–12. For E. D. Hirsch, see "Gadamer's Theory of Interpretation," in *Validity in Interpretation* (New Haven, Conn.: Yale University Press, 1967),

245-64; and *Aims of Interpretation* (Chicago: University of Chicago Press, 1976), 17, 39-49. Hirsch has more recently qualified his critique; see his "Meaning and Significance Re-interpreted," *Critical Inquiry* 11 (December 1984): 202-25.

6. Martin Heidegger, *Die Grundprobleme der Phänomenologie*, vol. 24 of his *Gesamtausgabe* (Frankfurt: Klostermann, 1975), 167-68; in English, *The Basic Problems of Phenomenology*, trans. Albert Hofstader (Bloomington, Ind.: Indiana University Press, 1982), 118.

7. This is a prominent and central theme throughout Friedrich Nietzsche's work. See, for example, his question "whether all existence is not essentially actively engaged in interpretation" in *Gay Science*, trans. Walter Kaufmann (New York: Vintage, 1974), 336. See also his *Morgenröte* (Stuttgart: Kröner, 1964), 105-108 where to experience is to invent or fictionalize (*Erdichten*). Jean Granier argues that, for Nietzsche, Being as such is interpretive; see his "Perspectivism and Interpretation," in *The New Nietzsche*, ed. David B. Allison (New York: Dell, 1977), 190-200.

8. See Harold Bloom, *The Anxiety of Influence* (New York: Oxford University Press, 1973) and *Kaballah and Criticism* (New York: Seabury Press, 1975), especially "The Necessity of Misreading," 95-126. In this Bloomian sense, Richard Rorty is right to call Gadamer a "weak textualist"; see Richard Rorty, "Idealism and Textualism," in *Consequences of Pragmatism* (Minneapolis, Minn.: University of Minnesota Press, 1982), 139-59. In Gadamer's *Truth and Method* we find: "Interpretation does not seek to replace the interpreted work. It does not, for example, seek to draw attention to itself by the poetic power of its own utterance. Rather, it remains fundamentally accidental" (*WM*, 377; *TM*, 361).

9. Strauss, "Correspondence," 5.

10. See Hans-Georg Gadamer, "Text und Interpretation," *GW* 2: 330-60; as well as "Destruktion und Dekonstruktion," *GW* 2: 361-72 and "The Hermeneutics of Suspicion," *Man and World* 17 (1984): 313-23. It is not accidental that in the brief exchange between Gadamer and Jacques Derrida two closely related themes are at issue: (1) the appropriateness of psychoanalysis as a model for interpretation in general, and (2) the significance of Nietzsche. Gadamer denies that psychoanalysis is an appropriate model and second, that Nietzsche provides a fruitful understanding of the hermeneutical experience. As Paul Ricoeur points out, Nietzsche and Freud are the contemporary

progenitors of the hermeneutics of suspicion. For the exchange, see *Text und Interpretation*, ed. Philippe Forget (Munich: Fink, 1984), 56–77.

11. This is Rosen's argument in chap. 1 of *Hermeneutics as Politics*.

12. In assessing his own work, Gadamer comments that there is a clear line of development from Edmund Husserl's concept of passive synthesis and anonymous intentionality to hermeneutical experience; see Hans-Georg Gadamer, "Zwischen Phänomenologie und Dialektik: Versuch einer Selbstkritik," *GW* 2: 16.

13. The concept of *mimesis* is central to Gadamer's understanding of art and poetry. See especially Hans-Georg Gadamer, "Kunst und Nachahmung," *KS* 2: 16–26, and "Dichtung und Mimesis," *KS* 4: 228–33; in English, "Art and imitation" and "Poetry and mimesis," in *The Relevance of the Beautiful and Other Essays*, trans. Nicholas Walker, ed. Robert Bernasconi (Cambridge: Cambridge University Press, 1986). See also Gadamer, *WM*, 287ff.; *TM*, 371ff. *Mimesis* for Gadamer is *Darstellung*, "presentation"; *Darstellung* is misleadingly translated in *Truth and Method* as "representation."

14. Gadamer, *WM*, 422; *TM*, 404.

15. Gadamer, *WM*, 423; *TM*, 406.

16. Gadamer, *WM*, 423; *TM*, 405.

17. See, for example, Robert Bernasconi's "Editor's Introduction" to *Relevance of the Beautiful* as well as his *The Question of Language in Heidegger's History of Being* (Atlantic Highlands, N. J.: Humanities Press, 1985), especially 1–2 and 32; and his "Bridging the Abyss: Heidegger and Gadamer," *Research in Phenomenology* 16: 1–19.

18. Gadamer, *WM*, 278; *TM*, 262; translation modified.

19. Gadamer, *WM*, 261; *TM*, 245.

20. Gadamer, "Philosophie und Poesie," 242; in English, "Philosophy and poetry," in *Relevance of the Beautiful*, 132.

21. Gadamer, "Destruktion und Dekonstruktion," 369; my translation. In "Der Tod als Frage," Gadamer offers a definition of philosophy in terms of *anamnesis*: "These are questions that philosophy must put to itself in its own way. For the task of philosophy is to wish to know what one knows such that one does not know he knows it. [Denn ihre

Aufgabe ist, das wissen zu wollen, was man so weiss, ohne es zu wissen.] This is an exact definition of what philosophy is and a good description of that which Plato first recognized—namely, that the knowing with which we are here concerned is *anamnesis*, a fetching up out of the inner self and a raising to consciousness." See vol. 4 of his *GW* (Tübingen: J. C. B. Mohr, 1987), 163–64; my translation.

22. Gadamer, *WM*, 279; *TM*, 262–3; translation modified.

23. A section of vol. 4 of *GW* has the subtitle "Das Rätsel der Zeit." It includes four essays: "Die Zeitanschauung des Abendlandes" (1977), "Über leere und erfüllte Zeit" (1969), "Das Alte und das Neue" (1981), and "Der Tod als Frage" (1975).

24. Martin Heidegger, *Being and Time*, trans. John Macquarrie and Edward Robinson (New York: Harper and Row, 1962), 465ff.

25. Hans-Georg Gadamer, "Die Aktualität des Schönen" (Stuttgart: Reclam, 1977), 12; in English, "The relevance of the beautiful," in *Relevance of the Beautiful*, 10.

26. Hans-Georg Gadamer, "Die Universalität des hermeneutischen Problems," *GW* 2: 224; in English, "The Universality of the Hermeneutical Problem," in *Philosophical Hermeneutics*, trans. David E. Linge (Berkeley, Calif.: University of California Press, 1976), 9. The succeeding sentence to the one cited is the following: "Here we have learned from Heidegger, for he exhibited precisely the primacy of the futurity for our possible recollection and retention, and for the whole of history."

27. Gadamer, "Über leere und erfüllte Zeit," *GW* 4: 139–40; in English, "Concerning Empty and Ful-filled Time," *The Southern Journal of Philosophy* 8 (Winter 1970): 343.

28. Jürgen Habermas, "A Review of Gadamer's *Truth and Method*," in *Understanding and Social Inquiry*, eds. Fred Dallmayr and Thomas McCarthy (Notre Dame, Ind.: University of Notre Dame Press, 1977), 358, 360.

29. Gadamer, *WM*, 265; *TM*, 250.

30. Nietzsche, *Gay Science*, 280 (aphorism 343).

31. Gadamer, "The relevance of the beautiful," 10.

32. Gadamer, "The relevance of the beautiful," 10.

33. Gadamer, *WM*, 274–75; *TM*, 258.

34. Gadamer, *GW* 2: 224.

35. Gadamer, *GW* 4: 149.

36. See especially Gadamer's essays "The relevance of the beautiful" and "The festive character of theatre" in which the notions of tarrying (*Verweilen*), eternity, the *nunc stans*, and the contemporaneity of the three dimensions of time all play an important role (*Relevance of the Beautiful*, 3–53, 57–65). See also Gadamer, *GW* 4: 462.

37. Nietzsche writes: "With the smallest as with the greatest happiness, however, there is always one thing which makes it happiness: being able to forget or, to express it in a more learned fashion, the capacity to live unhistorically while it endures. Whoever cannot settle on the threshold of the moment forgetful of the whole past, whoever is incapable of standing on a point like a goddess of victory without vertigo and fear, will never know what happiness is, and worse yet, will never do anything to make others happy"[*On the Advantage and Disadvantage of History for Life*, trans. Peter Preuss (Indianapolis, Ind.: Hackett, 1981), 9].

    In the same spirit, we find later in the essay: "But there we will also find the actuality of an essentially unhistorical culture and a culture which is nevertheless, or rather therefore, unspeakably rich and full of life" (46). We must acknowledge that Nietzsche calls not only for such forgetting (that is, the unhistorical) but also for the suprahistorical (that is, the eternal) as well as for a critical historical sense. As for the last, it is the willfulness of Nietzsche's position that distinguishes it from that of Gadamer or Heidegger.

    In this same essay we find: "Only from the standpoint of the highest strength of the present may you interpret the past . . ." (37) and ". . . now it is proper to know that only the builder of the future has the right to judge the past" (38). Because of the central place of the will in Nietzsche's thought, it is appropriate to characterize it as a philosophy of subjectivity which, in any of its versions, Gadamer takes great care to avoid.

38. See especially the "Appendix" to Jürgen Habermas, *Knowledge and Human Interests*, trans. Jeremy Shapiro (Boston: Beacon Press, 1971), where Habermas distinguishes the empirical-analytic sciences, the historical-hermeneutic sciences, and the critique of ideology. Concerning the second Habermas writes: "Thus the rules of

hermeneutics determine the possible meaning of the validity of statements of the cultural sciences" (309). The footnote to this sentence reads: "I concur with the analysis in Part 2 of Hans-Georg Gadamer, *Wahrheit und Methode*" (348).

39. Hans-Georg Gadamer, "The Eminent Text and Its Truth," *Bulletin of the Midwest Modern Language Association* 13 (Spring 1980): 5.

40. Gadamer, "Eminent Text," 6.

41. See Gadamer's essay "The Hermeneutics of Suspicion" and my "The World Never Lost: The Hermeneutics of Trust," *Philosophy and Phenomenological Research* 47 (March 1987): 413-34.

42. Hans-Georg Gadamer, "The Problem of Historical Consciousness," *Graduate Faculty Philosophy Journal* 5 (1975): 3. Much in the same spirit, the concluding line of "Text und Interpretation" reads: "Der Interpret, der seine Gründe beibrachte, verschwindet, und der Text spricht" (*GW* 2: 360).

43. Gadamer, *GW* 2: 339-40.

44. Gadamer, "The relevance of the beautiful," 52: "When the complete experience of a work of art is genuine, however, what amazes us is precisely the unobtrusiveness of the performers."

45. Hans-Georg Gadamer, "Über den Beitrag der Dichtkunst bei der Suche nach der Wahrheit," *KS* 4: 221; in English, "On the contribution of poetry to the search for truth," in *Relevance of the Beautiful*, 109: "Now it is not only the poetic word that is 'autonomous' in the sense that we subordinate ourselves to it and concentrate all our efforts upon it 'as a text.' " He adds that both religious and legal texts call for this subordination as well.

46. Hans-Georg Gadamer, "Zur Problematik des Selbstverständnisses," *GW* 2: 127; in English, "On the Problem of Self-Understanding," in *Philosophical Hermeneutics*, 50-51. See also Gadamer, *WM*, 317; *TM*, 299: "Understanding is possible only if one forgets oneself." ("Nur der versteht, der sich selber aus dem Spiele zu lassen versteht.")

47. Gadamer, "Philosophy and poetry," 132.

48. Gadamer, "The relevance of the beautiful," 43.

49. Gadamer, "Philosophy and poetry," 137.

50. Gadamer, "Philosophy and poetry," 133.

51. Gadamer, *WM*, 450; *TM*, 432: "Sein, das verstanden werden kann, ist Sprache."

52. See Plato's *Republic*, trans. Paul Shorey in *The Collected Dialogues of Plato*, eds. Edith Hamilton and Huntington Cairns (Princeton, N. J.: Princeton University Press, 1961), 511c.

53. Gadamer, "Philosophie und Literatur," 42.

54. When Gadamer selects those distinctive modes of discourse that call for subordination he does not mention philosophy. See note 42 above.

55. Here, too, Gadamer paraphrases Plato, who characterizes the distinctiveness of philosophy as finding what is common among many. What allows the philosophical conversation of the dialogues to continue is agreement. See, for example, *Republic* 484b: "Since the philosophers are those who are capable of apprehending that which is eternal and unchanging, while those who are incapable of this, but lose themselves and wander amid the multiplicities of multifarious things, are not philosophers. . . ."

Part II

The Practice of Hermeneutics

4

Hermeneutics and Justice

Fred Dallmayr

Alles ist Spiel, aber Spiele . . . .
— Rilke

*P*aying tribute to a major intellectual figure such as Hans-Georg
Gadamer is an exhilarating and difficult task — exhilarating and
difficult for the same reasons: the vast scope and pervasiveness of his
work. In my own case, this work has served as a guidepost for so
many years that today I find it difficult to sort out precisely his
thought from my own (modest) endeavors. In a way, I was carried
along by his voice and example — and voices akin to his — so steadily
that, at some point, they ceased to be "influences," turning instead
into an imperceptible ambiance. Yet, I cannot call myself his student or disciple, never having received formal training under his
guidance. Instead of replicating or explicating his work, I prefer to
pursue (in an Oakeshottian vein) the subtle "intimations" of his
thought — its implications and relevances in domains not always central to his concerns. In the course of these explorations, I also
became aware of certain differences of accent and orientation, differences having to do with certain "postidealist" and poststructuralist leanings on my part — but that were never able to cancel a
deeper affinity. Even among its chief spokesmen, poststructuralism
(I believe) is not nearly as hostile to continuity as is sometimes
assumed. As Michel Foucault noted in 1970 — in a passage I find
deeply congenial — he would have liked at the time "to perceive a
nameless voice, long preceding me, leaving me merely to enmesh
myself in it, taking up its cadence, and to lodge myself, when no one
was looking, in its interstices as if it had paused an instant, in
suspense, to beckon to me."[1]

90

Given the scope of Gadamer's work, my tribute has to be selective. As it happens, the focus of my interests has for some time been placed not so much on general philosophical speculation but instead on issues in political theory or philosophy; thus, Gadamerian hermeneutics primarily attracted and preoccupied me from this angle or under these auspices. In fact, my first personal encounter with Gadamer carried strong political overtones in that it occurred in a politically highly charged situation. The encounter happened two decades ago, at the height of the academic turmoil associated with the Vietnam War and the waves of student demonstrations both in America and in Europe. I was a visiting professor then in Hamburg and decided at one point to utilize my stay in Germany to travel to Heidelberg. I should interject that I was in some ways mentally prepared for the visit. Gadamer's *Truth and Method* had appeared in 1960 and was the topic of intense debates both inside and outside of Germany. At least obliquely, these debates had entered my field of vision for a number of reasons. As a student and then academic teacher in America, I had been exposed to relentless efforts of colleagues bent on transforming the study of politics into an empiricist methodology devoid of historical moorings and experiential significance. Among some political theorists, this outlook had spawned a countermovement aimed at the restoration of classical, and especially Platonic, teachings — a revival promising "absolute" truth and whose claims seemed equally far removed from contemporary experiential dilemmas. In this situation, Gadamer's *Truth and Method* was a beacon: by recommending a dialogue between present and past, between readers and classical texts, in which present concerns were by no means dismissed but recognized as an integral part of a learning process. At the same time, the study deemphasized methodology (empiricist or otherwise) in favor of an open-ended search for truth, a search that remained ever mindful of the intermeshing of knowledge and ignorance and thus seemed wedded less to finished doctrines than to the Socratic model of inquiry.

So far, these perceptions were for me only pale intuitions, still tainted with the "greyness" of theory; nothing really prepared me for the actual encounter. When I arrived in Heidelberg, the university — including the philosophy institute — had been occupied by students, and classes and seminars had been cancelled; for all practical purposes, life at the university had come to a standstill. When I inquired about Gadamer's classes, I was at first reminded of the shutdown of academic activities; through further probing, however, I discovered that the shutdown was not entirely complete: the notable exception being Gadamer's course in contemporary philosophy. At the appointed hour I went to the lecture hall, located near the river; I found the large hall filled nearly to capacity by students quietly reading books and awaiting the appearance of their teacher. Needless to say, the contrast between the hall's hushed silence and the turbulence raging throughout the rest of the university was stunning. In due course, Gadamer appeared and proceeded to lecture for nearly two hours without interruption—or only interrupted by questions directly pertinent to his talk.[2] As I was told, the lecture was made possible by the respect and affection enjoyed by Gadamer among virtually all of the contending factions at the University. On me—reared in the heady ideological climate of the Cold War and its aftermath—the lecture had a profound effect, as it seemed to symbolize the precariousness but also the promise of philosophical reflection in public life. As a teacher, Gadamer appeared to me then (and still does) as the personification of the Socratic spirit: a spirit relentlessly committed to lively conversation in which all fixed positions are dissolved or transformed—though a conversation that is not aimless chatter but dedicated to the common search for a "truth" that never is allowed to congeal into a finished doctrine.

Since that first encounter in the midst of turmoil, I have been fortunate enough to meet and interact with Gadamer repeatedly over the years, both in his native surroundings and in America (where he was a frequent visitor during the 1980s). Still under the impact of the Heidelberg lecture, I returned immediately to a renewed reading of *Truth and Method*—where I found ample confirmation of Gadamer's conversational civility and of the political texture of his "philosophical hermeneutics." What particularly captured my attention on renewed study was the critique of aesthetic subjectivism, the vindication of the "common sense" tradition, the dialogical structure of interpretation, and the tensional correlation of communal beliefs (or *doxa*) and critical judgment. Not surprisingly, many of these themes resurfaced in my own fledgling investigations and "exercises" during the ensuing period; thus, bending the themes to my own concerns, I explored the role of "understanding" in social science inquiry, the experiential character of *praxis* or political action, and the interdependence of ethics and aesthetics—paying tribute to Gadamer as mentor steadily along the way.[3] However, the point of these pages is not merely retrospective—as if my debt was in the past tense; instead, I want to highlight the continuing and impending salience of Gadamer's thought both for myself and for intellectual discussions in our time. As it happens, the past few years have seen the publication of Gadamer's collected works—volumes noteworthy particularly for containing a wealth of materials antedating *Truth and Method* (and previously accessible in their entirety only to a narrow circle of experts). Thus, students and friends of Gadamer find themselves in the curious position of discovering, at a relatively late date, many new and youthfully engaging facets of his work—facets which are not simply preambles or prolegomena to *Truth and Method* but have a claim to independent attention.

For my purposes here, I want to single out for consideration two of Gadamer's early writings: namely, the 1934 essay, "Plato and the Poets," and the 1942 essay, "Plato's Educational State."[4] The selection is guided by several motives. First of all, both writings are exegetic commentaries on Plato's *Republic* and thus on a canonical text in political philosophy. More explicitly than in later phases, Gadamer's approach at that point has the character of a political or moral-political hermeneutics (in contradistinction to the philosophical-ontological variant). The political thrust of these writings is dramatically underscored by their historical context: both were conceived and published during the Nazi regime. Their import, however, exceeds this particular timeframe. In contemporary discussions, Gadamer's conversational outlook is sometimes equated with a shallow pragmatism and even with a *laisser-faire* liberalism devoid of normative yardsticks. This portrayal—already dubious against the backdrop of *Truth and Method*—is entirely disavowed in "Plato's Educational State" with its emphasis on a virtuous citizenry and especially on the overriding political virtue of justice. With regard to the latter issue, incidentally, his essay still contains lessons worth pondering today—when justice is often seen either as an abstract rule divorced from common practices or as a rhetorical ploy in the service of power. The essay's focus on *idiopraxis*, in particular, seems a useful way to highlight the differential or differentiating quality of justice — which does not coincide with role segregation or reciprocal indifference. In light of contemporary tendencies to approximate and even fuse philosophy and poetry, on the other hand, Gadamer's "Plato and the Poets" raises an important caveat — a reminder entirely predicated on considerations of political virtue or a virtuous *polis* and ultimately rooted in the contest between ethical-political action and "mimetic" reproduction.

The prominence of Plato in Gadamer's early writings was hardly fortuitous nor due to merely academic-philological interests. As to many German intellectuals, the Weimar period appeared to him as a difficult transitional era if not a time of profound malaise — an era when time-honored traditions had eroded or vanished without being replaced by new and stable moral-political practices. To this extent, the period resembled the situation of classical Athens at the time of Socrates and Plato when older moral bonds had disintegrated and the future of the city seemed to hang in the balance. The parallel has been stressed by Gadamer himself on several occasions. Thus, a 1930 essay dealing with Greek ethics contained these lines: "Classical Greek philosophizing occurred in the midst of a pervasive crisis of culture. How in the dissolution of the old this philosophy seeks to preserve tradition, how in the midst of divisiveness and discord [*Entzweiung*] it attempts a reconciliation with an older way of life — this aspect is congenial and intelligible to us due to the divisiveness of our own moral condition." Almost one-half century later, Gadamer in a partial autobiography referred to the ferment and malaise of his youth. "In the disarray unleashed by the first World War and its outcome in German life," he wrote, "the placid acceptance of a continuing tradition was no longer an option. Thus, confusion and lostness became primary impulses for philosophical questioning. . . . What we — the younger generation — were looking for at the time was a new (philosophical) orientation in a disoriented world."[5]

This sense of lostness and disorientation was undoubtedly intensified by the rise of the Nazi regime and the installation of a dogmatic ideology totally averse to philosophical reflection. Gadamer's turn to Plato's *Republic* during this time should be seen in this context. Contrary to charges of a collusion between Plato and "totalitarianism"—charges later advanced by Karl Popper and others—Gadamer found in Plato (or the Platonic Socrates) a profoundly oppositional figure—although, for purposes of self-preservation, this oppositional role was carefully disguised in the garb of classical scholarship.[6] Irrespective of personal caution, however, Gadamer's writings explicitly stressed the *political* background and significance of Plato's text, and, in fact, of all Platonic dialogues. Following the lead of other philologians, Gadamer took seriously the account in Plato's *Seventh Letter*: the account of his political misfortunes and frustrations and of his subsequent decision to seek a revival or rejuvenation of his city through philosophical means. Seen from this angle, Plato's *Republic* and his other writings were eminent modes of political action or practice at a time when all other modes were blocked due to the corruption of public life. More important, given this corruption, political revival in Plato's view could not be pursued naively or dogmatically but only reflectively or through philosophical awakening. In Gadamer's words: "The text of the *Republic* has its place not only in the philosophical but also in the political biography of Plato and must be defined in its character from this angle." This approach stands in stark contrast to the claim—defended by Leo Strauss and others—that Plato's philosophy marks basically an exit route from politics and that for Plato philosophical life was a higher and preferable alternative (reserved for the few) to the necessarily polluted life of the *polis*.[7]

Although stressing Plato's political biography, Gadamer did not mean to assert the immediate practical relevance of the *Republic* or its ready adaptability to Athenian conditions. Instead, the *Republic* was for him a "city in speech," an ideal and even "utopian" image—but an image that precisely as *eidos* could serve as yardstick (though sometimes only in an ironic sense) for any possible city. As he observed: "This state is a state in thought, not a state on earth. That is to say: its purpose is to illuminate something and not to provide an actual blueprint for an improved order in real-political life. Plato's state is an '*eidos* [*Urbild*] in heaven' for anyone wishing to properly order himself and his own constitution; its sole point is to allow self-recognition in this *eidos*." According to Gadamer, however, self-recognition at this point should not be construed in a modern individualist or subjectivist sense—which would suggest the withdrawal of the self from the state; rather, what was recognized by the "self" was its character as a citizen or political being. Only because of the internal multiplicity or "intersubjectivity" of the self was it possible for Plato to present the state as a large-scale mirror of the "soul." Whoever recognizes himself in the *eidos*, we read, "does not recognize himself as an isolated, stateless or apolitical individual: he discovers in himself the ground upon which the state is built (however deformed or degenerate the actual state may be)." To underscore the communal or civic character of self-recognition Gadamer pointed to the concrete backdrop of Plato's educational state: the experiential context of the Platonic academy as a "community of investigators." For this academy, he noted, was not merely an "apolitical society of scholars" but rather a community whose rigorous investigations were meant to lead to a result that was unattainable for sophistic types of education: namely, to "a rediscovery of justice in one's own soul and thus to the formation of citizenship or *political human beings*."[8]

These comments touch on the crucial nerve of Plato's *Republic*: the centrality of justice or *dikaiosyne* as primary political virtue—where justice does not merely stand for legal rule or distributive arrangements but denotes more broadly fairness, right-mindedness and civic conscience. In Gadamer's account, Plato's basic message or counsel could be boiled down to this: "[O]nly justice can secure the stability and continuance of the state; and only one who is a friend to himself can gain the solid friendship of others." These two sentences, he noted, "contain the whole of Plato's political philosophy, by disclosing the essential correlation between state and soul, and also between politics and philosophy." The linkage of politics and philosophy at this point is due to the fact that justice is not simply a natural gift or native talent but a difficult achievement requiring the transcendence of narrow selfishness and the ability to perceive oneself in a larger communal context; this opening or transcendence, however, is the result of educational seasoning, preeminently the work of philosophical reflectiveness (where philosophy means "love of wisdom" and thus still carries erotic connotations). Given the situation in his native Athens, the initial impulse propelling Plato's political philosophizing was the stark question: "How was Socrates possible, the just man in an unjust city?" For, under the influence of sophistic teachings, *dikaiosyne* had lost its quality as a civic bond and had turned into a ploy or counter in the unbounded contest of self-seeking interests. More than anyone else, it was Socrates who revealed the core of sophistic education: namely, "that justice is only the prudential agreement among the weak; that *ethos* does not prevail on its own account but only as a form of reciprocal distrust and policing; and that 'right' is observed only out of mutual fear"—and not because rightness is a medium of self-recognition. Against this corruption of the city and civility, Plato's *Republic* intoned the encomium of justice in its genuine sense: to the effect that rightness or justice denotes not "the right one has *against* others" but rather a mode of "being just" (*Rechtsein*), which is a being of each by himself and of all jointly. To wit: "Justice does not mean a state where each watches and guards against the other, but one where each guards and watches over himself and over the 'being just' of his own constitution."[9]

Again, this kind of self-guarding or self-regard should not be confused with a simple concern for inwardness. In his essays, Gadamer is careful to differentiate "being just" from the cultivation of private morality—a point that, no doubt, reflected in part his own effort to distance himself from his neo-Kantian background in Marburg. Although radically opposed to merely prudential maxims, *dikaiosyne* in Plato's sense was a public rather than an inner-private virtue. "In contradistinction to Kant," he noted, "Plato's purpose is not to erect an inner-moral world of the unconditionally good will beyond or outside the realm of political *praxis;* instead his aim is to demonstrate the politically creative and *polis*-sustaining potency of the human soul, its political fertility [*gonima*] as it were, out of which arise the state and what is right and just." The distinction is reiterated in other passages with even greater sharpness and poignancy. "The inwardness of justice," we read at one point, "is certainly not an inwardness of disposition, not that good will which

97

'alone of all things in the world may be called good' (Kant). On the contrary, Plato's inwardness is both the measure and the origin of all genuine outward manifestation in human *praxis*; thus, it is not a sanctified realm of the heart known only to God but rather an order of governance and an ontological constitution of the soul which maintains and fulfills itself in every action." As can readily be seen, Gadamer's exegesis carries distinct overtones of Hegelian *Sittlichkeit* — although the concept is nowhere explicitly invoked in this context. Likewise, his comments evoke the Aristotelian legacy of *ethos* seen as an ontological framework undergirding the notion of man as "political animal." "The ontological status or genuine being of man," Gadamer observes in a counterindividualist vein, "is not of the sort that he promotes his own welfare and advancement in opposition to the state and that right and justice only are functions of reciprocal vigilance and distrust. Instead human existence is so constituted that the very being of the state — that which renders the state possible and which persists minimally even in its most corrupt forms — is anchored in the soul of its citizens, that is, in the 'idea' of justice."[10]

Moving beyond general considerations, Gadamer's essays proceed to a detailed discussion of the various opinions or arguments regarding justice advanced in Plato's *Republic* — a discussion whose complexity exceeds my aim in these pages; a few highlights must suffice. Starting from the opening of the *Republic*, Gadamer initially comments on the view of Simonides — "telling the truth and paying one's debts" — noting both the time-honored status and the vacuity of the definition, at least when judged by the reflective needs of the classical age. Carefully differentiating between living tradition and a shallow traditionalism he states: "Being so uncritically at home in the simple dictates of cult and custom is no longer possible for [Polemarchus], the son and heir [of Cephalus]. . . . Rather, he is forced to account for what he claims to know." Radically in contrast with cult and custom stands the sophistic claim of Thrasymachus that justice is nothing but the advantage of the stronger. Probing and critically dissecting this claim, Gadamer shows the basic untenability of the thesis, not as a theory of power or domination but as an account of justice — because the advantage of the powerful or the ruler consists precisely in the right-mindedness and justice of the ruled (which thus is presupposed): "The advantage of the stronger resides exactly in not being perceived as such [that is, as brute advantage] but as being a just or rightful position. The imposition of justice through mere power does not explain why the imposition is viewed not as coercion but as rightful and just." More subtle but no less defective than the coercive claim is the view of conventionalism (or contractarianism) advanced by Glaucon in the second book of the *Republic*. Gadamer at this point reiterates his and Plato's opposition to a purely "pragmatic" or liberal-utilitarian approach to politics. Here justice is assumed to derive from an agreement or convention among individuals predicated on "prudence and an awareness of one's own weakness"; the status of justice in this case remains purely conditional "for it obviously depends on a correct assessment of [fluctuating] power relations."[11]

In light of the historical context of Gadamer's essays, another thesis deserves particular mention: the view, derived from Simonides's arguments, that justice means helping one's friends and hurting one's enemies. As one may recall, Carl Schmitt in 1932 had published *The Concept of the Political* in which politics was identified with the stark division between friend and enemy.[12] Given the continuing repercussions of this thesis in our time, Gadamer's comments have more than academic relevance. Together with Plato he questions first of all the restriction of justice to warfare or war-like contests — noting that in peacetime the distinction of parties is not nearly as clear-cut, as little as is the meaning of "helping" and "hurting." However, even in warfare or war-like situations, the friend-enemy dichotomy is not nearly as univocal or unambiguous as claimed. Above all, it is far from clear that "being a friend" involves only a common front against an enemy and whether justice can at all be equated with a utility (or disutility) function or an instrumental capacity (to help or to hurt). Although "hurting one's enemy" may seem an unequivocal maxim, we must ask "whether this is the same as being just and whether justice consists in the superior exercise of a capacity" — that is, "whether it involves not much more a being than an ability." Differently phrased: the question is "whether the idea of justice does not imply a shared orientation toward the Good or the order of the Good — an orientation that, where it obtains, embraces even the enemy as one whom we do not actually wish to harm but only to set right by force?" This orientation, Gadamer adds, applies not only to domestic factions but possibly also to international politics or relations between states. Written during World War II and in the face of Hitler's brutal military expansionism, these lines acquire special resonance: "Not accidentally the reformulation of Simonides's view is ascribed to tyrants such as Periander and Xerxes—men whose self-image is based on brute power or their domineering capacity and whose talk of justice always carries with it their presumed superiority over all others. *Tyrants have no friends.*"[13]

These lines are a proper foil to the centerpiece of Gadamer's essays: the discussion of genuine justice in the *Republic,* focussed on the parallel or analogy between *polis* and the soul. As will be recalled, justice in the *polis* is portrayed by Plato as the balanced correlation between different public bodies or estates, each characterized by a distinct kind of excellence or virtue. "The ancient normative table of *patrios politeia,*" Gadamer comments, "recurs in Plato's so-called cardinal virtues—virtues which are curiously interwoven or interlaced and all permeated by a Socratic reflectiveness." While to the rulers is ascribed wisdom or the readiness of "thinking for everyone," courage is the proper quality of the warriors or auxiliaries—but "not the brute animal-like courage of the fighter, rather the political courage of the man using weapons for the sake of all and never for himself." Temperance, in turn, is assigned to all classes, rulers and ruled alike, namely, as the unison of the "thinking for everyone" and the "fighting for everyone" carried on by the governing groups. Justice of the *polis*, finally, consists in something "presupposed in all these estates and their distinctive virtues: namely, in doing one's own thing or '*idiopraxis*' which is required in the laboring estate as well as in the ruling groups and which alone secures the unity of the *polis.*" A similar harmonious relationship of elements is found by Plato in the properly constituted human soul—which, as indicated, is the seat and origin of justice in the *polis.* According to the *Republic*, three basic parts of the soul correspond to the three civil estates: reason (or love of knowledge), spiritedness, and desire. While desire involves an "attraction to something" and reason a grounded discrimination between "yes" and "no," spiritedness denotes an "engagement" in the alternatives of "yes" and "no." For Plato, the proper ordering of the parts of the soul "becomes a metaphor for the structure of the cardinal virtues," and justice appears "as the same kind of excellence as in the state: namely, as *idiopraxis* of the parts of the soul matching that of the estates." An action accordingly is just which reflects this order of the soul in a both creative and preserving manner.[14]

As Gadamer is careful to note, *idiopraxis* or "doing one's own thing" should not be misconstrued as the mere juxtaposition or segregation of functions after the model of the industrial "division of labor." In such a functional model, the unity of the whole derives in a quasi-organic or quasi-mechanical fashion from the functioning of the various parts, with each part remaining a self-contained unit unconcerned with the operation of other parts. Regarding the "wholeness" of the *polis* and the soul, Gadamer insists, "it is of decisive importance that 'doing one's own' does not gain its political sense of justice as a mere instance of the principle of the division of labor" or of a technical-mechanical correlation of parts. In functional-economic terms, we may speak of the simple coordination and integration of productive forces in a larger mode of production. In contrast to this economic model, doing one's own as "being just" involves precisely self-transcendence or self-transgression of parts in the direction of others and a political community; to this extent, *idiopraxis* is simultaneously an *allopraxis* — not in the sense of meddling in others' affairs, but in that of an opening to the "otherness" of the *polis* (which turns out to be not simply an "alien" otherness but constitutive for the own or self). In Gadamer's words, the ruling group in the *polis* is engaged in "thinking and acting for all," where both action and inaction are permeated by "holistic" concerns. Similarly, every worker or artisan in the *polis* is not simply a cog in the productive apparatus, but relates as a "citizen" directly to the whole of the state, through participation in or attunement to the web of political relations. On the other hand, perversion of *idiopraxis* through meddlesomeness, selfishness, or exploitation is the sure path to the corruption and disintegration of the city — as illustrated by the decay of Athenian democracy. In a similar vein, confusion of its internal parts sets the soul on the road toward pathology, that is, toward schizoid conflict and divisiveness (*Selbstentzweiung*). Recovery in this case depends on the restoration of inner balance, that is, on the soul's ability "in the diversity of its drives and strivings to achieve harmony and friendship with itself."[15]

According to Plato (and Gadamer), however, psychic wholeness and public justice are not simply the result of natural endowments operating on their own accord. Contrary to the regenerative power of physical nature and of the bodily organism, psychic and public "health" or well-being requires deliberate nurturing and cultivation. As Gadamer writes: "The healthy soul is not simply in the hands of a benevolent nature or in possession of a naturally good constitution prevailing on its own. Rather, the soul knows of the danger of dissonance because it must deliberately aim at self-harmony—which means that the latter is a constant task." This is the reason why Plato's *Republic* is an "educational state" or a state of *paideia*—where education means both character formation and citizenship training. Education in this context denotes both a deliberate molding or transformation and a restoration to wholeness or *restitutio in integrum.* To achieve well-being and justice, the parts of the soul and of the state must overcome selfishness or self-enclosure; that is, they must accomplish self-transcendence or self-transgression—but a transcendence that does not simply equal self-destruction or radical "alienation." Rather, precisely by exiting from self-centeredness, the soul and the citizen discover what is most properly constitutive of the self and the city: namely, well-being and justice, which means friendship with self and others. Plato's theory of the parts of the soul and their correlation, Gadamer comments, seeks to correct "a *dissonance* inherent in the 'nature' of man"; it attempts "a reconciliation of the irreconcilable: the conflict between wildness and peaceful civility." The guardians of the state—whose education is the focus of the *Republic*—are not "just by *nature*, so that one would only need to develop their native potential." Rather, "*paideia* [*Bildung*] is necessary precisely in order to blend the strife of their natural dispositions into a harmonious *ethos.* To this extent, the guardian class is *the proper estate of human beings*"—because guardianship of self or self-guarding is constitutive of being human.[16]

Seen against this background, Plato's doctrine of the soul is not a part of empirical psychology but an eminently ethical and political theory. Inseparable from the notion of cardinal virtues, the doctrine recounts the drama of inner divisiveness and the recovery of wholeness. "Whether the soul is one or many," Gadamer states, "whether it is uniform or a multi-headed monster, this is not a question of scientific psychology but a task for the proper conduct of life." Not being a natural gift (nor being against "nature"), *idiopraxis* requires careful training and seasoning—which in large measure is the work of thoughtfulness or reflectiveness. This accounts for the role of philosophy in Plato's *Republic*, a role not rigidly restricted to a narrow caste but permeating all parts of the soul and the state. As Gadamer notes, Plato strikingly compares the philosopher with the "lover" and philosophical reflection with the workings of "eros"—an apt comparison because both are peculiarly lodged at the intersection of self and other, of immanence and transcendence. As with reflection, love extricates the self from its native prison and opens it to the "other"—who turns out to be not a total stranger but the beloved or friend. At the same time love, unlike and transcending desire, does not seek the possession or absorption of the other, but rather nurtures and cherishes the other's autonomy (in a mode of "letting be"). In preserving the intersection of self and other, love just as philosophical reflection also respects the correlation of knowledge and ignorance—by never claiming perfect or absolute knowledge (of self or other). Political education in Plato's sense, we read, is "anything but indoctrination in a finished or predetermined ideology. Precisely by inquiring behind or beneath traditional moral conceptions it offers a new experience of justice; thus, this education is not an authoritative manual based on an ideal structure but rather lives from questioning alone."[17]

Plato's assessment of poetry needs to be seen in the framework of this "educational state." As Gadamer insists, the proposed banishment of poets implies not a general critique of art or artistic training, but derives its sense solely from the educational aims of the *Republic*. In his words: "The meaning and intent of this critique of the poets is determined entirely by its context: it is advanced in Plato's work on the 'state,' as part of an educational program for the state's guardians—a state which is erected before our eyes in speech alone out of its required or suitable building blocks." Plato's *Republic*, in turn, was predicated on the assumption of the erosion of traditional moral bonds or a communal *ethos* and hence on the need of reconstructing the city and public justice through reflective means. The question that arose at this point was whether traditional poetry—a poetry content with the mimetic portrayal of ordinary life—was adequate for this reconstructive task, a question Plato answered negatively. At a time when public spirit was moribund or decayed, Gadamer comments, "the possible educational role of poetry was turned into its opposite. For citizens captivated by the teachings of Thrasymachus and other sophists, the world of poetry—which for generations had provided exemplars of a higher life to young people—came to attest the perversion of spirit itself." Mimetic poetry, in Plato's view, merely imitated prevailing abuses, without any effort to differentiate between virtue and vice and without advancing beyond prudential-utilitarian construals of ethics: starting from heroic and Homeric times, no one had bothered "to condemn injustice or to praise justice for its own sake." Against this background, Plato's *Republic* was meant to inaugurate and exemplify a new kind of poetry or literary-philosophical genre: namely, as an encomium or hymn of praise to justice. His city in speech, Gadamer states, was designed to "intone the true praise of justice which would remain victorious over the sophistic corruption of its meaning." More generally, Plato's dialogues pursued a therapeutic or recuperative goal in the midst of cultural and political malaise. For, where justice is reduced to an "inner sense no longer corresponding to a shared reality" and where its status requires deliberate legitimation, there philosophical dialogue about the *polis* "becomes the only genuine praise and account of justice. The Platonic dialogue constitutes this song of praise"—a song that "in its playful portrayal of the educational state does not forget the serious issue of the formation of citizenship and the cultivation of justice."[18]

As Gadamer admits, Plato's indictment of poetry may seem to betray intellectualist hybris or a moralistic conceit; the attack on Homer and his legacy, in particular, may appear as an excess of puritanism. What renders this "excess" tolerable or at least intelligible, however, is the educational and profoundly political aim of Plato's *Republic*: the aim of rebuilding the *polis*. In light of this practical-political goal, his indictment cannot be dismissed blandly—especially not in our own age of mass culture and commercialized art. For, where commercial productions limit themselves to the imitation of existing behavior patterns, including violence and corruption, how can their effect be otherwise than humanly and politically demeaning? Only in the mode of *catharsis* (in Aristotle's sense) can art and poetry regain its ethical and political status—a mode where violence is portrayed *as* violence (rather than as routine behavior), corruption *as* corruption (rather than as "the way of the world"), and human misery and suffering *as* misery and suffering, whose depiction serves as catalyst for empathy and moral-political engagement. Without this cathartic effect, imitation becomes readily an invitation to apathy or self-indulgence. In Gadamer's words: "The experience of delusory imitation is in itself the incipient ruination of the soul. For, as made evident by the depth analysis of the soul's 'inner constitution': aesthetic self-oblivion grants to the sophistry of desire entry into the human heart." Against this background, Plato's critique can be translated into a vindication of a different type of art and poetry—one mindful of its catalytic and transformative role: "Exemplary art, in revealing a common *ethos*, is more than an external dramatization, more even than the descriptive portrayal of a model: it is a way of giving efficacy to the model in and through the artistic presentation."[19]

Gadamer's commentary on Plato's *Republic* has lost none of its stirring quality since its first publication. No doubt, the urgency of his observations was heightened by their immediate political context: the total destruction of public justice brought about by Nazi tyranny and ideological manipulation. In his later writings, his general outlook has somewhat mellowed and his comments on public life have tended to be more subdued—which may be the result both of personal intellectual maturation and of the decreased urgency of political conditions in the postwar period. Yet, despite changes in mood and philosophical formulation, many of the themes in Gadamer's early essays are still present in his later work, and especially in *Truth and Method*. Thus, the attack on imitation or on a purely receptive-reproductive type of art resurfaces in the critique of "aesthetic consciousness" seen as self-abandonment to the flow of sensual images, and the latter's subordination to ethical praxis or practical life-conduct. Similarly, the vindication of cathartic art recurs in the endorsement of Greek tragedy (especially the tragedies of Aeschylus), and more generally in the conception of art as the playful-serious enactment of existential or ontological predicaments, particularly of the interplay of finitude and transcendence. In terms of the ethical themes of Plato's *Republic*, Gadamer's later work tends to underscore the affinities between self-recognition and the Hegelian "struggle for recognition" and also between *paideia* and the experiential path of the "phenomenology of spirit." Above all, the early focus on *idiopraxis* held open the possibility of an ontological construal of justice in line with Hegel's *Sittlichkeit* — although this orientation remained more implicit than explicit in the later opus.[20]

To be sure, despite underlying continuities, some of the accents emerging in later writings were bound to affect and perhaps even jeopardize some earlier assumptions or arguments. A prominent case in point is the emphasis of the early writings on "wholeness" and on the integration of the parts of the soul and the city into a comprehensive "unity." In this respect, Gadamer's later explorations of Plato's ontology, especially of the complex relationship between the "one" and the indeterminate "two," have introduced considerations no longer strictly compatible with a unitary focus. A similar decentering effect has been entailed by his reflections on language (partly inspired by Martin Heidegger) — that is, the realization that language and cultural traditions form an inexhaustible background that can never be represented or made intelligible as a whole. Obviously, notions of this kind cast doubt on the rational unity of the state and thus invite a reformulation of the Platonic *polis* — a task Gadamer has bequeathed to his students and friends. Guideposts for this task lie abundantly ready in his later writings. As he writes in his 1968 essay, "Plato's Unwritten Dialectic": "If we are indeed forbidden to seek a fixed deductive system in Plato's teachings and if, on the contrary, his doctrine of the indeterminate 'two' establishes precisely the impossibility of completing such a system, then Plato's conception of ideas presents itself as a general theory of relationships which convincingly entails the infinite and unending character of the dialectic." What this insight yields is not a sophistic collusion or undecidability of truth and falsehood, but awareness of the interminable character of the search for truth which can never be summed up in a univocal doctrine. "Plato," he adds, "views the finitude of searching human beings from the vantage of the distance from an all-knowing God, a view which apart from its religious significance bears on dialectic as well. Yet, the incompleteness characterizing all human thinking and knowing, just as all earthly existence, does not diminish the magnificence and wonder of the path of human inquiry which always occurs in a field of openness [or nonclosure]."[21]

Notes

1. Michel Foucault, "The Discourse on Language," in *The Archaeology of Knowledge*, trans. A. M. Sheridan Smith (New York: Pantheon Books, 1972), 215. For a discussion of some of the mentioned differences, see my "Hermeneutics and Deconstruction: Gadamer and Derrida in Dialogue," in *Critical Encounters* (Notre Dame, Ind.: University of Notre Dame Press, 1987), 130-64.

2. The topic of the lecture, as I recall, was the relation between Husserl and Heidegger, a theme liberally enriched by references to classical Greek philosophy. I might add that it was chiefly Gadamer who facilitated my access to Heidegger's work (which subsequently became quite crucial to my own development).

3. See Fred Dallmayr and Thomas McCarthy, eds., *Understanding and Social Inquiry* (Notre Dame, Ind.: University of Notre Dame Press, 1977), esp. 285-365; also my *"Praxis* and Experience," in *Polis and Praxis* (Cambridge, Mass.: MIT Press, 1984), 47-76; and my "Hermeneutics and Deconstruction: Gadamer and Derrida in Dialogue."

4. See Hans-Georg Gadamer, "Plato und die Dichter" (1934) and "Platos Staat der Erziehung" (1942), in *Griechische Philosophie I*, vol. 5 of *Gesammelte Werke* (Tübingen: J. C. B. Mohr, 1985), 187-211, 249-62. *Gesammelte Werke* will be abbreviated hereafter as *GW* followed by volume number and page. The volume also contains Gadamer's longer habilitation thesis written under Heidegger's direction and entitled "Platos dialektische Ethik" (1931); but the thesis is mainly a commentary on Plato's *Philebus*. For an English translation

of the two essays, see Gadamer, *Dialogue and Dialectic*, trans. P. Christopher Smith (New Haven, Conn.: Yale University Press, 1980), 39–92.

5. Hans-Georg Gadamer, "Praktisches Wissen" (1930), in *GW* 5: 230, and "Selbstdarstellung" (1975), in *Hermeneutik II*, vol. 2 of *GW* (Tübingen: J. C. B. Mohr, 1986), 479–80.

6. The 1934 essay was preceded by these lines from Goethe: "Whosoever philosophizes is in disharmony with the opinions of his predecessors and contemporaries; thus the dialogues of Plato are directed not only *at* something but also *against* something." Commenting on the essay Gadamer observed later: "The publication documented my position regarding National Socialism already in its chosen motto: 'Whosoever philosophizes is in disharmony with the opinions of his time.' To be sure, the statement was disguised as a citation from Goethe and continued with his characterization of Plato's writings. Yet, short of becoming a martyr or of going voluntarily into exile, such a motto signaled to the perceptive reader at a time of ideological conformism the assertion of a differential stance." See *GW* 2: 489 and *GW* 5: 187.

7. See Gadamer, *GW* 5: 249, and *Dialogue and Dialectic*, 73 (in this and subsequent citations I have slightly altered the translation for purposes of clarity). Regarding Leo Strauss, see his *What is Political Philosophy?* (Glencoe, Ill.: Free Press, 1959), 92–94; also my "Political Philosophy Today," in *Polis and Praxis*, 15–46; and "Politics Against Philosophy: Strauss and Drury," in *Political Theory* 15 (1987): 326–37. In my view, Strauss's thesis is marked by a modernist bias—the preference for individual privacy—which is distant from both Plato and Gadamer.

8. Gadamer, *GW* 5: 194, 197, 249; *Dialogue and Dialectic*, 48–49, 52, 73. The phrase "community of investigators" is taken from Peirce and is not actually used by Gadamer.

9. Gadamer, *GW* 5: 195–96, 251–52; *Dialogue and Dialectic*, 50–51, 75–76.

10. Gadamer, *GW* 5: 256, 258–59; *Dialogue and Dialectic*, 82, 86.

11. Gadamer, *GW* 5: 253, 255–56; *Dialogue and Dialectic*, 78, 81–82.

12. See Carl Schmitt, *Der Begriff des Politischen* (1932; new ed., Berlin: Duncker and Humblot, 1963); for an English translation, see *The Concept of the Political*, trans. George Schwab (New Brunswick, N.

J.: Rutgers University Press, 1976). Cf. Paul Hirst, "Carl Schmitt's Decisionism," in *Telos* no. 72 (Summer 1987): 15-26.

13. Gadamer, *GW* 5: 253-54; *Dialogue and Dialectic*, 79-80 (italics mine).

14. Gadamer, *GW* 5: 257-58; *Dialogue and Dialectic*, 83-86.

15. Gadamer, *GW* 5: 257-58; *Dialogue and Dialectic*, 84-86.

16. Gadamer, *GW* 5: 198, 260; *Dialogue and Dialectic*, 54, 88. As Gadamer adds, *paideia* is not merely a natural process—nor is it simply unnatural. For, although some talents or dispositions must be "naturally" given, "man becomes a political being only *insofar as he resists the temptations of power arising from flattery.* This means: he must learn to distinguish the true friend from the false one and the truly just from flattering appearances. This, however, is the work of philosophy: to love the true and resist the false." See *GW* 5: 200; *Dialogue and Dialectic*, 56-57.

17. Gadamer, *GW* 5: 197, 259, 261; *Dialogue and Dialectic*, 52, 87-88, 90. In the above I have inserted some Heideggerian notions or considerations into Gadamer's account.

18. Gadamer, *GW* 5: 193, 195-96, 207; *Dialogue and Dialectic*, 48, 51, 66-67.

19. Gadamer, *GW* 5: 195-96, 206-207; *Dialogue and Dialectic*, 50-51, 65-66. Regarding the status of art and poetry, compare also Hans-Georg Gadamer, *The Relevance of the Beautiful and Other Essays*, trans. Nicholas Walker, ed. Robert Bernasconi (Cambridge: Cambridge University Press, 1986).

20. See Hans-Georg Gadamer, *Truth and Method*, trans. Sheed and Ward Ltd. (New York: Seabury Press, 1975), 10-19, 80-119, 316-24; also his *Hegel's Dialectic*, trans. P. Christopher Smith (New Haven, Conn.: Yale University Press, 1976), and my "Rethinking the Hegelian State," in *Margins of Political Discourse* (Albany: SUNY Press, 1989).

21. Hans-Georg Gadamer, "Platons ungeschriebene Dialektik," in *Griechische Philosophie II*, vol. 6 of *GW* (Tübingen: J. C. B. Mohr, 1985), 151-53; See *Dialogue and Dialectic*, 152, 154. He concludes: "The indirect tradition which informs us of the principles underlying Plato's teachings is not evidence of some esoteric dogma concealed behind his written work which could possibly undermine our understanding of

Plato's dialectic. Rather, it articulates and confirms the limited contingency of all human knowing and thus shows why the highest possibility of such knowing must be called not *sophia* but *philosophia*." See *GW* 6: 155.

5

Legal Hermeneutics: Recent Debates

David Couzens Hoy

1. Law as the Hermeneutical Paradigm

*H*ans-Georg Gadamer maintains in *Truth and Method* that the law provides us with the best example for thinking about how interpretation works.[1] His theory, however, has received more attention from other disciplines. In the United States, extensive interest in Gadamer's hermeneutics first came from those who worked primarily in literary studies. Yet, the law is in many ways unlike literature. In particular, the law must be applied by judges to present cases, and it must be applied in decisive ways that make a real, material difference not only to the disputing parties, but to anyone in a related situation. Interpretation always involves *application*, argues Gadamer, and as the clearest example of the interconnection between understanding and application, legal interpretation becomes the paradigm for Gadamer's construction of his hermeneutical philosophy.

Not only does the law provide the primary exemplar of application, it also serves to illustrate his notion of *Wirkungsgeschichte*. The judge's application of the law to a present case depends not only on an understanding of the language of the statute, but of the intervening history of interpretation of that statute or precedent. The practice of maintaining consistency with precedent, which in the law is known as the doctrine of *stare decisis*, illustrates Gadamer's notion that a tradition of interpretation always conditions our understanding, whether we know it or not. However, interpreters can fail to recognize this point, and they can thus fail to cultivate the hermeneutical self-consciousness that Gadamer calls *wirkungsgeschichtliches Bewußtsein*.

Recent debate about the Supreme Court's powers in interpreting the Constitution provides an excellent example of a theoretical position, called *originalism*, that fails to manifest this hermeneutical self-consciousness. Held mainly by conservatives, originalism is the view that judges should rule only in conformity to the original intentions and norms of the framers or ratifiers of the Constitutional provisions. Because hermeneutics is the area of philosophical debate in which one issue is the relation of interpretation to the original intent, it should take the legal controversy seriously. Some theorists who could be called hermeneutic theorists do subscribe to the theory that intent determines meaning (for instance, Schleiermacher or E. D. Hirsch). However, the major tendency of hermeneutic theorists since Martin Heidegger and Gadamer has been to drive a wedge between textual meaning and authorial intent. In the second section of this chapter, I extrapolate from Gadamer's theory and formulate the major hermeneutical arguments against originalism.

Once the text is cast off from the original intentions of its creator, though, the question arises whether it can constrain its interpretation and application, or whether anything goes. Hermeneutics as formulated by Gadamer denies that textual meaning can be reduced to the *author's* intentions, but it also denies that textual meaning is therefore determined by the *interpreter's* intentions. Interpretation cannot be willed arbitrarily, but is constrained by both the text and the context. To suggest only one argument hermeneutics can advance for this claim, a text is unlike a single sentence or utterance in being a more complex phenomenon than is accounted for by the usual tendency to take the interpretation of isolated speech acts as the paradigm of interpretation. Within a text, a sentence is constrained by its inherence in a context formed by the other sentences. Interpretation of a text requires the double activity of maximizing its coherence and intelligibility without minimizing its internal tensions, polysemy, and the possible undecidability of some of its parts.

Textual interpretation of the U. S. Constitution supplies an example of this point. Interpreting the Constitution requires an interpretation not of each part in isolation from the other parts, but rather of the entire document. One interpretation could be superior to another, for instance, if it showed that a particular part normally thought to be empty or redundant had a specific use. Coming to recognize that specificity might entail restricting the interpretation of other clauses that had previously been thought to be doing the work now attributed to the clause formerly thought to be redundant.[2]

Gadamer's denial that textual meaning is a function of intention (whether the author's or the interpreter's) thus stands in opposition to the thesis of recent intentionalists (such as Attorney General Edward Meese and Robert Bork in the law, and Walter Benn Michaels and Steven Knapp in literary theory) that the best interpretation is best simply because it captures authorial intention. Gadamer's own thesis about what makes the best interpretation best can be stated loosely as the claim that the best interpretation captures what the text has said that is true about the subject matter (*die Sache*) at stake in the text.

His position thus differs to some extent from the recent theory of legal interpretation developed by Ronald Dworkin in his latest book, *Law's Empire*.[3] Dworkin's theory agrees with Gadamer's on more points than they disagree, but I will suggest in criticism that although Dworkin has argued against reducing interpretation to authorial intention, as has Gadamer, he has not freed himself sufficiently from intentionalism, and has come too close to reducing textual meaning to *interpreter's* intention. As a result, I suggest that his own thesis that the best interpretation is the one that interprets the text in its "best light" does not serve him well in his attempt to distinguish his own position from that of the critical legal studies movement in his attack on the movement.

Critical legal studies and hermeneutics have both been criticized by opponents who fear that freeing interpretation from the constraints of intention will lead to interpretive nihilism, where interpreters are free to impose arbitrary readings on an indeterminate text. I believe that hermeneutics does not lead to nihilism, and I suggest some ways in which critical legal scholars could avoid the charge as well. But what I emphasize (in section three) is that critical legal scholars could borrow arguments from hermeneutics and resist the tendency in Dworkin's theory of interpretation to espouse what I call *critical monism*. Intentionalists are usually

critical monists because they think that there is a single interpretation that is correct because it captures the author's intention. But
critical monism is conceptually distinct from intentionalism, and I
define it, for now, as the view that all the questions about all the
features of a text must be postulated as being resolvable, at least
ideally. For critical pluralists, interpretation need not aspire to such
an ideal, and interpretive disagreements can be reasonable without
being univocally resolvable. Dworkin rejects intentionalism, but at
times he seems to subscribe to critical monism. Gadamer's theory
parts ways with Dworkin's (correctly, I believe) in avoiding critical
monism. After the following section in which I present the
hermeneutical critique of intentionalism, I show in the concluding
section how hermeneutics should steer an admittedly tortuous
course between the shoals of monism and nihilism.

2. The Hermeneutical Critique of Originalism[4]

Gadamer's and Dworkin's theories share an interest in
mediating between the past and the present. They both
acknowledge that interpretation of texts must be aware of the origin
of the text in a particular time and place. Yet, they both think that
texts address us from within the present context and not merely
from a dead past. Dworkin shows his affinity to hermeneutics in that
he appeals more than once to Gadamer, "whose account of interpretation as recognizing, while struggling against, the constraints of
history strikes the right note."[5] But he cites Jürgen Habermas in ex-
plaining where he parts ways with Gadamer. Habermas thinks that
Gadamer is too conservative, and too respectful of the authority of
the text. In contrast to Gadamer's supposedly "too-passive" and one-
directional attitude, whereby the interpreter must finally defer to
the text, Dworkin allies himself with Habermas's insistence that "the
author could learn from the interpreter."[6] Dworkin proposes that
his own theory of constructive interpretation best accounts for the
possibility not only of interpretation, but more importantly, of
criticism.

Instead of dwelling on these differences at the start, however, I
suggest we consider Dworkin and Gadamer mainly as allies in that,
like Dworkin, Gadamer develops his theory from a rejection of a
narrow intentionalism. Given the current legal debate, Gadamer

would be opposed to originalism for he thinks that a text has a life of its own once it has left the author's hands. However, his theory does not support the belief sometimes attributed to antioriginalist views that a text can be interpreted exclusively in the light of present-day concerns, disregarding its history. Gadamer's claim is not primarily about the question whether the interpreter should disregard anything other than either the original intentions or our present values. His view entails that either attempt would fail in any case. A text is not a thing-in-itself, but has meaning by virtue of inhering in a *Wirkungsgeschichte*, the intervening history of the interpretations a text has had. On Gadamer's theory, we can understand a text only through this intervening history. This history, more than some abstract theory, forms the context for our understanding of the text. We may not be aware of this history, and may think that we are understanding the text in an unmediated way, or as it was originally intended, or in the only way it could possibly be understood. But we can also develop our hermeneutical awareness of how our understanding is influenced by an intervening history. Gadamer's term for this hermeneutical awareness is *wirkungsgeschichtliches Bewußtsein*. We are better off becoming explicitly aware of how the intervening history conditions our interpretation, and this can be done by historical study, for example, of precedent. In any case, our reading is conditioned by the document's history of interpretation, even if we try to disregard it. The belief that one has returned to the original understanding is inevitably in error.

If we can be shown some ways in which our understanding differs from the original understanding of the U. S. Constitution, Gadamer thus would insist that from those particular differences it does not follow that we could ever free ourselves from this history of intervening interpretations and see the Constitution exactly as it was originally seen. At most, we can see how some intervening interpreters misinterpreted the original document, but we do this because we now see why that intervening interpreter had purposes that led to a misreading. We no longer share those purposes, and therefore can see the intervening mistake. But this fact does not entail that we are returning to the purity of the original understanding of the text. For one thing, we can now see how the language of the document could have led to that intervening misreading, and we thus read the document differently than it could have been read originally when that misreading was not foreseen. For another, we can assume that our own purposes may be coloring even our best interpretation, and that later interpreters will come to perceive mistakes that we cannot now perceive.

This recognition of our fallibility does not make our position irrational, and need not lead to nihilistic conclusions. We can say that although the intervening interpretation was mistaken, we can think that the mistake was a reasonable one. We might even say it was the best interpretation that could have been given at the time, despite being mistaken in a particular respect. If we think that future interpreters could grant us the same acknowledgement, we need not be insecure or indecisive in our best interpretive efforts. Interpretation can be reasonable and fallible at the same time.

Looking at the present legal scene, then, Gadamer's theory clearly has affinities with Justice William Brennan's liberal understanding of interpretation, precisely because on that view the central moment of interpretation involves this *wirkungsgeschichtliches Bewußtsein*. If interpretation is always conditioned by the intervening history of interpretation, then Attorney General Meese's conservative insistence on sticking to the original intentions represents an impossible task. I would even argue that the view that really leads to an irrational relativism or nihilism is not hermeneutics but originalism, because it is irrational to try to do what is known to be impossible (for instance, trying to find the last value of π).

But there is a further, more subtle contrast between Gadamer's theory and Meese's originalism. Meese's theory is perscriptive, in that it says that original intention is the only proper criterion for correct interpretation. It demands, therefore, that the interpreter adopt originalism. Gadamer is not making the same claim about the *wirkungsgeschichtliches Bewußtsein*. While the criterion of "connection to the tradition" can be a central one for an interpreter in justifying the preferred interpretation, it is not the only one. Hermeneutics should not be taken as advocating a doctrine of strict precedent, and it could recognize the occasional need to overrule precedent because of conflicts with contemporary norms.[7] The authority of precedent is not claimed by hermeneutics to be indefeasible, as the authority of original intention is by originalism.

So I would differentiate between the "prescriptive" or "commanding" character of originalism, and the merely "commendatory" character of the hermeneutic emphasis on developing an explicit awareness of the intervening tradition. By *commendatory* I mean that hermeneutic awareness comes in degrees and can be used to distinguish degrees of better and worse (more reflective and less reflective) interpretation. But these appraisals of interpretations are only matters of degree, and no claim can be made to be the "single best" or the "only correct" result. In contrast to the commendatory account that suggests at its strongest a recommendation about what would be better to do, I am using "prescriptive" not in its legal sense, but in its moral or medical sense to mean a strict command that something must be done to get the right result.

The hermeneutical claim is the recommendation that we are better off understanding how we came to have the particular reading of the text and the situation that we do. More reflection on the intervening history would make us in general less dogmatic. Acquiring this hermeneutical awareness may also benefit us in specific ways, because it could show us that we are not as frozen in one understanding of what the problem is as we might think. But the historical study necessary to understand the intervening history of interpretation is inevitably going to remain incomplete, and we will never uncover all the presuppositions or *Vorurteile* that condition our understanding. At most, then, increasing our hermeneutical awareness of the connection to the intervening tradition is a recommendation, not a command or a strict prescription. Hermeneutics is not offering a single criterion, or even a lexically ordered set of criteria, as guaranteeing the validity of interpretations.

If legal hermeneutics were to make the *wirkungsgeschichtliches Bewußtsein* and the connection to the tradition prescriptive, the effect would be similar to strict precedent in British law, where judges are radically constrained by the closest prior case. But in a judicial system such as ours without such constraint hermeneutics properly understood could argue that strict adherence to immediate precedent to the exclusion of all other factors involves the same misunderstanding of interpretation as originalism does. Even if the prior decision is much closer to us in time than the original intentions, it would still need to be interpreted in the light of *both* the new situation and the history of the development of the current reading. Hermeneutical awareness would focus on the prior history as a developmental one. The normative force is the recommendation that the judge consider how this development leads to the current situation and how the decision makes explicit certain features of the development that were only implicit before. This process of the implicit becoming explicit is one aspect of the hermeneutic circle of understanding.

Precedent on this hermeneutical account is not a rule that determines its future applications, but itself comes to be reinterpreted. Precedent is thus an important norm, but not a strict prescription determining the next application. Gadamer's account of precedent thus has some affinities with Dworkin, who insists that history matters in his conception of law as integrity, and that the doctrine of strict precedent is too narrow. Dworkin's argument depends on a special distinction, however. He insists that although history matters, consistency with the past is a value for law "only so far as and in the way its contemporary focus dictates."[8] Dworkin thinks it is possible for integrity of *principle* to trump consistency in *policy.*

Gadamer's theory has no comparable distinction between principle and policy, and while his hermeneutics would not deny that considerations about principle are important, the distinction could not be as decisive as Dworkin thinks. Most important, the distinction could not help in bringing about Dworkin's claim that there must be a right answer as to what is the correct and best interpretation. While hermeneutics does not want to abandon the idea that interpretations can be said to be right, its stress on the historical evolution of interpretation prevents it from asserting that there must be only one interpretation that is right.

Gadamer's more Aristotelian and less Kantian view about moral judgment does not appeal to the formulation of principle as much as Dworkin's does. Gadamer emphasizes instead Aristotle's notion of *phronesis,* or practical wisdom, which is a matter more of perception than principle. Knowing principles is one thing, but something more is required to perceive the situation as one in which right action is needed. On Gadamer's account, the history of intervening interpretations (i.e., precedent), is conditioning the way we even see the situation and the way we understand the conflict involved, including what kind of conflict it is. Reflecting on principle may be required by confronting a situation calling for a legal decision, but reflection alone does not determine practical perception.

To explain Gadamer's point, commentators such as Dagfinn Føllesdal and myself have stressed the similarity between the hermeneutic circle of understanding and what John Rawls has called *reflective equilibrium*, the attempt to understand a moral situation by balancing our principles and intuitions. This analogy will become problematic later when I turn to questions about law's authority and its criticism. For now I wish to note only that sometimes we will change our understanding of our principles and their force, but sometimes we may also find that our intuitions change. There is no priority here, and no drive to articulate all our intuitions or our prejudgments as explicit principles, an impossible task anyway. Achieving equilibrium is never a final affair, for new situations may disturb the equilibrium.

Phronesis or practical wisdom cannot be taught, nor can it be explained to those who do not have it. With it, however, one gets better at seeing what the situation calls for, and what counts as appropriate or inappropriate responses. Obviously, this description of practical wisdom does not tell us how to judge cases, but that does not mean it lacks a philosophical point. The description is intended to cut against other philosophical pictures that misrepresent how understanding and interpretation work in practice. But the description is not prescriptive and will not legislate how to make a specific judgment. On the contrary, its intent is to make us suspicious of any theory such as originalism that purports to prescribe exactly how judgments must be made.

In addition to these theoretical problems with originalism, practical problems occur as well. For one thing, the author's or authors' intention may not be available. In such a case, to identify the reading with the intention would be an empty stipulation. For another, legal clauses are not simply authored, but they must be legislated or ratified. What would be important, therefore, would be the intention not of the authors but of those who gave the language authority. Clearly, however, different ratifiers could have understood the clause differently, so there is no reason to believe it means only one thing.

This issue about why intentionalists generally speak of the intention or the meaning in the singular comes up again when it becomes necessary to ask whether the framers would have wanted constitutional clauses to apply only to cases they envisioned and not to unanticipated cases as well. The generality and abstractness of some clauses in the Constitution (in contrast to other, carefully detailed ones) suggests that the framers intended them to be interpreted to cover cases and situations unlike any they would have immediately known how to decide themselves. Hence, a hermeneutical judge who recognized that she was "supplementing" the Constitution in considering cases that the framers could not have anticipated, such as wiretapping, would not thereby have to believe she was "changing" rather than simply "interpreting" the law.

Originalists might reply that the clause is general only if it was intended to be general, but they would then need to specify exactly what can go into an intention. Does the intention include simply the words of the statement, for example, "due process of law," or does it include tacit provisos such as "due process in a procedural sense" or "due process in a substantive sense"? There are different kinds of intention involved in any single act. This complexity suggests that even intentionalism does not necessarily entail critical monism.

Hermeneutics tries to describe the conditions for the practice of interpreting the law rather than legislating a "method" or "theory" that will stand outside the practice of legal interpretation, grounding and guiding it. Therefore, it must account for the fact that judges and lawyers sometimes look to legislative histories for evidence about the original intention, and that precedents have been overruled to restore the original understanding.[9] Such cases might suggest that hermeneutics should not deny intention any role in interpetation, but should at least recognize that the features of the original situation can be taken into account in constructing an interpretation.

More radically, however, I believe that the idea of interpreting the original meaning of the text is too vague an idea to supply even a regulative ideal for interpretation. At best, we can say that a particular meaning could not have been intended at the time, but that does not tell us much about what really was understood at the time. And what do we mean by "at the time"? There is no better reason for including only the biographical authors and not their contemporary audience. Such an audience is itself an interpretive construct because we are not talking about what distinct historical individuals *did* understand, but of what they *could* have understood. Constructing such an ideal model is not radically different from what we do ourselves in coming to our own understanding of the text.

I can now summarize the hermeneutical critique of originalism, a critique to which not only Gadamer, but also Dworkin and his opponents, the critical legal scholars, could agree. In contrast to the originalists' isolation of questions of understanding from questions of application, hermeneutics maintains that understanding cannot abstract entirely from its present context of application. Interpretation always occurs in a current context that is conditioned by the history of the prior interpretations leading up to it and giving it a particular perspective. A text is invariably seen through the lenses of the intervening history and tradition of interpretations. Hermeneutical theory suggests only that an interpretation that was more conscious of this intervening history would be better and less dogmatic than one that was less conscious of it. Hermeneutics is thus less prescriptive than the constitutional theory that identifies original intention as the only criterion for correct interpretation. Hermeneutics is not saying that connection with the tradition is the only relevant criterion. It can recognize that precedents are sometimes overruled because they conflict with contemporary norms.[10] The authority of precedent is not indefeasible both because other criteria exist for preferring some interpretations over others, and because no single lexical ordering of such criteria will provide an algorithm for deciding between interpretations.

3. Steering between Nihilism and Monism

Given the likelihood of agreement on these basic hermeneutical tenets, I now turn from the controversy between conservative and liberal legal theorists to that between liberal and radical legal theorists, using Dworkin's recent book to focus the issues. In *Law's Empire*, Dworkin spells out a general theory of interpretation that he then applies to the special case of legal interpretation. His conclusion is that, "Law is an interpretive concept."[11] The interpretive character of the law should not lead, he believes, to skepticism about the possibility of reaching right answers on questions of interpretation. Skepticism leads in turn to nihilism, the view that "theoretical disagreement is only disguised politics."[12] Nihilism is, however, a hasty inference from the failure of philosophers to prove that lawyers all use "the same factual criteria for deciding when propositions of law are true and false."[13] With the movements of both legal realism and critical legal studies in mind, Dworkin says, "Some academic lawyers . . . say that past institutional decisions are not just occasionally but almost always vague or ambiguous or incomplete, and that they are often inconsistent or even incoherent as well. They conclude that there is never really law on any topic or issue, but only rhetoric judges use to dress up decisions actually dictated by ideological or class preference."[14]

Whereas nihilism is the view that no interpretation can ever be justified, and all are only ever arbitrary, intentionalism insists that there is a final justification for interpretation, and that this justification comes from the extent to which the interpreter has captured the authors' intentions. Although Dworkin criticizes intentionalism, I want to suggest that certain traces of it find their way into his own theory of constructive interpretation. Toward the end of the book he argues that the law should be construed as having an ideal integrity, including conceptual coherence and moral purpose. This integrity is achieved only by postulating that the law is written by a single author, the community personified: "The adjudicative principle of integrity instructs judges to identify legal rights and duties, so far as possible, on the assumption that they were all created by a single author—the community personified—expressing a coherent conception of justice and fairness."[15] Of course, the community personified would be a different author from the original framers, and is more obviously a construct of the interpreter. The effect of Dworkin's theory is intended, I believe, to shift attention from the author to the interpreter, thereby opening his theory to the charge of relativism.

To deflect relativism, as well as its attendants, skepticism and nihilism, Dworkin maintains that a formal or structural feature of interpretation is that the interpreter must be showing the object of interpretation *in its best light*.[16] This is the core of what he calls *constructive interpretation*. Initially specified as being appropriate for the special case of the "creative" interpretation of literary works, this feature is then generalized to *all* interpretation: "The constructive account of creative interpretation, therefore, could perhaps provide a more general account of interpretation in all its forms. We would then say that all interpretation strives to make an object the best it can be, as an instance of some assumed enterprise, and that interpretation takes different forms in different contexts only because different enterprises engage different standards of value or success." So Dworkin claims that constructive interpretation is the best general account of interpretation in *all its forms*.[17] Constructive interpretation on Dworkin's view is necessarily optimistic about the final success of achieving integrative coherence in a body of law that is admittedly produced in a haphazard manner.

Why should we think, however, that the law is a coherent whole? If it is, why should we think that practical interpretation succeeds in approximating it? Would a moderate skepticism be healthier than Dworkin's imperialistic optimism? Could we remain open to doubt about the final convergence of interpretation on a single, complete, and coherent doctrinal whole? An alternative to law's optimism is "law's cunning," which Dworkin says is "only another name for the ability of good judges to impose whatever order they can . . . on a historically haphazard process."[18] Although Dworkin implies that insisting on law's cunning would necessarily lead to nihilism, I can think of at least three attitudes toward law's cunning, and not all would entail nihilism.

1. The first attitude would be that of optimistic pragmatists. Their hope would be that well-trained, well-intentioned judges would do reasonably well in imposing doctrinal order. The expectation might be that, as in Kant's notion of the cunning of nature or Hegel's idea of the cunning of reason, the order might come about as a result of the overall efforts of all judges, despite the relative success, failure, or deviations of particular decisions.

Such a view, for instance, would hope that despite the great gaps and discontinuities in the history of the U. S. Supreme Court, such as the divide between the Lochner era and the Warren Court, or the abyss that might open in the future with the Rehnquist Court, there would still be a progressive story that could be told about emergent doctrine and the cunning triumph of judicial reason.

2. A second attitude would be more negative, and even nihilistic. This attitude is often attributed to the critical legal studies movement. Where the first attitude sees order emerging from proper legal training, the second sees legal education as a euphemism for a cunning ideological indoctrination reinforcing the unjust institutions of a perpetually divided society. The appearance of legal order might be a mask over social forces that if unleashed would show the underlying social reality to be something resembling war or even chaos.

3. If this is the attitude of some critical legal scholars, however, it is not that of all of them. Roberto Unger is one such scholar who is incredulous about the hopes of the first attitude, but his superliberalism does not convey the pessimism of the second attitude. A third attitude is thus possible that would be less negative than the second. Given incredulity about finding order in the haphazard history of the legislative process, but optimism about judges' abilities to produce a better society, judges could be advised to use the interpretive strategy of interpreting the law not to reinforce the existing institutions that stratify society, but to subvert them. Instead of valuing social stability, such judges will value social change. Their ideal would be the "cumulative loosening of the fixed order of society."[19] Change comes about by breaking up the reified divisions and thereby multiplying social and political options. The critical judge could therefore try to "recognize and develop the disharmonies of the law: the conflicts between principles and counterprinciples that can be found in any body of law."[20] This attitude apparently would be trying to maximize incoherence instead of coherence. But it would still be optimistic that in the long run justice (and perhaps coherence between legal doctrine and social reality) thereby would be produced.

So law's cunning need not lead to a nihilistic attitude. But the more general hermeneutical issue that emerges concerns what happens when the constructive, optimistic interpretive attitude espoused by Dworkin falters or fails. Are critical judges no longer interpreting if they share any of these three attitudes toward law's cunning? Unlike Dworkin, I still call their activity "interpretation" because, as I understand the word, it does not necessarily entail the constructive optimism about the object and values being interpreted. On my view, although achieving the best fit for its own sake is not all there is to interpretation, the best interpretation is not necessarily one that sees the particular text or object in the best or most favorable light.

Could someone believe that our current society was, if not wicked, at least wildly erratic in its interpretive applications of justice and fairness? The critical legal scholars do not seem to share Dworkin's belief that one can take the constructive interpretive attitude toward current law. Their view, if I understand it correctly, is that doing so is self-deceptive. Therefore, the following suggests some probable rejoinders to Dworkin from their perspective, before drawing some hermeneutical conclusions about the debate.

Dworkin's theory of legal interpretation argues for his optimistic belief in the correctness of decisions by supposing that an ideal interpreter would be able to see the coherence and completeness of the law, even if we finite interpreters cannot. He calls this ideal interpreter *Judge Hercules*. The proponents of law's cunning could argue against Dworkin that modelling legal reasoning on an ideal judge such as Hercules is illegitimate. Dworkin is certainly right that too much is claimed when some critical legal scholars urge that the law is shot through with contradictions, and those contradictions invalidate the entire legal process. Because in legal interpretation we are not dealing with abstract principles of formal logic but with concrete principles of morality and legality, propositions that sound contradictory can always be shown to be merely competing by adjusting the context. However, because Unger speaks more cautiously of "disharmonies," the issue is not settled by Dworkin's dismissal of "contradiction." The issue is better joined by asking whether critical legal scholars would need to admit Dworkin's stronger claim that in the limit these competing principles always can be reconciled in the harmonious whole that Hercules can see, even if we cannot. Dworkin's holistic optimism would supply metaphysical comfort to those who shared it, but the critical scholars could resist the argument that every interpretation must share it. They could follow Nietzsche in being suspicious of attempts to provide metaphysical comfort by methodological means.[21]

Contrary to Dworkin, I think that an interpretation that identified principles that were deeply disharmonious could count as an interpretation. Dworkin's view seems to entail that such an interpretation would be incomplete until it went on to explain how to reconcile the competing factors. However, while an ideal judge such as Hercules "can aim at a comprehensive theory," Dworkin admits that the interpretations of real judges "must be partial."[22] Even Hercules is said to "know that the law is far from perfectly consistent in principle [and thus not merely in policy] overall."[23] Hercules is himself forced finally to distinguish between what Dworkin calls *inclusive integrity* and pure integrity to compensate for tensions between the demands of due process and fairness in policy as well as the principles of justice. As opposed to *pure* integrity, which is the coherence the law as a whole would have if judges could attend only to principles of abstract justice, *inclusive* integrity is the maximal coherence of present law, taking into account not only justice, but also both fairness (consistency with past practices) and procedural due process.[24] However, knowing that there are tensions in the law as it stands now and maintaining nevertheless that interpretation must aim at holistic coherence seems to force even Hercules into bad faith. Hercules is saved from bad faith only by the further distinction between consistency (with the past) and coherence, or integrity as the expression of the ideal will of the community in "a single, coherent scheme of justice and fairness in the right relation."[25] Only Hercules, however, can know that this single scheme and therefore this ideal will obtain. For the rest of us these would be metaphysical postulates, or at least methodological regulative ideals for interpretations that remained optimistic only because their final redemption and success could be indefinitely deferred.

Dworkin's apparent assumption that real interpretations are always only ever partial or incomplete because they approach, but never achieve, the ideal limit of completeness measures human understanding and interpretation against hopeless ideals. If any interpretation could be said to be complete only if we had reached the final synthesis that Hercules envisions, then interpretation is an activity that aims to eliminate itself by shading off into absolute knowledge. But I think interpretation is not a poor cousin to knowledge and is not forced to think of its practical results as deficient because they are only ever partial. While interpretations always can be adjusted and expanded, I doubt that incomplete ones can be distinguished from complete ones in any definitive way, because I think the idea of a *complete* interpretation is not one that can be made sufficiently clear. How could we know that we had captured all the features of anything? Distinguishing complete from incomplete interpretations builds into the concept of interpretation an unnecessary and counterproductive commitment to an exaggerated idealism and holism.

I think the critical legal scholars could resist Dworkin's argument in one more theoretical issue. Dworkin admits that the major threat of the critical movement is that it "aims to show, not merely that different ideologies produced different parts of the law, but that any competent contemporary justification of these different parts would necessarily display fundamental contradictions of principle, that Hercules must fail in imposing a coherent structure on law's empire as a whole."[26] This does express a central objection to Dworkin's optimism, but his response is to shift the burden of proof: "Nothing is easier or more pointless than demonstrating that a flawed and contradictory account fits as well as a smoother and more attractive one. The internal skeptic," he adds, "must show that the flawed and contradictory account is the only one available."[27] On Dworkin's own account of interpretation, however, controversy is always inevitable. So *no* account, not even Hercules's, could be shown to be the only one available.

The critical scholars might therefore shift the burden back to Dworkin. They could point out that all attempts to prove complete coherence and integrity have failed so far, so there is no reason to believe that Hercules could succeed. Inevitability of failure in practice is as damaging a result as failure in theory. So if the holism built into the assumptions about what Hercules can do are beyond our reach, that in itself provides us with a reason for not trying to imitate him. Not even the greatest optimist can rationally try to do the impossible.

Instead of arguing against Dworkin further, however, I suggest another tactic critical legal scholars could try: subverting Dworkin's theory precisely by accepting it. They need not admit that they were trying to see the statute in its worst light. They could claim that because they believed they lived in a stratified society the laws of which preserved social division, by seeing the law as disharmonious rather than harmonious, they *are* seeing it in the best light. The best we could do, on their account, might be to see existing law as lacking "inclusive integrity," or complete coherence. The project of the critical scholars would be to make this lack of inclusive integrity as apparent as possible, perhaps in the interest of better achieving the "pure integrity" of abstract justice in the end. They would thus be doing to Dworkin what Marx claims to do to Hegel, namely, to put Hegel's dialectic, which is said to stand on its head, back on its feet.

If this strategy of reversal were possible, however, I would point out to both parties in the dispute that there would not then seem to be a necessary connection between the theory of interpretation and the political uses to which it could be put. I raise this point to question whether the method of constructive interpretation entails the political commitment to the substantive, optimistic belief that our existing law expresses our personified will as a community of principle. However attractive this belief is, I have trouble convincing myself that it is more than a useful fiction, or that it could follow necessarily from a theory of interpretation in general, or of legal interpretation in particular. Interpretive *method* and substantive *politics* may not necessarily entail each other.

Do we need to believe that by using methods such as optimistic construction or nihilistic deconstruction in reading a "sacred" legal text such as the Constitution we must be either blindly perpetuating or else completely undermining its authority? These alternatives do not seem to be the only possible ones, but the question raises the disturbing thought that because interpretations reflect social divisions and political commitments, there may be no right answers about the interpretation of legal texts and no likelihood of consensus. This point brings me back to the distinction between critical monism and critical pluralism. *Critical monism* is the view that all the questions about all the features of a text must be postulated as being resolvable, at least at the ideal limit. *Critical pluralism* is a response to this view and maintains that monism represents philosophical overkill. For pluralists, disagreements can be reasonable without necessarily being resolvable. Dissent can be rational without presupposing ideal convergence or consensus.[28]

Given this distinction, which cuts across that between constructive and deconstructive interpretation, how should critical legal studies and Dworkin be classified? Critical legal scholars might be tempted to imitate deconstructionists who go beyond pluralism toward the explicit nihilism of the claim that an infinite number of interpretations are possible and that conflicts of interpretation can never be rationally adjudicated. Thereby, they may be assuming that deconstruction will work every time because textuality is inevitably duplicitous. But the a priori thought that deconstruction will reveal textual incoherency *in every case* seems no more defensible than the claim that construction optimism will be able to reveal some ultimate unity in the law as a whole.

What about Dworkin? His insistence on right answers appears monistic, yet his acknowledgment of genuine disagreement in legal practice suggests critical pluralism. I consider his theory's great virtue to be its insistence on the *critical* potential of interpretation. Despite his insistence on the drive of interpretation toward monistic coherence, and toward right answers, there is a (perhaps contradictory?) recognition and affirmation of the inevitability of disagreement and dissent. Dworkin argues that the ideal of law as integrity does not preclude political disagreement, but on the contrary, holds to the idea that some disagreement is a good thing.[29] Law as integrity "not only permits but fosters different forms of substantive conflict or tension within the overall best interpretation of law."[30] So although he holds that legal judgments are "pervasively contestable,"[31] he does not conclude from the essential contestability of interpretive concepts to the standard conclusion that there is therefore no single, right answer. On the contrary, he thinks that denying there is a right answer is a mistake resulting from overestimating the force of skeptical arguments.[32]

By arguing indirectly against the denial of right answers rather than directly for such a postulation, Dworkin has not fully explained how he can have both contestability and correctness. The question is whether asserting that judicial reasoning is right or wrong entails believing that there is only one right way for the reasoning to go, or that there is a single "best light." I also do not object to Dworkin's claim that our interpretations are always colored by our evaluations of what is required by the subject matter. Dworkin cites Gadamer, who maintains that our understanding of a text will be guided by our preunderstanding of the subject matter. But Gadamer's view, I have suggested, is that we will not necessarily force the text to bear out our preunderstanding, and we sometimes do *learn* from texts, that is, we change our own preunderstanding of the subject matter.

This point does not entail, however, respect of the text to such a degree that when the eminent text's understanding of the subject matter conflicts with one's own understanding, one must concede authority to the text. In drawing this consequence from Gadamer's theory, Habermas and Dworkin may be misconstruing Gadamer and overstating their own claims for constructive interpretation. Gadamer may want to "save the text" as much as possible, whereas Habermas has a different case and a stronger point in mind. The object of interpretation may be a text, but Habermas is thinking in particular about cases in anthropology where the rationality of the self-understanding of the tribe being interpreted is in question. When the agent's understanding conflicts with ours, Habermas wants to hold open the possibility that it must be criticized, and its competing claims to correctness, rationality, and authority rejected.

I think Gadamer could reply to Habermas that invalidating another's understanding is not the primary goal of interpretation. Gadamer could claim instead that efforts must be made to grasp whatever is being interpreted in an appropriate way, exercising caution about imposing inappropriate features of "our" context on others. Clearly, however, the appropriateness of context is itself a matter of interpretation. What does guide any interpretation, according to Gadamer, is some understanding of the *subject matter* or *die Sache* at stake in the interpretation. So if the legal statute concerns abortion or private sexual acts, the interpreter will invariably have some commitments to what is permissible, either for the agents or for the law's regulation of the agents. But the understanding of

130

die Sache could be modified by the confrontation with situations not previously imagined.

This circular, hermeneutical process of reaching understanding resembles Rawls's description of attaining reflective equilibrium between the preunderstanding, or one's intuitive sense of the issue, and the conceptual articulation of this understanding. Rawls offers some qualifications, however, that I think should be remembered. The goal of reflective equilibrium in his book is to reach a conception of justice, but not one that is deduced from self-evident premises. Instead, the conception is to be justified through "the mutual support of many considerations, of everything fitting into one coherent view."[33] However, Rawls also remarks that the reflective equilibrium is not necessarily stable, but is always subject to disruption by further examination of principles and cases. I assume that Hercules's reflections could always be destabilized as well. Is there then a *final* reflective equilibrium at which Hercules could intelligibly aim? Rawls mentions some difficulties with the notion of reflective equilibrium conceived as being "presented with all possible descriptions to which one might plausibly conform one's judgments together with all relevant philosophical arguments for them"; he remarks: "To be sure, it is doubtful whether one can ever reach this state. For even if the idea of all possible descriptions and of all philosophically relevant arguments is well-defined (which is questionable), we cannot examine each of them."[34] He then raises further questions: "Does a reflective equilibrium (in the sense of the philosophical ideal) exist? If so, is it unique? Even if it is unique, can it be reached?"[35] But he refuses to take a stand on these questions, probably because he finds them unanswerable in principle.

If Rawls hesitates on the limited problem of specifying a conception of justice, I see all the more reason to be less optimistic about what even a Hercules could achieve in the much broader task of justifying the entire body of law. In my view, Dworkin has imposed too strong a requirement even on Hercules. I conclude by supplementing his arguments in one limited way, however. For me it is significant that he thinks that he can have *both* contestability and correctness. The reason is that, unlike Habermas in one crucial respect, he does not make agreement or consensus a central condition of justified interpretation. While he thinks we want to be a single community, he also recognizes that a community of principle is not always of one mind, even ideally. Hence, coercion through law might still be necessary under a fully legitimized rule of law. Justice is what the law aspires to in the ideal, and whether agreement follows is another issue. So an outcome of Dworkin's theory (and also, I believe, of Gadamer's) is that we can hold to our interpretations, and think they are right (or at least reasonably well justified), without presupposing (in Habermas's fashion) that everyone else would accept them, even under ideal conditions.

The concept of an ideal community does not seem to require the strong principle of ideal convergence and consensus, but only the weaker principle of respecting and reflecting dissent and disagreement. Where Gadamer and Dworkin might be agreeing on this issue, however, they could still part ways on whether to set as a condition of understanding the strong requirement that there be ultimately only one right interpretation. This idea seems to require having a complete and coherent account of a clearly delimited domain of facts. But if we can carve up our contexts differently, and if some contexts are too large or complex to delimit sufficiently, the requirement threatens to condemn us to permanent irrationality.

Rationality in my view does not require interpreters to infer that each of their interpretations is the only possible right one. There is nothing unreasonable about both believing one's own reading and at the same time believing that there are probably some features, perhaps central ones, that must be revised. These considerations make me hesitate to impose critical monism as a methodological presupposition on all interpretation. They also lead me in reading Dworkin to value most those moments in his theory showing that interpretation thrives best in a climate of significant and substantial disagreement.

At the same time, if denying critical monism entails that one is a critical pluralist, I also want to distinguish critical pluralism from relativism and nihilism. Critical pluralism implies that interpretations can legitimate themselves sufficiently by claiming that they are better than other competing interpretations. Critical pluralism does not see the need to insist more strongly that insofar as the interpretation is the best that one now has reason to accept, it is the best in general, or that it is correct because it comes closest to what the ideal best interpretation would be. If interpretations are always underdetermined by the evidence, then the idea of the *single* best interpretation goes by the board. But by insisting on the possibility of distinguishing better from worse interpretations, critical pluralism shows that it does not avow relativism, however pessimistic it may be about arbitrating particular disputes. Relativism, after all, is uncritical. Even critical legal nihilism could not accept the idea of uncritical tolerance of all possible positions, because it objects precisely to what it takes as the dominant and presumably repressive strategies of current legal interpretation. I conclude that both monism and nihilism go beyond what is required to make sense of the adjudication of conflicts of legal interpretation, and that a more moderate, hermeneutical pluralism suffices.

Notes

1. See Hans-Georg Gadamer, "Die exemplarische Bedeutung der juristischen Hermeneutik," in *Wahrheit und Methode* (Tübingen: J. C. B. Mohr, 1965), 307–23; for English, see *Truth and Method*, trans. Sheed and Ward Ltd. (New York: Seabury Press, 1975), 289–305. Portions of the following article have been excerpted from my longer essay, "Dworkin's Constructive Optimism v. Deconstructive Legal Nihilism," *Law and Philosophy* 6 (1987): 321–56, and are used here with permission of that journal. Research for this article was supported with a National Endowment for the Humanities Fellowship for College Teachers.

2. See John Hart Ely on the ninth amendment in *Democracy and Distrust: A Theory of Judicial Review* (Cambridge, Mass.: Harvard University Press, 1980), 34–41.

3. Ronald Dworkin, *Law's Empire* (Cambridge, Mass.: Harvard University Press, 1986).

4. *Originalism* is the term in law for intentionalistic approaches to legal meaning, and here I use *intentionalism* and *originalism* interchangeably. For a detailed discussion of originalism in legal theory, and particularly of Michael Perry's account of it in *Morality, Politics, and Law* (Oxford: Oxford University Press, 1988), see my "A

133

Hermeneutical Critique of the Originalism/Nonoriginalism Distinction," *Northern Kentucky Law Review* 15 (1988): 479–98, as well as my "Interpreting the Law: Hermeneutical and Poststructuralist Perspectives," *Southern California Law Review* 58 (1985): 135–76.

5. Dworkin, *Law's Empire*, 62.

6. Dworkin, *Law's Empire*, 420.

7. This need is reflected in the case of the Supreme Court on *Harper v. Virginia State Board of Elections* (1966).

8. Dworkin, *Law's Empire*, 227.

9. See *Erie R. R. v. Tompkins* (1938).

10. See the Supreme Court on *Harper v. Virginia State Board of Elections* (1966).

11. Dworkin, *Law's Empire*, 410.

12. Dworkin, *Law's Empire*, 10.

13. Dworkin, *Law's Empire*, 43.

14. Dworkin, *Law's Empire*, 9.

15. Dworkin, *Law's Empire*, 225.

16. Dworkin, *Law's Empire*, 52–53.

17. Dworkin, *Law's Empire*, 53.

18. Dworkin, *Law's Empire*, 409.

19. Roberto Unger, *Critical Legal Studies Movement*, 96 *Harvard Law Review* (1983): 563, 584.

20. Unger, *Critical Legal Studies Movement*, 578.

21. See the conclusion of Friedrich Nietzsche's later preface (called "Attempt at a Self-Criticism") to *The Birth of Tragedy* where he criticizes his early work for seeking metaphysical comfort. *Basic Writings of Nietzsche*, ed. Walter Kaufmann (New York: Modern Library, 1968), 26.

22. Dworkin, *Law's Empire*, 265.

23. Dworkin, *Law's Empire*, 268.

24. Dworkin, *Law's Empire*, 405.

25. Dworkin, *Law's Empire*, 219.

26. Dworkin, *Law's Empire*, 273.

27. Dworkin, *Law's Empire*, 274.

28. Whether consensus is a necessary presupposition of communicative discourse, as Habermas argues, is challenged by Jean-François Lyotard, who celebrates dissensus in *The Postmodern Condition: A Report on Knowledge*, trans. Geoff Bennington and Brian Massumi (Minneapolis, Minn.: University of Minnesota Press, 1984).

29. Dworkin, *Law's Empire*, 88–89.

30. Dworkin, *Law's Empire*, 404.

31. Dworkin, *Law's Empire*, 411.

32. Dworkin, *Law's Empire*, 412.

33. John Rawls, *A Theory of Justice* (Cambridge, Mass.: Harvard University Press, 1971), 21.

34. Rawls, *Theory of Justice*, 49.

35. Rawls, *Theory of Justice*, 50.

6

Walzer, Rawls, and Gadamer: Hermeneutics and Political Theory

Georgia Warnke

> Once again I appeal to Gadamer whose account of interpretation as recognizing, while struggling against, the constraints of history strikes the right note.
>
> — Ronald Dworkin

*A*t first glance, Ronald Dworkin's appeal to Hans-Georg Gadamer in *Law's Empire* for an account of interpretation that not only recognizes the constraints of history but struggles against them seems odd.[1] Surely Gadamer's philosophical hermeneutics encourages us not to struggle against those constraints but to accept them. We are situated within historical traditions and subject to the "effective-history" (*Wirkungsgeschichte*) of the ideas, norms, and standards they develop. Even our attempts to escape these criteria remain conditioned by them; on Gadamer's view, either we accept much more than we admit from the tradition we are trying to reject or we reject it for its failings with regard to standards it itself has fostered. Thus, Dworkin's own recourse to the idea of "abstract justice" as a critical standard uninfluenced by our legal decisons and capable of providing a relatively "objective" assessment of our political arrangements seems to represent a problem; it seems to overlook precisely the authority of historical traditions on what we count as abstract justice. The same seems to hold true of the Kantian approach to political theory taken by such theorists as John Rawls, Jürgen Habermas, and Bruce Ackerman. From a hermeneutic point of view, the attempt to find some unconditioned "Archimedean point" for assessing the norms and principles of a given society fails to account for the limits of its own historical perspective. We are, in Gadamer's view, thoroughly historical and this means that our history penetrates even those critical designs or procedures through which we try to provide for a critical distance from our own beliefs and political traditions.

This analysis of the thrust of Gadamer's hermeneutics is the one that Richard Rorty has introduced into contemporary political theory. In his view, Gadamer's insight into tradition and history can be combined with Dewey's pragmatism to lead to a kind of "postmodernist bourgeois liberalism."[2] For Rorty this means that we cannot and need not justify our political beliefs by showing them to correspond to independent standards of "abstract justice" or to a formal, universally valid procedure for generating norms and principles. To take hermeneutics seriously is rather to recognize that our political ideals are radically contingent; they are the product of a specific history that might have been different and any of the terms in which we might try to justify them are part of that same history. Hence, we cannot "justify" liberalism in politics any more than we can, say, "justify" our aesthetic tastes. All we can do and all we need do is "start from where we are," from the common standards and beliefs of our tradition, affirming what democratic politics these allow us to confirm.[3]

By now, Rorty's particular combination of Dewey and Gadamer is well-known. This chapter examines the way in which some of the themes Rorty emphasizes in Gadamer's work, particularly those involving the authority of our political tradition and the commonality of the norms embedded in it, also support two other approaches to politics — the approach Michael Walzer takes in *Spheres of Justice*[4] and *Interpretation and Social Criticism*[5] and the tack John Rawls has pursued in recent essays such as "Kantian Constructivism"[6] and "Justice as Fairness: Political not Metaphysical."[7] Neither Walzer nor Rawls refer explicitly to Gadamer's hermeneutics;[8] still it seems to fortify the political perspective each now offers. As Rorty does, Walzer and Rawls abandon the search for moral or metaphysical foundations to our political conceptions; both, instead, try to articulate the shared understandings of distributive justice already developed by our political traditions. The approach of each is thus staunchly interpretive. Political philosophy, as they practice it, is an attempt to clarify, for the democratic culture to which they belong, its own political norms and values, and to resolve for it the apparent contradictions in its beliefs and practices. What such a "hermeneutic" political theory accomplishes, then, is not the "erection of a beyond supposed to exist" that Hegel already criticized.[9] It rather works out a conception of justice meant to correspond more faithfully to the common notions of citizenship, equality, and liberty that we already possess. Indeed, echoing Hegel, Walzer argues: "Justice and equality can conceivably be worked out as philosophical artifacts, but a just or an egalitarian society cannot be. If such a society isn't already here — hidden, as it were, in our concepts and categories — we will never know it concretely or realize it in fact."[10]

Many questions might be raised about this kind of Hegelian-hermeneutic political philosophy as interpretation. *Is* there a coherent social vision hidden in our concepts and categories or, as Alasdair MacIntyre has argued, are the norms of modern pluralistic democracies simply remnants of competing attempts to rescue a shattered tradition?[11] Are "our" shared understandings really shared and, if so, by whom? Cornel West has posed these questions with regard to Rorty's reference to "us" Western intellectuals[12] and in this chapter, I shall consider an analogous set of issues by focussing on the problem of subjectivism. If the political philosophy Walzer and Rawls now pursue is an interpretation of our shared understandings, nonetheless, their accounts of this shared understanding differ. Both claim to be clarifying to us the political ideals we already possess, but the ideals they claim we share are not the same. Should we, then, take seriously their interpretive claims or are their differing views of our mutual understandings simply views each would like us to share? What makes either of their articulations of our political heritage the right or even a right interpretation? Might there not be *other* possible interpretations of our shared understandings and, if so, how might we choose between them? Does giving up the attempt to find an objective standpoint for assessing principles of justice mean that any standpoint will be subjective?

Gadamer's hermeneutics seems to me to offer a more penetrating examination of these questions than hermeneutic political philosophy has yet provided. In the following, therefore, I want first to show how the problem of subjectivism arises for Walzer and Rawls and then turn to Gadamer's consideration of it. Doing so should help clarify the grounds for Dworkin's recourse to Gadamer, because it also becomes clear that Rorty's appropriation of Gadamer is only partial. If Gadamer's work suggests the limits of universalistic and foundationalist political theories, it also offers an alternative to subjectivism.

1. Walzer and the Problem of Subjectivism

Walzer begins his *Spheres of Justice* with a criticism of Rawls's approach to the issue of distributive justice. On his view, the Kantian strategy that Rawls pursues in *A Theory of Justice* in imagining what principles of justice rational individuals would choose under suitably universalizing conditions starts at too late a point. It overlooks the fact that before just principles can be formulated for the distribution of goods, the goods must first be "conceived and created"; moreover, they are conceived and created in historically specific ways. Whether and how education, property, and political office are considered "goods" are questions differently decided by different societies and decided differently at different points in their histories. Walzer admits that "certain key goods have . . . characteristic normative structures reiterated across the lines (but not all the lines) of time and space." Nevertheless, his essential point is that goods are socially and historically constituted, that although a good may be a good for many different societies it is not always a good in the same way. Bread, for instance, is variously conceived as of "the staff of life, the body of Christ, the symbol of the sabbath, the means of hospitality and so on." Moreover, "if the religious uses of bread were to conflict with its nutritional uses . . . it is by no means clear which one would be primary."[13]

Walzer's claim here is one that has been more exhaustively elaborated not only in the hermeneutic tradition from which Gadamer comes but also in the so-called neo-Wittgensteinian philosophy of the social sciences. Both perspectives argue that the meaning of something as a good is a social creation, that goods are goods within a nexus of values, norms, and social practices, and that understanding what a particular good is, therefore, requires understanding the context within which it is a good. For the hermeneutic tradition in literary interpretation this means that understanding moves within a circle of part and whole. In understanding a text, one has to see how its various parts are connected with one another to form a coherent whole; at the same time, one's interpretation of each part is guided by one's expectation of the meaning of the whole. One can therefore use one's initial understanding of the whole as the context within which to interpret the parts and revise this understanding of the whole in terms of the vantage point or context each of the parts supplies. The neo-Wittgensteinian tradition claims that the same circumstances hold of social understanding; again, understanding involves making sense of a particular practice or norm as part of the larger context that gives it the meaning it has; in turn, one's understanding of this context is composed of and corrected by one's understanding of the particular meaning in question together with other social meanings. As Charles Taylor puts the point in his "Interpretation and the Sciences of Man": "Things only have meanings in a field, that is in relation to the meanings of other things. This means that there is no such thing as a single, unrelated meaningful element. Meanings cannot be identified except in relation to others."[14]

Both Gadamer and neo-Wittgensteinian philosophy of the social sciences originally employed this insight into the contextual character of meaning and understanding to criticize positivist social science. The claim was that social practices, actions, and norms could not be explained simply in terms of general laws of behavior; rather, the contexts that made them the practices, actions, or norms they were had first to be understood. One could not subsume the Christian practice of baptism and pagan purification rituals involving water under the same causal generalization because to do so would miss the cultural particularity and, hence, the meaning of each of the practices under study.[15] Practices, in other words, could not be ripped out of their social and historical context and equated with different practices in different circumstances possessing superficially similar features; the particular social context, it was argued, rather gave the practices their sense as the practices they were. The claim here, however, was not that certain generalizations might not be possible or that scientific language could never replace the language of action and participation. Still, both hermeneuticists and neo-Wittgensteinians argued that scientific generalization and language had to retain some connection to the language of action or risk misidentifying the very meaning they sought to explain.[16]

Walzer pushes this claim in a political direction. If a hermeneutic understanding of meaning remains essential to social science, this same hermeneutic understanding has normative consequences. For, once the meaning of a particular social good is clear, so too is the proper mode of its distribution. The meaning of a particular good for a given community already includes principles for its just allocation. If we understand what a good is, he writes, "what it means to those for whom it is a good, we understand how, by whom and for what reason it ought to be distributed. All distributions are just or unjust relative to the social meanings of the goods at stake."[17] This "internal" meaning of social goods serves as a critical principle. A hermeneutic understanding of meaning shows both how a good, according to its meaning, ought to be distributed and when it is being unjustly distributed: namely, when its distribution conflicts with its meaning. In this case, distributive practices have to be reformed to conform to the meaning the good already has. The distribution of medical care in the United States serves Walzer as a case in point.

On his view, the meaning medical care has in this society is constituted by the meaning of such federally funded programs as Medicare and Medicaid, by the significance of using tax dollars to support medical research, by the point of mandatory vaccination programs for children, and so forth. Such practices indicate that medical care is, for us, a "need." In other words, it is a good that our society considers necessary for all its ill members and therefore undertakes to provide for them. To conceive of health care as a need is to presume that no other criterion enters into its distributive norms. There is no wealth- or achievement-requirement for receiving care; rather, it is to be distributed equally to all those who need it *because* they need it.

This understanding of medical care is a relatively recent one. During the Middle Ages, care of the body was considered a private affair while care of the soul was a socially recognized and supported need. Therefore, there were churches in every parish, catechism classes, and regular religious services so that "every Christian had an equal chance at salvation and eternal life."[28] In modern societies, the assessments of the importance of medical care and salvation have been reversed and the new interpretation given health care now requires the state licensing of physicians, state medical schools, public hospitals, general vaccination and health-care programs, and so forth.

Because of this new interpretation, Walzer claims that the United States has a shabby system for health-care provision. Given the meaning medical care has come to possess, it should be given to anyone who needs it to the extent that the technology is publically supported and available. But it remains the case in the United States that citizens with money can buy better and more extensive care than those without money, even though the care they buy is subsidized by the society at large. "Were medical care a luxury," Walzer writes, the discrepancy between the care the rich receive and that provided the poor "would not matter much; but as soon as medical care becomes a socially recognized need and as soon as the community invests in its provision, [it] matter[s] a great deal." It matters, moreover, not only because the poor are sicker than the rich, but because unequal access to care affects their status as full members of the society: "For then deprivation is a double loss—to one's health and to one's social standing. Doctors and hospitals have become such massively important features of contemporary life that to be cut off from the help they provide is not only dangerous but degrading."[19]

As Walzer's critics have suggested, this analysis of the social meaning of medical care poses a problem. We have seen that Walzer's is a contextualist account of social understanding; in order to understand the meaning of a particular good we must understand the context in which it is a good. Walzer thinks that the meaning of medical care in the United States is to be understood in the context of the modern history of the idea of health care, on the one hand, and certain more specific practices such as state support for medical research, aid programs, and state licensing of health-care workers, on the other. But why is this the only appropriate context for understanding the meaning of medical care? Why focus on just the practices on which Walzer does? Why are not those practices that he thinks *conflict* with the distributive principles internal to their meaning instead equally *constitutive* of that meaning? As Dworkin points out, one can look to public support for medical research and care as evidence that some Americans consider health care a need; but surely the very facts that Walzer criticizes, namely that health care can also be privately purchased and is, in any case, unequally provided to rich and poor are also social practices that ought to "count" in interpreting its social meaning.[20] Why emphasize some of these practices over others?

In his reply to Dworkin, Walzer admits that social meanings might be interpreted in different ways and, indeed, that definitive interpretations are probably impossible. Nonetheless, he argues that we can still distinguish between better and worse interpretations of a given norm or practice and that what marks the former off from the latter is that they are "deep and inclusive" rather than "shallow and partisan."[21] His point here seems to be that social interpretation has to be more than a superficial reading of disagreements in our political opinions and social perceptions. One cannot simply point to conflicting views to argue that medical care in the United States has no consistent meaning. For Walzer, a "deep and inclusive" interpretation is distinguished precisely by its ability to dig below surface disagreements and to unearth the understandings we really do share. Crucial in this connection is his claim that we no longer conceive of disease as a plague, that we rather regard it as both curable and preventable and, for this reason, are willing to spend public money on cures and preventions. It is this shared understanding, beneath, as it were, our disagreements on the just distribution of cures, that underlies his criticism of current health-care practices. The point is that we share a common general view of health and disease, and it is this common understanding that requires reform in the distribution of medical care.

Still, this account of the understanding we really do share seems only to remove the problem Dworkin raises to another level. For if some warrant for Walzer's criticism of health-care practices can be found in a deeply shared understanding of health and disease, alternative interpretations also of this understanding seem possible. Why not, for example, offer an interpretation that categorizes only certain diseases as ones for which cures are socially supportable needs? Do we really conceive of all disease as a problem from which our society should try to deliver us? Must we underwrite either spas that cater to what some might interpret as real physical health or psychic centers offering spiritual health? Dworkin seems to have questions of this sort in mind in claiming that health care might be most illuminatingly understood as a hybrid combining commodity and welfare spheres.[22] One might argue that while we consider certain aspects of health care as needs—a cure for AIDS, for example, or vaccinations for all children—we see others still as luxuries, available only to those who can afford them.

The question here, then, is how, given two versions of the meaning of health care, we are to choose between them. Why should health-care practices be reformed in the direction Walzer proposes? Why not say, as Dworkin imagines one might say, "that justice requires leaving medicine to the market but insists on just the qualifications and exceptions that we have made."[23] Are not both proposals one-sided and even partisan interpretations of our shared understandings? At a more fundamental level, is not the view of citizenship that informs each version one-sided and partisan? Walzer contends that current distributions of medical care are discriminatory in excluding the poor not only from decent health care but from full participation in the community as equally valued members of it. But the alternative view of the meaning health and disease have for us could invoke an alternative understanding of the meaning of citizenship: an understanding stressing, not membership and inclusion, but rather the protection of an individual liberty that requires leaving as much as justly possible to the distributive mechanisms of a free market.

Although this proposed reliance on free-market mechanisms and, accordingly, the picture Dworkin imagines of just health-care distributions are more privatistic than any conception Rawls (or Dworkin himself) would endorse, Rawls's political theory offers an analysis of the meaning of membership in a democratic society that differs in important ways from Walzer's own. I therefore want to sketch this alternative conception and to show how the same problem that arises for Walzer also arises for Rawls: namely, that of justifying his particular interpretations of our shared social meanings.

2. *Rawls and the Problem of Subjectivism*

Despite the criticism of a Rawlsian approach to political theory with which Walzer begins *Spheres of Justice*, in recent works Rawls has articulated a conception of political philosophy quite close to Walzer's own. According to this conception, the task of political theory is not to discover an Archimedean point outside of any particular society for assessing the justice of its basic structure. Rawls admits that this might have been a plausible interpretation of *A Theory of Justice*.[24] There it might have seemed that the principles of justice chosen in the "original position" were supposed to be principles of justice for any community; they were the principles that any agent would choose if he or she had to choose behind "a veil of ignorance," without the kind of knowledge that might lead him or her to favor a particular social position or conception of the good in formulating principles for the basic structure. Hence parties in the original position were supposed to be ignorant of their social class or economic situation as well as of their aims, ideas of the good, and fortune in the distribution of natural assets. They were also supposed to be ignorant of the kind of society or historical generation to which they belonged so that the principles they chose could have universal application. Not only were these principles therefore supposed to supersede the pluralism of distributive criteria *within* a society, on which Walzer insists. They were also meant to supersede the pluralism of principles of justice *among* societies, cultures, and traditions. Rawls's principles of justice were rather "those which rational persons concerned to advance their interests would accept in this position of equality to settle the basic terms of their association."[25]

A Theory of Justice is open to another interpretation as well, according to which Rawls was not concerned in it to discover an unconditioned standpoint for formulating principles of justice; rather, his concern was to articulate the conception of justice already corresponding to our deepest beliefs and settled convictions. To this extent, it was not meant as the only rational theory of justice, but rather one that clarifies for us our own fundamental social understandings and resolves the contradictions they might involve. This Walzerian view of the task of a theory of justice is the one that emerges from the conception of "reflective equilibrium"[26] and is also that which Rawls has emphasized in recent works. Hence, he writes in "Kantian Constructivism in Moral Theory" that the point of such a theory is "to articulate and to make explicit those shared notions and principles thought to be already latent in common sense, or, as is often the case, if common sense is hesitant and uncertain, and doesn't know what to think, to propose to it certain conceptions and principles congenial to its most essential convictions and historical traditions."[27]

According to this analysis, political philosophy must do what Hegel said it must do: not construct ideal social structures but rather articulate the principles and priorities already immanent in our own traditions. While Walzer emphasizes shared social understandings, Rawls writes, "What justifies a conception of justice is not its being true to an order antecedent to and given to us, but its congruence with our deeper understanding of ourselves and our aspirations and our realization that, given our history and the traditions embedded in our public life, it is the most reasonable doctrine for us."[28]

As Rawls conceives of the theory of justice then, it need not deny its location within the context of specific political norms and beliefs; his interest is rather precisely *what* these political norms and beliefs are and what theory of justice they entail. The original position is not meant to provide a neutral standpoint for choosing principles for the basic structure of society; it rather serves as "a device of representation." That is, it is supposed to represent, in a particularly lucid form, what we already think about the question of designing basic institutions and distributive arrangements: namely, that any such design must follow a rational procedure that is fair to all the parties the institutions and arrangements are meant to serve. It thus "models what we regard as fair conditions" and serves "as a unifying idea by which our considered convictions at all levels of generality are brought to bear on one another so as to achieve greater mutual agreement and self-understanding."[29]

This account of the original position requires a clarification of the description of the parties to it. The account of representatives behind a veil of ignorance, stripped of various forms of knowledge, and choosing in ignorance of their ends, talents, and attachments is not supposed to characterize a theory of the self. Such a theory would be open to the criticism Michael Sandel makes in his *Liberalism and the Limits of Justice* that it reduces the self to the point of a wholly disembodied noumenon, devoid not only of all attributes and interests but also of any possibility of choice in the choice situation.[30] But the account of the parties behind the veil of ignorance is meant simply to represent our conception of moral persons under fair conditions of choice. Rawls's concern, in other words, is not what the self is *essentially* but, instead, how persons are to be viewed from the point of view of our considered conception of justice or, in other words, how they are to be considered as citizens. What matters in this connection is not the particular ends, attachments, and assets they have but their freedom to pursue their ends and their moral equality with one another.

The principles of justice that Rawls thinks follow from these "model conceptions" of the original position and moral persons justify distributive arrangements that diverge markedly from those we now possess. According to Rawls, the two principles of justice are, first, that "each person is to have an equal right to the most extensive basic liberty compatible with a similar liberty for others"[31] and, second, that "social and economic inequalities are to be arranged so that they are both (a) to the greatest benefit of the least advantaged and (b) attached to offices and positions open to all under conditions of fair equality of opportunity."[32] At least the first part of the second principle requires reforms in the economic arrangements and practices we now have, but this necessity raises the same question that we raised with regard to Walzer's political reforms. The two principles are not supposed to follow from rational choice in an original position that is conceived of as representing an Archimedean standpoint for assessing principles of justice. They follow instead from a model conception of what we consider fair conditions of choice by what we consider free and equal moral persons; but what justifies just this model conception? Since it requires changes in our practices, it can surely not be viewed as a *self-evident* implication of them. But then can Rawls's understanding of our deep convictions and political traditions not be viewed as just as selective and therefore as partisan as Walzer's social interpretations?

If one compares Walzer's and Rawls's accounts of the meaning of the liberty and equality of democratic citizens, one can see just how partial Rawls's account might be considered.[33] Rawls claims that, for our conception of justice, the particular ends persons have at a given time and their particular social or economic situation are meant to be irrelevant to the question of their fair treatment. What is crucial about citizens from the standpoint of justice is rather their equal ability to *have* ends and to revise and pursue them. In recent works Rawls has, therefore, emphasized two moral powers: (1) the capacity for a sense of justice and (2) the capacity "to form, to revise and rationally to pursue a conception of the good."[34] But for Walzer the freedom and equality of democratic citizens do not lie only in these capacities. Freedom rather involves participation in the shared deliberative life of the community to which one belongs, while equality means that the significance of natural differences in assets and interests is made secondary to what Taylor calls "the balance of mutual indebtedness" in sustaining a common way of life.[35]

To be sure, Rawls also attempts to account for the value of community, and has even argued that supporting the good of political democracy functions as a common goal and project on the part of its citizens.[36] Still, his starting point remains the model conception of free and equal persons where their freedom consists in the capacity to form, revise, and pursue their own conception of the good, and their equality lies in the sense of justice that allows for this capacity on the part of all others.[37] The question here is why begin with free and equal moral persons as opposed to beginning with the free and equal participation of mutually dependent citizens? Why propose two principles of justice that follow from our supposed "model conceptions" and are to be enforced in all distributions of goods; why not propose different "spheres of justice" where appropriate principles of distribution will be pluralistic, differing with the different meanings goods such as medical care, education, wealth, and office supposedly have for us?

Both Walzer's and Rawls's accounts of the meaning of freedom, equality, and citizenship might be contrasted to a libertarian conception according to which they involve primarily the equal protection of everyone's right to property.[38] Indeed, it may be that viewed from a libertarian perspective, Walzer and Rawls are more alike than they are different in their general social interpretations. Still, to the extent that their understandings of our shared meanings and their corresponding visions of just distributive practices differ at all, they seem to indicate a problem with an interpretive political theory. For, if Rawls's reliance on an equal liberty to form, revise, and pursue one's own conception of the good reflects only his interpretation of our conception of justice and citizenship, and if Walzer's emphasis on participation in a shared form of life reflects only his, both are *equally* partisan and selective. Can an interpretive political theory avoid, then, the criticism that it is inevitably subjectivistic, that it simply articulates the different meanings different theorists find in our goods, political traditions, and deep convictions? To explore this question, I turn to Gadamer's work.

3. Gadamer and the Problem of Subjectivism

Gadamer's hermeneutics may seem less a solution to the problem of subjectivism than an endorsement of it. In attempting to rescue the status of prejudices from their Enlightenment devaluation, Gadamer emphasizes that assumptions and prejudgments are part of all attempts to understand. Following Schleiermacher, Dilthey, and others in the hermeneutic tradition, he argues that any understanding of meaning—whether of a text or text-analogue such as a social practice or norm—depends upon expectations that need not be explicit but that nonetheless project the context within which meaning can emerge. One comes to one's object from within the "horizon" offered by certain practices, purposes, and concerns and its meaning is thus initially anticipated to fall within a range of possible meanings and contrasts. Hence, understanding always has the "forestructure" Martin Heidegger delineated. The meaning that is understood is always the product of, first, the specific context within which it is understood. Heidegger calls the process here a fore-having (*Vorhabe*) of understanding. Second, it is a result of the specific perspective from which it is approached. Heidegger refers here to a fore-sight (*Vorsicht*). Finally, it is a result of the specific way it is conceived (a preconception or *Vorgriff*).[39]

For the hermeneutic tradition, this forestructure constitutes only an initial orientation to the meaning in question, and a guide for further interpretation and revision. The process of interpretation moves in the hermeneutic circle mentioned earlier. One projects a meaning for the whole of one's text or text-analogue, uses this interpretation as a guide to the meaning of its individual parts or aspects, and then employs the interpretation of these individual parts or aspects to reassess one's understanding of the whole. To this extent the notion of prejudice is simply that of an interpretive projection. One projects onto one's object an interpretation that necessarily goes beyond the evidence that is initially available to one, but what such a projection provides is a preview of possible meaning that allows for a more penetrating consideration of the text or text-analogue at issue. Hence, Gadamer notes, literally a prejudice (*Vorurteil*) is simply a pre-judgment (*Vor-urteil*), a judgment offered tentatively before all the necessary evidence is available in order to provide a basis for further interpretation and judgment.[40] Indeed, for the hermeneutic tradition, such interpretive projections are supposed to lead ultimately to an "objective" or unconditioned understanding. By assessing one's projection of the meaning of the whole of a text in light of one's interpretation of the parts and, conversely, by assessing one's interpretation of individual parts in light of the coherent meaning they compose for the whole, one is meant to be led to an understanding in which all discrepencies between the interpretation of the parts and the interpretation of the whole have been eliminated. The aim here is a complete knowledge of the meaning of a text, a knowledge, which however "infinite" a task, still meets the criteria of scientific objectivity.

It is at this point, however, that Gadamer parts company with the hermeneutic tradition. Following Heidegger, he denies that understanding ever escapes the conditioned character of the hermeneutic circle. Correction, reassessment, and revision of one's initial prejudices or anticipations remain themselves prejudiced by the concerns and aims one has, by the practice in which one is engaged, and, moreover, by what else one knows or considers true. The meaning of any text or text-analogue, then, is always circumscribed by an interpreter's particular circumstances and perspective. For this reason, Gadamer stresses not only the relatively innocuous connection between prejudice and interpretive projection or prejudgment but also the more radical contrast between prejudice (*Vor-urteil*) and judgment (*Urteil*). "The prejudices of the individual," he claims, "far more than his judgments constitute the historical reality of his being."[41] No understanding achieves the objectivity the hermeneutic tradition once sought; all rather remain particular *interpretations* and arise out of particular interpretive horizons.

Gadamer's rehabilitation of the status of prejudices thus seems to support subjectivism. He seems to argue that one understanding of textual or social meaning can never be less prejudiced than any other and hence that all interpretation is as unjustifiable as critics have found Walzer's interpretations of social goods. Hence, a Gadamerian defense of Walzer's analysis would have to claim that his account of the meaning of medical care in the United States is partial and partisan but that all interpretation is guilty of this defect. No interpretation grasps meaning impartially because all interpretations — and all socioscientific surveys — reflect the interpreter's involvement in particular practices, concerns, and contexts. The same might serve as a defense of Rawls's later work. Naturally his view of the meanings of citizenship, liberty, and equality is a partisan one, and naturally this view contrasts with both Walzer's and a libertarian position. Still no account can be any more objective given the prejudiced and subjective character of understanding and interpretation in general.

I think that Gadamer's analysis does lend some credence to this kind of approach — a dissolution of the problem of subjectivism by way of endorsement. Nonetheless, the account of prejudice is also meant to indicate the weight of a history that in a sense *undermines* subjectivism. By stressing the prejudiced character of understanding, Gadamer does not mean simply that our views are always idiosyncratic biases; neither is his emphasis on the more radical force of prejudice concerned merely to situate our views in our own antecedent expectations; he wants also to situate our expectations in history: they are *not* ours alone but those of the culture and tradition to which we belong. Central here is Gadamer's notion of effective-history: the idea that who we are and what we think is the product not of self-determination and reason, as the Enlightenment might have us think, but rather of our past. Gadamer, of course, does not deny the possibility of revising our traditions; his point is that in doing so we remain, not only within a hermeneutic circle, but within a historically situated hermeneutic circle, within, in other words, the province of an effective-history that influences the lines and terms of such revision. His example in this regard is the idea of the classical.

For Gadamer, the idea of the classical is significant because, despite historicist attempts to reduce it to the concept of a certain historical style, the classical retains normative force for our contemporary judgments. If something is considered classical, this does not primarily mean that it belongs to the art and architecture of a certain age; it means rather that it has evaluative authority, that it is a standard to which we ought to aspire. Thus, for example, Gadamer suggests that the idea of a classical education means not simply that students receive training in Latin and Greek, but that they receive a good education, the education everyone ought to receive.[42] Indeed, the normative authority of the classical extends even to our rebellions against it; the notion of its excellence and importance remain the criterion against which the results of those rebellions are measured. The idea of the classical, then, indicates the hold of historical tradition over our contemporary assessments and even over our attempts to escape that hold. Insight into this hold, moreover, serves Gadamer as a critique of what he considers the "subjectivism of modern philosophy."[43] In assuming an ability to rise above authority and tradition and to judge things according to the tenets of reason alone, the Enlightenment simply allows our historical prejudices to operate over our "subjective" opinion in all the more unchallenged a way.

How does this criticism of the "subjectivism of modern philosophy" support the different interpretations Walzer and Rawls offer of our shared meanings? From a Gadamerian perspective it supports them the only way they can be supported: namely, by grounding them in history. Walzer and Rawls may offer contrasting interpretations of our understandings of liberty, equality, and citizenship; still, their interpretations are not for that reason alone arbitrary. Rather, they represent the articulation of different traditions of interpretation and are justified by the authority of these traditions. Whereas Rawls emphasizes a liberal understanding of our political traditions, relying on such theorists as Locke and Mill, Walzer moves in a more communitarian direction represented by such theorists as Rousseau, Montesquieu, and Hegel.

Of course, this solution to the problem of subjectivism may seem no great bargain. In the first place, we seem to have provided only a historical reformulation of the problem already raised in the discussion thus far. Walzer's critics seem to assume that his interpretations of goods and of democratic citizenship in general are simply idiosyncratic. But, suppose they have their roots in a wider understanding of our political tradition? If this understanding contrasts with a more liberal gloss on our political understandings, then the question simply becomes which traditional understanding of our beliefs, convictions, and so forth is more appropriate? Which historically grounded account of our shared social meanings are we to adopt? The recognition that our differing political views reflect differing strands of our sociopolitical heritage does not seem to provide an answer to this question.

In the second place, the insistence of Walzer's critics on the entirely subjective character of his interpretations at least attributes originality to them. In dissolving this subjective character into the force of effective-history, a Gadamerian approach seems to deprive them even of this value. Walzer's views become simply a more recent articulation of traditional positions. But obviously their oldness cannot make them legitimate interpretations of the tradition any more than the historical roots of Rawls's liberalism legitimate it. The question arises, then, as to what, in a Gadamerian view, does legitimate interpretation? How do we choose between positions that are equally historically rooted and developed—in Walzer's words between equally deep and inclusive accounts?

A Gadamerian answer to this question can be found, I think, in his conception of hermeneutic dialogue. Gadamer argues that the point of any serious conversation or any serious attempt to understand a text or text-analogue is to arrive at a better understanding of the subject matter at issue. In other words, if we are concerned really to understand the meaning of a certain text or social practice, the underlying premise of this attempt has to be that we might learn from it, that the text or practice may have something to teach us

153

about issues we confront. Indeed, according to what Gadamer calls an anticipation of completeness (*der Vorgriff der Vollkommenheit*),[44] if a text or text-analogue appears to have no coherent meaning, if we can make no sense out of it, this can indicate not as much a problem with the "text" as the inadequacy of the interpetation. We must at least provisionally expect our "texts" to tell us something "true," to illuminate a subject matter for us and hence offer us a way of revising our knowledge of it; otherwise, we have no standard for revising inadequate interpretations and no way of distinguishing between ultimately incoherent texts and merely partial interpretations. It may be that interpreters have failed to allow a text or text-analogue to test or question the prejudices they bring to it; hence, they cannot uncover the coherence and "truth" it nonetheless has. We always come already prejudiced to the project of understanding and these prejudices affect our understanding of a text or text-analogue. Still, if we are hermeneutically serious, if we assume the possibility of learning from what we are studying, we can illuminate our prejudices and test the legitimacy of our beliefs.

Naturally, such illumination and examination of beliefs and prejudices do not render the new interpretations to which we come prejudice-free. Still, the result of dialogic encounter for Gadamer is a development of our initial views. We need not agree ultimately with the text or text-analogue we are studying. It may not be an option for us to adopt Zande beliefs in witchcraft, for example, and we may decide to reject a particular philosophical argument. But Gadamer's contention is that whatever the outcome of conversation—whether we finally agree or disagree with what we have understood—the result is an achievement of understanding in which each of the initial positions is refined and enriched. Our initial expectations and assumptions are changed by the encounter with other perspectives even if we have finally to reject them for ourselves. In rejecting them, we affirm our own perspective in a new way, a way more differentiated and aware of its own partiality and potential deficiencies. For Gadamer, such revision, refinement, and enrichment is, in fact, the process of tradition. Traditions of interpretation remain vital because they are continually developed, affirmed, and reworked in line with the insights achieved in interpretive encounters with alien traditions and, indeed, with different aspects of themselves.

Now, it seems to me that this analysis helps clarify the importance of situating Walzer's and Rawls's accounts of citizenship, liberty, and equality in the history of the traditions of political thought from which they come. First, it becomes clear that in reformulating insights of the liberal and communitarian strands of our political heritage, neither is simply rehashing the old. The originality of each position rather lies in its articulation of new perspectives on old traditions and its extension of old traditions to deal with new problems. Second, and more crucial, each is able to do this *because* of the dialogic encounter with the other. In *Spheres of Justice,* Walzer undertakes a defense of a communitarian position explicitly in light of a criticism of the Kantian strategy that Rawls pursues in *A Theory of Justice.* In his later essays, Rawls interprets his own *A Theory of Justice* so that the conception of justice he articulates there can encompass communitarian concerns with history and political participation. Were we to adopt merely one of these alternative liberal or communitarian self-interpretations as the proper account of our political understandings, one could argue that the strength of each would be diminished and this might hold for the other possible interpretations of our political heritage as well. The cogency of each position, in other words, seems to depend upon the extent to which it has appropriated what it takes to be the insights of the others and protected itself against what it takes to be their mistakes. To discover what errors and insights are possible, however, each must continually engage the others in conversation.

One might argue, then, in general, that traditions survive and develop because they are not monolithic, because they include diverse self-interpretations and self-conceptions, and because these opposed self-understandings can educate one another. Traditions may acquire their authority through the interplay of competing interpretations in which the limits and merits of each can appear. In assessing the view of our political heritage offered by either Rawls or Walzer, then, the crucial question might not be which has captured the essence of our self-understanding; it might be, rather, whether either has exhausted it and how we might broaden our view of ourselves to include both the image of rational life-planners and that of citizens. The idea here is not to pick between interpretations of our political traditions, but rather to achieve a differentiated synthesis in which the merits and differences of alternative interpretations can be recognized and preserved.

Gadamer always claims that his philosophical hermeneutics offers no proposals for change or reform, that it simply tries "to correct false thinking";[45] but it seems to me that the correction of false thinking about what a tradition is here has practical consequences. In the debate between communitarianism and liberalism, we ought not to be trying to decide which is the more legitimate interpretation of "our" common political understanding of justice and democratic citizenship. We ought rather to accept both (and others) as part of a multifaceted tradition and to try to extend each to incorporate what we have learned in conversation with the others. The upshot of this dialogic approach to our tradition might be both a more differentiated understanding of ourselves and an attempt to establish a basic structure more sensitive to this understanding.[46]

But if Gadamerian dialogue thus sustains a kind of interpretive pluralism, what guarantees the rationality of the dialogic arena? It may be that a dialogue between competing interpretations of our political tradition is important both to the strength of the tradition and to the interpretive sensitivity of its fundamental institutions. Still, political positions and historical perspectives exist from which we, perhaps, should not learn and social groups exist whose voices have not always been heard. Why then begin with the premise that political conversation can be educational and that the basic structure of society should adequately reflect its pluralistic or differentiated results? Why not begin instead with the premise that political dialogue is ideologically distorted and its rationality undermined by social and economic relations of power? This, of course, is the starting point of Habermas's critique of Gadamer; he claims that Gadamer simply assumes the rationality of hermeneutic conversation and ignores the effect on it of social conditions of labor and domination. For Habermas, it is not enough simply either to acknowledge the conflict in interpetations or to foster dialogue between them. Instead, one needs a critical social theory that can uncover the conditions constraining and perverting the process of dialogue itself.[47]

I do not intend here to recapitulate the stages of the debate between Habermas and Gadamer.[48] I think, in fact, that Gadamer does assume the general rationality of hermeneutic conversation and, hence, of the course of a tradition. Still, he assumes it because he assumes conversation can ultimately disclose the same ideological factors that constrain it. Just as Walzer does, Gadamer also rejects the Kantain move to idealized conditions of either discourse or rational choice. We are socially, culturally, and historically situated. The only means that we have for reaching clarity about our situation, on his view, lies in continued dialogue about it. Certainly such dialogue can be systematically distorted; but, for Gadamer, notwithstanding Rorty's interpretation of him, it is to see through such distortions and to develop our insights that we must continue to talk. If conversation is reason's only hope, in other words, reason is also conversation's point. This supposition connects Gadamer's account of hermeneutic dialogue to the goals of both Habermasian discourse and Enlightenment rationality, I think, and also indicates the truth in the remark by Dworkin with which we began. We struggle against history not by ignoring the limits it imposes on either who we are or the political positions we can take; we struggle against history rather by acknowledging the multiple meanings it can have for us and learning from their confrontation with one another.

Notes

1. Ronald Dworkin, *Law's Empire* (Cambridge, Mass.: Harvard University Press, 1986), 62.

2. Richard Rorty, "Postmodernist Bourgeois Liberalism," in *Hermeneutics and Praxis*, ed. Robert Hollinger (Notre Dame, Ind.: University of Notre Dame Press, 1985).

3. Richard Rorty, "Solidarity and Objectivity," in *Post-Analytic Philosophy*, eds. John Rajchman and Cornel West (New York: Columbia University Press, 1985), 12.

4. Michael Walzer, *Spheres of Justice: A Defense of Pluralism and Equality* (New York: Basic Books, 1983).

5. Michael Walzer, *Interpretation and Social Criticism* (Cambridge Mass.: Harvard University Press, 1987).

6. John Rawls, "Kantian Constructivism in Moral Theory," *Journal of Philosophy* 76 (Summer 1980): 515-70.

7. John Rawls, "Justice as Fairness: Political not Metaphysical," *Philosophy and Public Affairs* 14 (Summer 1985): 223-51.

8. But see Walzer, *Interpretation and Social Criticism*, vi.

9. G. W. F. Hegel, *The Philosophy of Right*, trans. T. M. Knox (Oxford: Oxford University Press, 1967), 10.

10. Walzer, *Spheres of Justice*, xiv.

11. See Alasdair MacIntyre, *After Virtue* (Notre Dame, Ind.: University of Notre Dame Press, 1981), esp. chap. 1.

12. See Cornel West, "The Politics of American Neo-Pragmatism," in *Post-Analytic Philosophy*, 259-75.

13. Walzer, *Spheres of Justice*, 8.

14. Charles Taylor, "Interpretation and the Sciences of Man," in vol. 2 of *Philosophical Papers* (Cambridge: Cambridge University Press, 1985), 22.

15. Peter Winch, *The Idea of a Social Science and its Relation to Philosophy* (New York: Routledge and Kegan Paul, 1973), 105.

16. See Taylor's "Interpretation and the Sciences of Man," 26-27; and Winch's *The Idea of a Social Science and its Relation to Philosophy*, 89. For criticism, see Richard Rorty, "Method, Social Science, and Social Hope," in *Consequences of Pragmatism* (Minneapolis, Minn.: University of Minnesota Press, 1982), 191-210.

17. Walzer, *Spheres of Justice*, 9.

18. Walzer, *Spheres of Justice*, 89.

19. Walzer, *Spheres of Justice*, 89.

20. Ronald Dworkin, "To Each his Own," *New York Review of Books*, vol. 30, no. 6 (April 1983): 4.

21. Walzer, "Spheres of Justice: An Exchange," *New York Review of Books*, vol. 30, no. 12 (July 1983): 43.

22. Dworkin, "To Each his Own," 4.

23. Walzer, "Spheres of Justice: An Exchange," 45.

24. John Rawls, *A Theory of Justice* (Cambridge, Mass.: Harvard University Press, 1971).

25. Rawls, *Theory of Justice*, 118–19.

26. Rawls, *Theory of Justice*, 20.

27. Rawls, "Kantian Constructivism in Moral Theory," 518.

28. Rawls, "Kantian Constructivism in Moral Theory," 519.

29. Rawls, "Justice as Fairness," 237–38.

30. Michael Sandel, *Liberalism and the Limits of Justice* (Cambridge: Cambridge University Press, 1982).

31. Rawls, *Theory of Justice*, 66.

32. Rawls, *Theory of Justice*, 83.

33. For help in this account of the one-sided character of Rawls's account of democratic citizenship, I am indebted to Paul Stern's unpublished manuscript, "Citizenship, Community and Pluralism: The Current Dispute on Distributive Justice."

34. "Kantian Constructivism in Moral Theory," 525.

35. Charles Taylor, "The Nature and Scope of Distributive Justice," in vol. 2 of *Philosophical Papers*, 299–300.

36. See John Rawls, "The Priority of Right and Ideas of the Good," in *Philosophy and Public Affairs* 17 (Fall 1988): 251–76.

37. See John Rawls, "The Basic Liberties and their Priority," in *Liberty, Equality and Law*, ed. Sterling M. McMurrin (Salt Lake City, Utah: University of Utah Press, 1987), esp. 16.

38. Taylor, "Distributive Justice," esp. 293.

39. An interpretation of paragraph 32 of Martin Heidegger's *Being and Time*, trans. John Macquarrie and Edward Robinson (New York: Harper and Row, 1962).

40. Hans-Georg Gadamer, *Truth and Method*, trans. Sheed and Ward Ltd. (New York: Seabury Press, 1975), 240.

41. Gadamer, *Truth and Method*, 245.

42. Gadamer, *Truth and Method*, 253.

43. Gadamer, *Truth and Method*, 228.

44. Gadamer, *Truth and Method*, 261-62.

45. Gadamer, *Truth and Method*, xiii.

46. One might argue that since Walzer proposes a pluralistic understanding of our social goods, the approach I am suggesting here is the same as his. I think, however, that there are two differences. First, Walzer never focusses on the problem of subjectivism. Hence, although he claims that our goods have distinct meanings, he assumes that we share a common understanding of both their meanings and the way they differ from one another. The pluralistic approach suggested here, in contrast, recognizes that different groups within our culture understand the *same* goods in different ways. This means, second, that the attempt to structure basic institutions and distributive arrangements in a way reflective of our interpretive pluralism cannot be one theorist's attempt. Walzer's account of our social meanings would have to be seen, rather, as one important contribution to a general public discussion.

47. See Jürgen Habermas, "A Review of Gadamer's *Truth and Method,*" in *Understanding and Social Inquiry*, eds. Fred Dallmayr and Thomas McCarthy (Notre Dame, Ind.: University of Notre Dame Press, 1977), 335-64.

48. See my *Gadamer: Hermeneutics, Tradition and Reason* (Stanford, Calif.: Stanford University Press, 1987), chap. 4 for one analysis of the discussion.

7

Poetry, Dialogue, and Negotiation: Liberal Culture and Conservative Politics in Hans-Georg Gadamer's Thought

Dieter Misgeld

*I*n one of his essays Hans-Georg Gadamer asks whether the art of conversation or dialogue (*die Kunst des Gesprächs*) is about to disappear. Can we not observe, he notes, an increasing tendency toward the becoming monological of human behavior? Are such developments, if they obtain, a general phenomenon of modern civilization arising from scientific-technical modes of thought? Is it not also possible that some of us may refuse to participate in the babble of voices magnified by the media, the incessant flow of communication and information in contemporary societies?[1]

Gadamer does not simply answer these questions by recommending withdrawal from public communication or by claiming that in economically and technically developed societies people are altogether losing their capacity to engage one another in conversation. Instead, he restates a central argument of *Truth and Method* by reaffirming that language only has its reality in conversation. It is the reality of language as spoken, the use of language for the purpose of one person addressing another, or for the purpose of establishing a common relationship to a subject matter under consideration, which, for Gadamer, can show us how basic solidarities between people are formed and maintained. Communication provided by the electronic media (the "mass media" as Gadamer says employing a phrase commonly used in Germany since the introduction of the radio) can never convey or institute this sense of solidarity. Thus, the question arises what resources there are for members of modern societies sufficiently sensitive to the problem to maintain and develop their capacity for dialogue in the face of the massive onslaught of highly publicized, anonymously directed modes of communication.

Generally, Gadamer is confident that cultural traditions of learning and education predating the Age of Industrialism and of "mass-democracies" continue to be sufficiently alive to sustain an interest in conversation among educated and highly literate people.[2] It is for this reason that he devotes so much attention to the *Geisteswissenschaften* and the arts, rather than, for example, education in the sciences. He regards the social sciences with a great deal of skepticism for similar reasons. For him they are very much part of a mode of social organization, which places primary importance on the constant refinement of techniques of administrative regulation.[3]

It is against this background that one can come to appreciate Gadamer's lifelong love for and devotion to poetry, his unique emphasis on modes of conversation, which presuppose an intact private sphere of communication as a secure background or which rely on the institutional security of the classical German university, founded on the Humboldtian principles of "solitude and freedom" (*Einsamkeit und Freiheit*), as his now deceased contemporary Helmut Schelsky once said.[4]

Gadamer wants to protect forms of intimate and deeply engaging conversation from the technologically reinforced invasion of culturally and intellectually still viable institutional spheres, capable, in his view, of maintaining the mentioned forms of communication. It is for this reason that he defends some central educational concerns of the German university manifest, in particular, in the humanities and usually derived from the principle of the unity of research and teaching (*Einheit von Forschung und Lehre*). In addition, all these reflections serve as a background to his appraisal of the possibilities of politics in our times. In the following, I therefore discuss three aspects of his thinking about conversation and three applications of the principle that language only has its *reality* in conversation. The concluding comments address the relation among these three dimensions of his philosophy of dialogue.

1. *Persistent Intimacy: The Voice of the Poet*

In his beautiful and most readable essay "Have the Poets Fallen Silent?"[5] Gadamer asks, what force of persuasion, what possibilities for being heard and being attended to poetry can retain in a world, in which the anonymous apparatus of the media rules social life and in which "the [living] word no longer brings about immediate communication."[6] He answers that the poets and poetry have not as yet fallen silent. For contemporary poets in particular speak in a low voice (*mit leiser Stimme*), their communications are discreet; they speak to those who are capable of listening. It is as if only the least intrusive words, words spoken with the greatest care, and with quiet insistence, can once again establish what you and I have in common or help us rediscover what we already have in common. Thus, Gadamer remarks, in a beautiful sentence concluding the essay, "We are hardly yet in a position to appreciate what capacities and what experiences of life in technical civilization have entered into these verbal [poetic] constructions and have been captured in them — such that we may suddenly encounter the alien power of the modern world in our own house and welcome it as something familiar."[7] We would have escaped the babble of electronically magnified voices and once again feel at home in the world.

This is not to say that Gadamer favors poets whose voices are easily accessible to us. Quite to the contrary. He has devoted an entire small book to the interpretation of one of the least accessible poets writing in German during the last decades, Paul Celan.[8] Gadamer values Celan because Celan has developed a style of lyrical writing that responds to the new conditions of mass communication. He has developed forms that are resistant to expectations created in the passive and frequently soothing reception of media messages. Poetry of this kind requires an engaged reading, an attentiveness that wrests itself loose from habitual and easily available modes of listening and speaking.

Therefore, he entitles an essay interpreting a poem by Paul Celan: "Meaning and the Concealment of Meaning in Paul Celan's Poetry."[9] With this title, he explains, "we only put into words what each of us experiences who becomes familiar with Celan's poetry. The reader senses the presence of a very precise meaning to which he [or she] is attracted. Yet, at the same time he [or she] becomes aware that this meaning withholds itself. It may even be artfully concealed."[10] And discussing poetry in more general terms, he remarks that when common consciousness is filled with nothing but science, and the idolatry of technical progress prevails, "can there still be such a joining of words that everyone will feel at home in them? Certainly the poet's word will have to be different in such times. It will have to show some similarity with the language of reports, with the casualness and coolness of technical language."[11] And he adds: poetry, of course, will not be transformed into scientific or journalistic reports. Rather, the existence of technical, technological language, and the insistent stream of information that reaches us through the media, can only be responded to poetically, so to speak, by the poet's retreating into a less insistent, into an almost noiseless form of communication.

Here Gadamer refers to a 1923 letter by Rainer Maria Rilke in which Rilke speaks of his relation to God and says: "There is an indescribable sense of discretion between us."[12] For Gadamer, such indescribable discretion is at the very heart of modern poetry. It makes us listen to the voice of the poet, and ultimately our own, beneath the level of slogans of all kinds and the unceasing stream of "information" to which we are exposed and which we can never assimilate.

No wonder, then, that brevity, elliptical phrases, and hermetic concealment are constitutive of and themselves thematic in much contemporary poetry (quite strikingly in German poetry of the post-World War II period). Gadamer has paid much attention to it. The concealment of meaning in contemporary poetry, far from being an artificial aesthetic or literary device, is demanded by a sociocultural situation, in which poetry can only survive by means of the most subtly and intransigently produced discretion. Thus, poetry provides for the possiblity of the soul's conversation with itself (to refer to a classical Greek formulation). The most intimate and seemingly private form of communication also makes us reach beyond ourselves and find a world beyond that of publicly approved, conventional meaning.

2. Reciprocity and Friendship: The Maintenance of Dialogue

Language has its reality in conversation (beyond our listening to poetry or reading it). A conversation in confidence (*unter vier Augen*)[13] is an example of dialogue, in which the participants are fully equal and interested in achieving a common understanding about something. When this dialogue takes the form of a cooperative search for a shared understanding, be it of a subject matter or of the right attitude to take with respect to an important decision, a growth of persons beyond their individual point of view or their singularity (*Einzelheit*) may occur. Each of the participants tests and probes the strength and extent of common convictions. The sense of self-sufficiency and self-importance are left behind, which nourish so many of our delusions of knowledge and personal significance. Thus, once again, an intimate form of conversation helps retain and strengthen forms of solidarity indispensable for broadly based public communication.

An essential condition for this form of dialogue is openness to the other as well as to what the other says. It is the condition most frequently violated in contemporary large-scale public communication. Openness of this kind is not a question of a conversational or communicational strategy; it is an attitude or even disposition deeply rooted in a definite sense of solidarity accompanied by holding fast to one's self.[14] Therefore, Gadamer frequently singles out friendship as an example of a condition enabling us to engage in conversation.[15]

Friendship is important because it helps us describe intimate forms of conversation and of the cooperative search for that kind of truth, which does not remain external to us such as bits of information. In discovering such truth, we are transformed as persons, not merely as knowers. Therefore, dialogue is constitutive of friendship. In dialogue, "one can become a friend to the other and build that form of commonality [*Gemeinsamkeit*] in which each is himself [or herself] for the other. For each discovers the other and himself [or herself] in the other."[16]

Gadamer largely associates the transformative power of dialogue with the conversation between friends or a conversation between those who have something in common that they love and honor, because in these cases dialogue frees us from egocentric preoccupations. A philosophy of dialogue is imaginable, Gadamer says, which unfolds the relationship between the perspective of individuals and the entire world, reflecting itself as one and the same, that is, as a common world, in a multiplicity of standpoints.[17] We may believe, therefore, that for Gadamer dialogue and conversation, in their various forms, are constitutive of what the world is for people. And nothing is more important than having a world in common. Having a world in common means living in solidarity, and living in solidarity means openness to conversation and dialogue. The other becomes indispensable for us in this openness and for it.

Readers of Gadamer's writings are aware of the centrality of these ideas for his hermeneutics and his interpretations of the philosophical tradition. Yet, these very same ideas underlie his skeptical attitude toward much of modern life, and his fear that the pace of technical, economic, and administrative progress (not to speak of the increase in military power) will overtake cultural resources contained in this tradition. A history and a world are to be remembered, indeed to be acknowledged in their continuing reality, which seem to have lent more support to dialogical attitudes and intellectually searching conversation than the current age. The humanist tradition, for example, once encouraged and required the cultivation of tact, of aesthetic and moral sensitivities in their conjunction;[18] there hardly seems to be much room for it in contemporary highly politicized, overadministered academic environments subject to the exigencies of the competitive politics of academic success and a corresponding emphasis on public relations. The loss of moral and aesthetic subtlety, of capacities of comprehension commensurate with it, can only bring forth a sense of uprootedness, accompanied as it is by the loss of spontaneous historical memory. It harbors "the danger of a loss of identity of people today." Gadamer adds: "The individual becomes incapable of identifying with society, if he [or she] feels dependent and helpless in the face of its technically organized forms of life. This has profound effects on society. And here lies the greatest danger for our civilization: the elevation of adaptation to a privileged status."[19]

For Gadamer, the social sciences favor modes of conduct rooted in the pressure toward external adaptation commonly required in developed modern societies. They are part of a managerial and administrative apparatus that demands responsiveness to externally established behavioral clues, be it in the form of media images, advertising, or bureaucratic regulation. As such, Gadamer's critique of contemporary society surely is radical, as Richard Bernstein observes.[20] The humanistic tradition and habits of classical learning are important, as Bernstein notes, because "they can still serve as an essential corrective to scientism and the obsession with instrumental technical thinking that is dominant today."[21]

Instrumental, technical thinking encourages an organization of habits of conduct not mediated by reflective knowledge or the subtle forms of understanding of self and others achieved in intensive and searching forms of conversation. It sanctions routinized and automatically unfolding forms of behavior that leave little space for an experienced and known integration of internal and external conditions of conduct.

When adaptation is favored over reflectively regulated modes of conduct, the members of modern society adjust to its "technically organized forms of life" as existing beyond their powers of understanding and control. They have no reason to want to make these forms of life known to themselves in conversation nor can they accept the unfamiliarity of what exists. The powers of comprehension are lost with the capacity for dialogue as well as the need to recreate the world for one's understanding in conversation. "Reaching agreement in dialogue implies, that both partners are ready for it and endeavor to recognize as valid for themselves what appears to be alien and opposed to them. If this happens, reciprocally, and each of the partners, while simultaneously holding onto his [or her] own arguments, considers the counter-arguments, they can finally attain, in an imperceptible and spontaneous reciprocal transference of points of view, a common language and a common statement."[22]

Dialogue as a form of communication, therefore, is the opposite of the imposition of categories on one's understanding, which are not derived from the process of understanding itself. Nor is it a process for which beginning and end are easily identified in advance. Neither external adjustment to the other's point of view nor the suppression of what is different from one's own identity can be regarded

167

as desirable for it. Rather, the very play of identity and difference gives dialogue the power to convey something to our understanding, while also making participants more present to themselves and each other as capable of understanding.

On all these grounds, the dialogical principle can be suitably regarded as the opposite of technical, technological making or of instrumental action. Engaging in dialogue also entails the absence of strategic thinking or of the strategic placement of words in conversation. Were I, for example, to attribute hidden motives to you, when you appear to speak with me openly and without withholding your own reasons for speaking with me, I would adopt a strategic attitude toward you and violate the condition of trust required for dialogue. Yet, this is what is commonly done in public life. Frankness itself is regarded as a step in a strategic game. Or were you to attempt to second-guess what I might mean without ever telling me how you interpret my utterances and why you attribute certain meanings to them, you would act strategically as well. There would be no possibility that we achieve an agreement with each other in an unnoticed and spontaneous transference of points of view. At most we could be said to engage in a process of negotiation where each of us is very conscious of our motives for the conversation, while not making these known to the other. We would remain most aware of what separates us from each other, while only being open to the possibility of agreement required for a "settlement." Negotiations, therefore, are not the process of noninstrumental communicative action that Gadamer has in mind, even if elements of a true acknowledgment of the other's interests may be part of them.[23]

Because acting strategically and acting in the form of external adaptation to the conditions of life are so prevalent in modern societies, and because the concomitant modes of behavior are deeply bound to institutions of the modern state, to a corporate economy, and to an increasing international military, financial, and economic competition, it is not surprising that Gadamer turns to the frequently enfeebled and undermined traditions of humanistic and literary studies in order to give some historical-cultural background to his conception of dialogue. However, in doing so, he also privileges a form of cultural learning not widely available, withheld from large sections of the population in modern societies. I am convinced that his ideas are mostly directed to cultural and educational elites still firmly rooted in traditions of classical learning. Gadamer hardly pays much attention to the forms of popular consciousness and popular political expressiveness, which also document the strength to resist the relentlessness of administrative and technical progress.[24] One also wonders, of course, whether Gadamer is at all aware of the potential, contained in modern institutions and social movements since the Enlightenment, for the extension of public debate, the creation of new discursive spaces and of cultures of criticism. Their sympathetic appraisal requires a vantage-point favorably disposed toward the development of modern democracies and of some mass movements carrying forward the claims of democratization and of the universalist emancipatory ideals of the Enlightenment.[25]

These questions, however, take us into the domain of politics and public negotiation. It is here that Gadamer makes prudent suggestions for the maintenance of minimal conditions of tolerance and understanding, rather than proposing that what he means by dialogue can become a measure of fully public communication.

3. *Politics as Management, the Prudence of Statecraft and Negotiation*

In a rarely discussed but important essay, "Notes on Planning for the Future," Gadamer approaches the contemporary world as someone fully aware of the exigencies created by the beginning formation of a world-order, or of "planning on a world scale."[26] Certainly his observations about the state of international affairs and about the difficulties attendant upon the search for solutions to the most pressing problems of our day do not conceal a deep-rooted skepticism with respect to the possibilities of planning. In his remarks, he concentrates on the limits of politics and the "art of statecraft as the ultimate expertise."[27] Following classical discussions, Gadamer denies that there can be such expertise. The politican cannot and may not be a scientific specialist, drawing upon available technical knowledge for the management of social processes: "The idea of making and craftsmanship represents a false model of cognition [when applied to political situations]." There is no generalizable, "rational model" that we can employ when at-

169

tempting to delineate possibilities of social improvement by political means.[28]

Gadamer turns to an older conception of politics and the politician in this context. He thinks of the "statesman"[29] as that public figure who always must make decisions under conditions of uncertainty. For him, such public figures will seek to maintain and establish an equilibrium among different and often conflicting forces. Following Plato, Gadamer compares the statesman's prudent adjustment of differences of perception and judgment to an always-to-be-reestablished fragile, common ground with the action of piloting or steering. *Piloting* means selecting a direction "within the oscillating equilibrium."[30] And he compares this form of the practice of politics to medicine, calling upon older conceptions of the healing arts. For here, just as in many cases of political action, the healer's intervention does not consist in the effort to completely control a process. The relevant interventions are merely meant to help the patient regain a natural state of balance. What does all this entail for a theory of politics and the place of conversation in it?

There is at least one very clear answer. Gadamer takes a strongly antiutopian position, which includes the rejection of emancipatory politics as a real possibility of social transformation. Gadamer clearly knows what he does *not* regard as possible or desirable. Any form of utopian politics aiming at the achievement of an *ideal* order or any form of planning (be it piecemeal or total planning) is suspect to him, as long as both forms of politics or administration and management do not respect the fact that political decisions are finite and that they are based on limited knowledge gained in the interpretation of situational constraints and subject to a great variety of standards of measurement and evaluation. Utopian politics and pragmatic social engineering are equally suspect to him, because, in his view, they confound politics with administration or tend to replace the former by the latter.[31]

Thus, the statesman's acts of piloting amount to a readiness to steer a course between incompatible interests, divergent worldviews, and conflicting opinions. The form of conversation adequate to politics understood in this sense — as the actions of persons acting on behalf of states, large power blocs or large groups, such as parties — can only consist in negotiation, in the formal process of weighing different interests and coming to an agreement about their respective legitimacy. It follows that major political conflicts and differences of opinion (for example, differences between the North Atlantic Treaty Organization and the Warsaw Pact countries regarding the meaning and significance of human rights)[32] can never be treated in the same way as differences of opinion or differently held convictions in a conversation between friends. For political differences may reflect deep divisions of public life, of organized collective interests. Solutions can only be found, if it is recognized that differences of belief and attitude are always intertwined with a possible resort to power and the exercise of force.

Those who argue that Gadamer has underestimated the place of power or coercion in social life and therefore has failed to address the phenomenon of domination as a social problem in modern societies are mistaken.[33] Gadamer is so much aware of the presence of these factors that he refuses to transform hermeneutics as a practical philosophy into a *critique* of domination. Critical theory as a critique of domination is incompatible with his hermeneutics, because, in his view, it fails to do justice to the phenomenon of power. Power, authority-relations, and differences between the major world powers and less politically and economically influential countries and nations are just as ineradicable from human history as are differences of intelligence, competence, and physical well-being among individuals. For him there always will be such differences, no matter how they may change or be alleviated and reduced in one or the other social and political domain. It is only by taking note of this element of skepticism vis-à-vis the overriding tendency, in modernity, to regard major social and political differences as potentially eliminatable that one can make sense of Gadamer's rejection of utopian and emancipatory politics as well as his aversion to social engineering and large-scale social planning.

In fact, Gadamer cannot distinguish between emancipatory politics, utopian social engineering, and pragmatic social engineering (on the premises of American liberalism let us say), because in each case a more or less egalitarian premise comes into play. He does not argue against this premise as such (even if he cannot make it his own). He simply believes that any politics pursuing its implementation will fail to come to terms with its own consequences, the creation of new differences and inequalities. In other words, history repeats itself, even if it is never exactly the same. Therefore, the "wise statesman" will respect the fact that inequalities, for example, are persistent features of the social order. *Disorder*, as he says in one case,[34] is the natural condition of a political world-order.

Political wisdom consists in the prudent acceptance of the relevant differences and inequalities. To give an example: Western Europe, in Gadamer's view, can no longer aspire to be a political "world-leader" nor can it expect to be economically predominant. It can best fulfill its "world-historical mission," if it restricts itself to a culturally civilizing role, recognizing fully well, at the same time, that there are cultural traditions outside the Western hemisphere, which are equal to it. Therefore, Europe is to enter into dialogue with Asia (India, China, Japan in particular).[35]

This sober appraisal of the possibilities of politics and of the limits to past European hegemony in particular matches quite readily with Gadamer's appraisal of other facts of our historical situation. Thus, he believes that we need to *accept* the fact of competing world-systems in a nuclear age: no one may strive for ultimate hegemony. Therefore, he concedes that differences between "Western" democracy (such as that found in Europe and North America) and democracy in primarily one-party states (such as the Soviet Union) are not absolute. As with other conservative Germans of his generation,[36] Gadamer fails to be impressed by the Enlightenment pathos of liberal democracy and its advocates, and he has never been attracted at all to the egalitarian and socially emancipatory *ethos* of European socialism or to the forms of grassroots mobilization characteristic of it. He can, therefore, assume that opposition, conflict, possibly enmity, or the *lack* of friendship are a *fundamental* condition of politics. Yet he does not regard politics in general and international relations in particular as merely consisting of relations among friends and foes.[37] For him, politics is the art of transforming enmity into a *negotiable* opposition of interests. But there is no raison d'être for politics as the effort to keep enmity under control, were we to assume that there can be a perfect harmony of interests. Opposition and competition between different interests and conflicting conceptions of the social good are the very element of politics, without which it would become mere administration. The displacement of politics by administration is rejected because it purports to offer solutions, which remove the irritation of having to come to terms with conflict as a reality. Politics as administration can only lead to an external adjustment of interests carried out by an all-pervasive authority, disguising itself as a functionally required form of administration. For these reasons, Gadamer fails to perceive the difference between emancipatory and technocratic politics.

As others of his generation, he agrees with Max Weber's critique of socialism: the pursuit of its egalitarian ideals can only lead to greater bureaucratic regulation. But he does not enter into an argument about the possible advantages of even this development for a great majority of people in the world,[38] nor does he examine whether there can be less harmful alternatives. Here his thinking is impeded by the fact that the major socially emancipatory movements of modernity always appear to him to lead to the creation of mass-democracies that only can be governed without much respect for liberty and individuality as principles. He does not see that there is a definite relation between the universal character of these principles and modern emancipatory movements (e.g., from the movements to extend the franchise to women, the propertyless, and so forth, to anticolonial movements and contemporary feminism). In other words, his most sensible political realism is accompanied by a somewhat passive and quietist attitude toward modern history. For, during this period, major social transformations were fought for with good reasons.[39] It follows, therefore, that Gadamer's views of the rationality possible in politics deeply reflect his advocacy of the prudent weighing of different courses of action as the right attitude to take toward matters of personal and public morality.

4. Negotiation, Dialogue, Poetry

Friendship cannot be made a fundamental condition of public decisionmaking nor can the conversation between friends or the open-minded pursuit of truth in intellectual conversation be the measure for possible agreement to be reached in public negotiation.[40] All that we can hope for in this domain is civility, the concerted effort to create conditions for the give-and-take of negotiations. The art of statesmanship consists in this effort. Philosophy in our times, therefore, pleads for "tolerance as the central civic virtue."[41]

Gadamer's plea for it follows from his entire philosophy as a philosophy of dialogue. The politician as functionary, manager, or social engineer can hardly be expected to be imbued with the spirit of dialogue, but the "wise statesman" (if there are such) can and may be. For Gadamer, public life outside educational institutions and the sphere of culture hardly is the realm of freedom. The necessities of collective life surface in it just as strongly as the necessities of the physical survival and of the decay of individuals surface in the case of health, illness, and disease. Therefore, there can be no political ideal, no public conception of justice or morality, which could be equally attractive to thoughtful human beings as the dialogue they freely and openly engage in, uncoerced by the need for compromise or the weighing of momentous economic, military, and ideological decisions. Gadamer follows Plato in favoring the philosopher over the statesman, while not at all expecting or even wanting to entertain the possibility (ironically or not) that philosophers can be statesmen.

Philosophers desire conversation for its own sake. Through it they discover whether their beliefs and convictions make sense. They require the other, the friend as opponent (or the reverse), for the sake of examining the limits of their beliefs. This is not the case with those holding central positions in public life. They will test the limits of the other's convictions in order to see where he or she can be overwhelmed and where his or her real *power* lies. Once this limit is identified, the power of the other side has to be respected or peace (at least in international relations) cannot be maintained.

Thus Gadamer has traced different forms of dialogue or conversation at home in different domains of social, political, and personal life. His is a view of world and history that includes what he believes we find sustenance in, friendship and the quiet intimacy of poetical speech. It also includes what we cannot escape from, the bonds, pressures, and restrictions of collective life in an ever more integrated international order (a form of organized disorder—in his view). Measured by contemporary expectations of what is possible *and* necessary (given the dynamics of modern history and the

174

legitimate aspirations of the world's peoples, especially of those so far largely taken for granted or having been used and exploited for the development of a few European and North American societies), Gadamer's position is deeply, even if prudently, conservative.

Not only can he not envisage a world free of the disturbing facts of power, but like conservatives of his generation deeply disturbed by World War I, the Soviet revolution, the defeat of German national power, the internal conflicts of Weimar Germany, and finally the Nazi seizure of power, he can only conclude that a prudent acceptance of the realities of power leaves room for the real interests of a liberal spirit: scholarly learning, humanist erudition, and sensitive intellectual conversation as well as a love and respect of the arts. Gadamer's *radicalism* manifests itself *most* clearly in his love for poetry and, in particular, his dedication to the work of a Holocaust poet such as Paul Celan. Here Gadamer realizes that real human hope cannot survive without facing utter hopelessness.[42] Somewhere underneath Gadamer's seigneurial and aristocratic defense of inherited "European" culture and his Bismarckian political realism inspired by a form of conservative institutionalist Hegelianism,[43] lies hidden a feeling for the deeply disturbing conflicts and contradictions of modernity.

This sensitivity comes to expression in his acceptance of the lonely figure of the poet writing under conditions of mass communication. It contrasts strongly with Gadamer's own public persona as a representative of powerful intellectual and cultural traditions. Many among us may not feel comfortable with the element of almost aristocratic liberalism present in his thought or the conception and theory of politics linked with it. We would do so for good reasons. For nowhere in Gadamer's work can we discover any careful consideration of even European democratic traditions or of Marxism and the history of socialism, of anticolonial movements or of social movements generally. Much of recent history reaching beyond the university and the arts has been screened from his thought. But we can hardly escape the truth and humanity of an intellectual disposition that gives the last word to the poet and poetry, especially a poet who never was on the side of power.[44]

And insofar as there are traces of this disposition to be found in all of Gadamer's reflections on dialogue and conversation, one can hardly claim that he does *not* speak to the situation even of those among us, who definitely have a more political and radical vision than he and who work and think in a different frame of commitments and obligations no longer accepting the centrality of "occidental Europe." Gadamer's hermeneutics is deeply formed by a distrust of *any* instrumental attitude toward truth, knowledge, or interpersonal relations. In this sense, his hermeneutics also contributes to the critique of instrumental reason, the voice of a weak and mostly defeated Enlightenment tradition,[45] which may, one day, be thought of as the best of the occidental tradition mentioned.

Notes

1. Hans-Georg Gadamer, "Die Unfähigkeit zum Gespräch," in *Hermeneutik II*, vol. 2 of *Gesammelte Werke* (Tübingen: J. C. B. Mohr, 1986), 207-18. *Gesammelte Werke* will be abbreviated hereafter as *GW* followed by volume number and page.

2. A sociological interpretation of Gadamer's reflections on language, *Bildung*, and *Gespräch* could easily show that his ideas are developed in the social space of the German *Bildungsbürgertum*. It is one of the strengths of his position, and a charming feature of it, that he never denies this. Jürgen Habermas has described Gadamer in these terms in his laudation; see his "Urbanisierung der Heideggerschen Provinz. Laudatio auf Hans-Georg Gadamer," in Hans-Georg Gadamer and Jürgen Habermas, *Das Erbe Hegels* (Frankfurt: Suhrkamp, 1979), 9-32.

3. Gadamer has never been impressed by efforts such as Habermas's to develop a critical social science. His skepticism may be justified, in many respects, and is confirmed by analyses of the role of the social sciences such as Michel Foucault's. However, Gadamer underestimates the positive and emancipatory effects of both the natural and social sciences, that is, with respect to the sexual emancipation of women (and men) in recent decades, changes in childrearing, and even in areas such as legal reform and the reforms of schooling. He has given little thought to the social transformations which have, for example, taken place in Western Europe since the 1950s, and especially in the Federal Republic of Germany.

4. See Hans-Georg Gadamer, "Die Idee der Universität. Gestern, Heute, Morgen," address on the occasion of the 600th anniversary of the University of Heidelberg (October 1985). See also Hans-Georg Gadamer, *Die Universität Heidelberg und die Geburt der modernen Wissenschaft* (Berlin: Springer, 1987), 5-21; and Helmut Schelsky, *Einsamkeit and Freiheit. Die deutsche Universität und ihre Reformen* (Hamburg: Reinbek, 1963).

5. Hans-Georg Gadamer, "Verstummen die Dichter?", in *Poetica* (Frankfurt: Insel, 1977), 103-18. Unless otherwise noted, all translations from German of this and other works are my own.

6. Gadamer, "Verstummen die Dichter," 103.

7. Gadamer, "Verstummen die Dichter," 118.

8. He is not unlike Theodor Adorno in this respect. Adorno quite explicitly defended the most esoteric forms of modern art in music, poetry, and literature, arguing that only avant-garde art possessed the features necessary for the survival of art as a form of objective spirit with critically illuminating powers. Gadamer, however, does not adhere to a general theoretical argument of this kind either in his reflections on poetry or in his interpretations of it.

9. Hans-Georg Gadamer, "Sinn und Sinnverhüllung bei Paul Celan," in *Poetica*, 119-34.

10. Gadamer, "Sinn und Sinnverhüllung," 119.

11. Gadamer, "Sinn und Sinnverhüllung," 105.

12. Gadamer, "Sinn und Sinnverhüllung," 105.

13. See Gadamer, "Unfähigkeit zum Gespräch," 219.

14. The analogy to Habermas's reflections on the relation between solidarity and individuation is striking. For an illuminating discussion of Habermas's arguments, see Seyla Benhabib, *Critique, Norm, and Utopia* (New York: Columbia University Press, 1986), 279-354.

15. Gadamer does not propose that we resurrect Aristotelian views of public and political life that refer to friendship as a condition for citizenship. He is less conservative (or radical) in this respect than Hannah Arendt. For he knows that the modern world cannot be held accountable to such a view and that the Greek *polis* was not simply a republic of friends or what Aristotle meant it to be. For the similarities

between Gadamer and Arendt, see Richard J. Bernstein, *Beyond Objectivism and Relativism* (Philadelphia, Penn.: University of Pennsylvania Press, 1983), 212-23.

16. Gadamer, "Unfähigkeit zum Gespräch," 211.

17. Here Gadamer refers to Leibniz and Goethe; see "Unfähigkeit zum Gespräch," 210.

18. See Hans-Georg Gadamer, *Wahrheit und Methode,* in vol. 1 of *GW* (Tübingen: J. C. B. Mohr, 1986), 20-24, 45-47; see also the entire discussion of *Bildung, sensus communis,* and taste, *GW* 1: 15-42. The humanistic tradition in ethics is essentially Greek, for Gadamer. And Greek ethics is "in a deep and encompassing sense an ethics of good taste" (*GW* 1: 45). For an application of the notions of tact and *sensus communis* to social theory, see my "Common Sense and Common Convictions: Scientific Sociology, Phenomenological Sociology and the Hermeneutical Point of View," in *Common Sense: The Foundation for Social Science,* eds. F. van Holthoon and D. R. Olson (New York: University Press of America, 1988), 235-74.

19. See Hans-Georg Gadamer, "What is Practice?", in *Reason in the Age of Science,* trans. Frederick G. Lawrence (Cambridge, Mass.: MIT Press, 1981), 73; translation modified.

20. Bernstein, *Beyond Objectivism and Relativism,* 163-64.

21. Bernstein, *Beyond Objectivism and Relativism,* 180.

22. Gadamer, *Wahrheit und Methode,* in *GW* 1: 390. See also Gadamer, *Truth and Method,* trans. Sheed and Ward Ltd. (New York: Seabury Press, 1975), 348; translation modified.

23. Gadamer, "Unfähigkeit zum Gespräch," 213.

24. Recent work in social history has contributed to an increased awareness of these themes, for example, the studies of heretical religious movements during the Middle Ages and in the early phases of classical capitalism, the studies of the beginnings of the working-class movement such as protests against industrialization, studies of the resistance, among women midwives, against the professional monopoly of male medical doctors, and studies of the role of carnivals and popular festivities among lower-class people throughout the centuries.

25. See Jürgen Habermas, *The Philosophical Discourse of Modernity* (Cambridge, Mass.: MIT Press, 1987), 336-67.

26. Hans-Georg Gadamer, "Notes on Planning for the Future," in *Daedulus* 95 (1966): 573.

27. Gadamer, "Notes on Planning for the Future," 578.

28. Gadamer, "Notes on Planning for the Future," 581-82.

29. I use this somewhat antiquated term with Gadamer to reflect traditions of politics reminiscent of a Talleyrand or Metternich, but not of our times. This term also has a definitely masculinist bias.

30. Gadamer, "Notes on Planning for the Future," 582.

31. Here Gadamer's thought is similar to that of Arendt and her praise of the purported Greek separation of economics from politics.

32. Gadamer expressed such views in the course of an extended interview conducted by Graeme Nicholson and myself during the summer of 1986 in Heidelberg. At one point in this interview, he warned against the United States being too insistent upon the Soviet Union's acceptance of conceptions of human rights which the United States regard as universally valid. Such insistence, according to Gadamer, would be bound to upset the delicate balance of power between the two countries.

33. See Bernstein's critique in *Beyond Objectivism and Relativism*, 156. The same critique is implicit in Habermas's critique of Gadamer's linguistic idealism; see Jürgen Habermas, *Zur Logik der Sozialwissenschaften* (Frankfurt: Suhrkamp, 1982), 306-10. For a discussion of the differences between Habermas and Gadamer, see my "Critical Theory and Hermeneutics: The Debate between Habermas and Gadamer," in *On Critical Theory*, ed. J. O'Neill (New York: Seabury Press, 1976), 164-83. See also Graeme Nicholson, "Answers to Critical Theory," and my reply, "Hermeneutics and Modernity. A Critical Theoretical Rejoinder," in *Gadamer and Hermeneutics*, vol. 4 of *Continental Philosophy*, ed. Hugh Silverman (London, New York: Methuen, 1989).

34. See Gadamer, "Notes on Planning for the Future," 574.

35. See Hans-Georg Gadamer, "Die Zukunft der europäischen Geisteswissenschaften," in *Europa. Horizonte der Hoffnung*, eds. F. König and K. Rahner (Vienna: Styria, 1983), 243-61.

36. I am thinking of Arnold Gehlen, Hans Freyer, Carl Schmitt, and Martin Heidegger, as well as Ernst Jünger. This is not to deny that

179

Gadamer is much more liberal than any of these men and also "durch und durch Zivilist," as Habermas once said. The others have — at one time or another — praised military discipline and/or an antiliberal esprit de corps. I have discussed aspects of the conservativism in question in my general introduction to *Modern German Sociology*, eds. Volker Meja, Dieter Misgeld, and Nico Stehr (New York: Columbia University Press, 1987), 1–30, and, in greater detail, in my "Modernity, Democracy and Social Engineering," *Praxis International* 7 (1987/1988): 268–85.

37. Thus Gadamer's views are clearly different from Carl Schmitt's much discussed critique of liberal politics. See *Telos*, no. 71 (Spring 1987): 37–110, and *Telos*, no. 72 (summer 1987), the entire issue.

38. Gadamer acknowledges that socialism may be necessary for many countries in the Third World. It is clear, however, that it is not his preferred choice for the part of the world most familiar to him. See his "Notes on Planning for the Future," 587.

39. Gadamer recognizes this insofar as he says that the "principle that all are free can never again be shaken"; see Gadamer, "What is Practice?", 80.

40. Thus Gadamer implicitly accepts Habermas's argument that modernity is characterized by a differentiation of questions of truth from those of justice, morality, and taste. See Habermas, *Philosophical Discourse of Modernity*, 336–67.

41. See Gadamer, "Notes on Planning for the Future," 588.

42. Here Gadamer's thought converges with the much more radical thought of either Martin Heidegger or Walter Benjamin.

43. See Habermas, *Philosophical Discourse of Modernity*, 51–74 for a brilliant, critical discussion of the conservative Hegelian tradition and the richness of its institutionalist views reaching from Hegel to Arnold Gehlen, Joachim Ritter, and, marginally, Gadamer.

44. See Hans-Georg Gadamer's wonderful little book on Paul Celan, *Wer bin Ich und wer bist Du?* (Frankfurt: Suhrkamp, 1973).

45. When considered from this perspective, Gadamer's thought converges with that of the Frankfurt school and its critique of the Enlightenment. However, Gadamer relies more strongly on the traditions of German Romanticism through his reception and critique of

historicism. Max Horkheimer and Theodor Adorno develop their critique of Enlightenment ideas of progress and scientific rationality out of the counterenlightenment thought of those "dark writers of the bourgeoisie" (from de Sade to Nietzsche); on this point, see Habermas, *Philosophical Discourse of Modernity*, 106-30.

Part III

Hermeneutics and the Challenges of Poetry and Postmodern Thinking

8

Paul Celan's Challenges to Heidegger's Poetics*

Véronique M. Fóti

---

*I*n his study of the interinvolvement of philosophical and political concerns on Martin Heidegger's path of thinking, Otto Pöggeler points out that a fruitful contemporary engagement with Heidegger must address, above all, his concrete analyses, notably those of art, especially poetry, and of technicity.[1] These analyses not only orient Heidegger's questioning of the self-understanding and contemporary task of philosophy but also provide a foothold for investigating the concealed and problematic political dimension of Heidegger's thought.

In the *Spiegel* interview of 1966, which constitutes Heidegger's only explicit discussion of his own political past, he indicates that his change of topic for his lecture course in the 1934 summer term (from "The State and Science" to "Logic," i.e., *logos*), together with his subsequent lecture courses on Hölderlin and Nietzsche, and with the "Poetizing and Thinking" problematic of the period from 1944 to 1945, constitute "a confrontation with National Socialism."[2] An *Auseinandersetzung* with totalitarianism and, most of all, with the totalitarian rhetoric that had enthralled him, inaugurates Heidegger's philosophical poetics and ushers in the analyses of art and technicity. These concerns, therefore, do not mark—as is sometimes assumed—a turning away from the political dimension; but rather, they make for the encrypting of Heidegger's political thought.

This essay does not engage in the long labor of tracing the labyrinthine configurations of this crypt—requisite and timely though such a labor may be—but will address, instead, the rather

---

*For Hans-Georg Gadamer who first introduced me to the poetry of Paul Celan.

surprising failure of Heidegger's poetics to extend itself, beyond Hölderlin, Rilke, Trakl, and George, to the poetry of Paul Celan.

Several considerations make this failure surprising. First, Celan's poetry is not only, like that of Hölderlin and Rilke, self-problematizing and focussed importantly on its own possibility and mandate in a "destitute time" but thematizes, with extraordinary complexity and precision of articulation, what Werner Hamacher and Evelyn Hünneke have called, respectively (with different emphases) the fissioning im/partment of language and "the realization of the real in the medium of poetry."[3] Not only is this concern of a piece with Heidegger's problematic of the poetic character of language (so that the exigencies of his own thinking should have involved him in dialogue with the poet); but it is indissociable in Celan from an agonized effort to articulate the possibilities of meaning and communion still open to a language that has been put into the service of totalitarianism and has passed through the Holocaust. A philosophical poetics, which is an encrypted meditation on the origins, the persuasive power, and the possible surpassing of totalitarian organization, can scarcely fail to engage with Celan's poetry.

Both Gerhardt Baumann and Pöggeler attest to Heidegger's familiarity with Celan's work, including the important prose text of the 1960s "Der Meridian."[4] Celan, for his part, was an assiduous reader of Heidegger's writings; yet the relationship between poet and thinker (on the occasions, particularly, of their meetings in 1967 and 1970) appears to have been strained, despite mutual regard. Baumann ascribes this, above all, to the fact that Celan's passionate desire for the "coming word" of atonement on Heidegger's part came up against the latter's stubborn refusal: "Heidegger sought to reserve a possible confession, a legacy over against the horizon of his entire path of thinking; that everything had to remain, in all respects, inadequate was something he was perhaps conscious of in the end."[5]

Because a fruitful engagement with both poet and thinker must take place at the level of intellectual and poetic articulation, this chapter bypasses further biographical and circumstantial considerations. It proposes, rather, to trace some exploratory paths into largely uncharted territory by considering some of the challenges which

Celan's poetry poses to Heidegger's poetics, and to develop their import.

I

A dialogue between thinker and poet consists, for Heidegger, in a thoughtful situating (*Erörterung*) of the poetic saying that proceeds by way of an elucidating (*Erläuterung*) of individual poems. The reciprocity between situating and elucidating opens up the space of such a dialogue. Situating involves the preliminary movements of indicating and heeding the site (*Ort*), followed by a questioning which seeks the locality (*Ortschaft*) of this site.[6]

Heidegger speaks of the site of a given poet's lyric saying as the point of a convergence that pulls together the dispersions, the multivalences, and polysemy of the poetry "at the tip of the spear," which is to say, in accordance with their "highest" and "utmost" inner necessity. This gathering *in extremis* configures a single but always "unsaid" or unachieved poem, which is at once the hidden source and the promised confluence of the saying. Because this single, originary poem remains unsaid, it calls forth the counterplay of situating and elucidating; for it can be indicated only through the elucidation of actual or said poems, while, at the same time, their elucidation must draw from the hidden source.

The point of opening up, through this interrelation, the interval of dialogue is, for Heidegger, to make manifest the very Being (*Wesen*) of language, so as to indicate the locality (*Ortschaft*) of human or mortal dwelling. In his essay "Language," Heidegger speaks of the "height" and "depth" opened up by the abyssal (and seemingly tautologous) statements that "language is language" and that "language speaks" (*die Sprache spricht*).[7] The locality of mortal dwelling opened up by these dimensions of height and depth is, at the same time, the essential site (*Ort*) of language: it marks the coming to pass of *Ereignis*.[8] Language here can be understood in terms of what Heidegger, in "A Dialogue on Language," describes as the unbinding hermeneutical bond that engages man both to receive and to respond to the "tidings" (*die Kunde*) of the Differing.[9]

The figure of the point of the spear recalls Hölderlin's notion of the *caesura* that gathers the conflicting forces of a dramatic action

186

through a "pure word" that "tears [man] from the midpoint of his inner life . . . and pulls [him] into the eccentric sphere of the dead," but which also thereby configures a living image of man.[10] The correspondences between Hölderlin's *caesura* and Celan's notions of an *Atemwende* or turning of breath and of the counterword (*Gegenwort*) have been insightfully discussed by Bernhard Böschenstein and Sieghild Bogumil;[11] but Heidegger's place in this interrelation still remains to be explored. With regard to this task, these remarks are preliminary.

For Heidegger, the locality of poetic dwelling is the rift of the Differing; yet the interpretive or dialogical path to this locality requires a double effacing of differences. It postulates, first of all, a convergence of the polysemy of poetic saying at "the tip of the spear," such that Georg Trakl's relentless ambiguities and reversals, for instance, become the complex unfolding of a single accord that remains withdrawn into the unsayable and marks the "inmost site" of his poetry. Heidegger contrasts such ultimately convergent ambiguity with the uncertain gropings of minor poets who abide in ambiguity because they lack "the ownmost poem and its place."[12] Although the place of convergence is the Differing, it resolves ambiguity and reconciles the differential im/partment of poetic articulation.

Second, duality and polarity, such as that of Celan's counterplay between "I" and "you" that has been richly explored by Gadamer,[13] or, in Levinasian terms, of encounter and the Face of the Other, is collapsed; for mortals are gathered into sameness in being considered strictly as such, as they are pulled into the draw of the Differing. By the same token, historical or political upheavals cannot be radically disruptive. Celan's poetry, however, resolutely resists these unifying moves. His poem "À la pointe acérée," whose title, notwithstanding acknowledged allusions to Baudelaire and Hoffmannsthal,[14] strikingly recalls the extreme point of the *caesura* and the tip of the spear, can open up some initial perspectives on this resistance:

> Es liegen die Erze bloss, die Kristalle,
> die Drusen.

Ungeschriebenes, zu
Sprache verhärtet, legt
einen Himmel frei.

(Nach oben verworfen, zutage,
überquer, so
liegen auch wir.

Tür du davor einst, Tafel
mit dem getöteten
Kreidestern drauf:
ihn
hat nun ein — lesendes? — Aug.)

Wege dorthin.
Waldstunde an
der blubbernden Radspur entlang.
Auf-
gelesene
kleine, klaffende
Buchecker: schwärzliches
Offen, von
Fingergedanken befragt
nach —
wonach?

Nach
dem Unwiederholbaren, nach
ihm, nach
allem.

Blubbernde Wege dorthin.

Etwas, das gehn kann, grusslos
wie Herzgewordenes,
kommt.[15]

If one adopts what Gadamer characterizes as "a fundamental principle of all interpretation," namely, to make a beginning where "the first light of understanding flashes forth"[16] (although such understanding must remain open to revisions), one may be led to approach this poem as a meditation on *legein*. The thematic of *lesen*, *legen*, and *liegen* (reading, laying, and lying) in the first four stanzas recalls Heidegger's concern with *logos* in its intimate connection with unconcealment. What lies unconcealed here, however, is not gathered together by a col-lecting (*Lese*) that remains "drawn and, at the same time, sustained by the fundamental trait of sheltering" (*des Bergens*).[17] It has been cast up, rather, from the sheltering depths by a cataclysmic upheaval that, in its unrepeatability, remains unwritten. Instead, the chaotic desolation and shameless exposure have hardened into language; and Celan's line break ("zu/ Sprache verhärtet") suggests, at the same time, an ensuing sclerosis of language. Bogumil has observed, with reference to Celan's poem "Sprachgitter" (*PC* 1: 167), that a pure origin is unthinkable for the poet because "in front of it there stands always the fencework of language."[18] This fencework or *Sprachgitter* is, at the same time, by analogy to the *Kristallgitter* (the structural matrix of crystals) the vital core of language that has been injured in the outcasting.

What is "laid/free" by the upheaval (recalling here that unconcealment is freedom) is "a sky" — not the single sky or heaven of Heidegger's Fourfold, but one whose identity is in question. Readers of Celan's poetry will recall the second verse of his poem "Unter ein Bild": "Welchen Himmels Blau? Des untern? Obern?" (Which sky's blue? That of the lower? The upper?) (*PC* 1: 155), together with his statement, in "Der Meridian," that one who walks on his head "has heaven beneath him as an abyss" (*PC* 3: 195). The *caesura* between the promise and the abyss, marked, in the poem just cited (with clear reference to Hölderlin's "Hälfte des Lebens"), by the concluding words "beide Welten" (both worlds) cannot be effaced or bridged by any unifying effort. Irreconcilable fissionings and redoublings have come about through the cataclysm and through the sclerosis of language.

The chalk star of the third stanza, considered literally, is the star of David chalked upon the ghetto door;[19] but it also indicates, together with the tablet that blocks the view, a "killed" representation of heaven. What can it mean now to "read" such a symbol?

The poem keeps itself on the "ways thither," the ways to the site of the death camp, following the trace of the gurgling "wheel-track."

On the one hand, the "woodland hour" and the trace hearken back to Heidegger's *Holzwege* (wood-paths) of questioning and to his thematization of the holy as trace;[20] but on the other hand, they point to the fact that the perpetrators of the Holocaust sought to camouflage all traces, for instance, by planting "pine trees that were three or four years old,"[21] thus restoring an appearance of the rustic calm valorized by the ideology of National Socialism. On the "ways thither," reading and writing become a "col-lecting" of traces, a multiple *auflesen* marked off from the *auslesen* (selecting, electing, singling out) that Heidegger emphasizes in his discussion of *legein*.[22] What gathers and reads is not the detached eye that can span the panoramic scene, but the close, searching touch of "finger-thoughts" that question the "blackish opening" of "beechnuts" (*Buchecker*) [or, by connotation, the openings found between the corners of books, (*Buchecken*)], encountering ruptures and clefts.

One can no longer, with Heidegger, interpret *legein* here as "lesendes beisammen-vor-liegen-Lassen [das] nichts anderes sein kann als das Wesen des Einen, das alles ins All des einfachen Anwesens versammelt."[23] Out of the disunity and mimetic failure (relating the repeated "nach" to *Nachahmung*, mimetic repetition), "something" (perhaps the poem or work of art) can still go forth; but it comes ungreeting. In elucidating Hölderlin's poem "Andenken," Heidegger focusses on the verse "Geh aber nun und grüsse" ("go now, however, and greet") and speaks of a greeting that brings tidings of that which holds itself in concealment.[24] Celan, however, must acknowledge that the obliterated dead remain infrangibly beyond greeting; yet perhaps no greeting is needed; for the unrepeatable origin of the poem has "become heart."

II

Unlike Heidegger's *Dichtung*, Celan's poetic diction does not open up a "world" that grants to things their presencing yet shelters them within its radiance; it does not reveal the (singular) rift of the Differing but rather foregrounds its own impartment. Disseminating, impeding, and perhaps, in Derrida's trope, "circum-cizing" itself,[25] it achieves a strange amalgam of classically ordered (hence decipherable) and abyssal complexity.

190

To bring to the fore certain non-Heideggerian aspects of Celan's understanding of poetic language, this chapter addresses, in particular, his poem "Engführung" (*PC* 1: 197–204), of which Peter Szondi has performed a pathbreaking exegesis.[26] Rather than moving sequentially through the ten sections of the poem, the analysis makes an initial incision at the beginning of the fifth part:

> Deckte es
> zu — wer?
>
> Kam, kam.
> Kam ein Wort, kam,
> kam durch die Nacht,
> wollt leuchten, wollt leuchten.[27]

The word that came through the night came (yet no longer comes) as inexorably as the sleep which overcame the victims ("Keines/ erwachte, der/ Schlaf/ kam über sie") and their speaking "of words";[28] yet it sought to dispel oblivion and darkness, to reveal and render manifest what has been, ambiguously, both covered in the exposure of its nakedness and covered over and up ("zudecken").

Szondi locates a sharp break, a (non-Hölderlinian) *caesura* between this stanza and the second stanza of the fifth section:

> Asche.
> Asche, Asche.
> Nacht.
> Nacht-und-Nacht. — Zum
> Aug geh, zum feuchten.[29]

The break indicates the failure of any "pure word" in the face of the "as yet unfathomable magnitude"[30] of the Holocaust; the disclosive power of the *logos* is not, as Heidegger took it to be, ahistorically secure. The rupture, nevertheless, is not as decisive as Szondi understands it, given that,[31] the rhyme of "leuchten" and "feuchten" links the two stanzas, and that it is the "night" of the first stanza that darkens into "night-and-night," whereas the "go" (which also echoes the "Look no longer — go!" of the first section) redirects the initial "came." The luminous word still seeks an eye for which to shine, although this eye is now, rather incongruously (given the incompatibility between fire and moisture) a "moist one," inclined to mourning and perhaps even to nostalgia for lost traditions.

Another rupture becomes evident with the first stanza of the sixth section:

> Zum
> Aug geh,
> zum feuchten —

Orkane,
Orkane, von je,
Partikelgestöber, das andre,
du
weissts ja, wir
lasens im Buche, war
Meinung.[32]

If the word fails to shine, this is not solely a matter of history; rather, what "was, was," but can hold its own no more is the "opinion" that dissembles the whirlwind of particles or what one might call, with Hamacher, "the self-disruptive, self-dispersive, and disseminating speaking of langage."[33] It is, of course, questionable whether such disarticulating and fissioning is indeed still a speaking. If language or "saying" cannot accomplish what Heidegger asks of it, namely "to show, to let appear, to let [something] be seen and heard"[34] in the manner of *phainesthai*, the reason is that language lacks inherent meaningfulness and an originary proper nature that would allow it, in Heidegger's words, to be brought "as language to language."[35]

Gadamer, in his essay "Celan's Schlussgedicht," comments similarly, albeit with broader focus:

> The postulate of harmony which we have so far kept intact as an assured expectation of meaning [*Sinn*] in every encountered obscuration of meaning, has withdrawn itself. . . . It is a breakdown of the expectation of meaning which, as a perseverance without projective agency and without belief in something inviolate [*ein Heiles*] has found its poetic expression in the poem.[36]

In "Engführung," the withdrawal of the expectation of sense or, to speak with Philippe Forget, of "a circularity which, in the end, would be without remainder, since it is primarily concerned with the (original) sense,"[37] is linked to the figure of writing. In its opening

192

and closing sections, the poem speaks of the trace that, although "undeceiving," is not to be read, of the conversations of "groundwater-traces," of lapidary and shadow-writing, of the "grass / written asunder." Dispersive writing and the trace, indeed, form the poem's own remainder in that its form, in opening and closing with these tropes, describes a failed circle; for the sparse and halting final stanzas approximate the fuller and more sonorous opening. The writ here repudiates the phenomenological and hermeneutical investment of *logos* and its tie to any pure origin. The datum of history (indicated by the "undeceiving / trace") is ineffaceable; yet it eludes representation while, nevertheless, it is accessible only in and as cipher and text. Thus, to quote Forget once more, "date and text are not to be brought back to an original donation of sense."[38]

The third stanza of the sixth section speaks, however, of a collusion (the stressed "we"), which has silenced and obliterated the writ:

> Es stand auch geschrieben, dass.
> Wo? Wir
> taten ein Schweigen darüber,
> giftgestillt, gross,
> ein
> grünes
> Schweigen, ein
> Kelchblatt, es
> hing ein Gedanke an Pflanzliches dran —
> grün, ja,
> hing, ja,
> unter hämischem
> Himmel.[39]

The stilling and silence recall Heidegger's description of language as the "resounding of silence" (*das Geläut der Stille*) in his essay "Language"[40] as well as his discussion, with respect to Rainer Maria Rilke, of a stilling of man's unprotectedness through interiorizing remembrance that effects a reversal (*die er-innernde Umkehrung*).[41] In contrast to dispersive writing, the resounding of silence consummates a gathering and enowning. Heidegger names "the calling gathered within itself and that, in calling, gathers to itself" as the speaking of language which both appropriates human being and brings it into its own.[42]

Heidegger's reading of Rilke is a critical *Auseinandersetzung* charging that Rilke's key notions, such as that of "nature" (also "the fullness of nature") or of "the open" remain metaphysical in that they envisage reality or the whole as totality and understand the Being of beings as self-willing will, which "ventures" beings and cradles them in the open, the balance of the draw. The critical focus is not so much on a return to the philosophical tradition as on what Heidegger takes to be the self-completion of that tradition in the self-absolutizing posure (*Gestell*) of technicity, in representationalism, in totalitarian political organization, and in the rhetoric of unconditional command.

Because Heidegger, however, insists on a "rounding uniting" as a fundamental trait of Being (interpreting the Parmenidean sphere as "unconcealing clearing uniting";[43] and on the gathering and propriative character of language, he neither abandons the Rilkean notions nor treats them as paleonyms in the Derridean sense. Instead, he seeks to recast and transform them, almost by a sleight of hand, in such a manner as to claim them for a postmetaphysical turn of thinking that, by that very self-inscription, becomes profoundly ambiguous. While Heidegger reads the Rilkean notion of a stilling within the open or the draw (a stilling more accessible to "plant and animal" than to man) to be a covering over of the Differing and of the nature of language, it is by no means clear that his own understanding of *physis* and *logos* have abjured a poisonous "green/ silence" that, by its inverted chalice or calyx (*Kelch*), conceals the dispersive and ultimately undecidable character of writing and linguistic articulation and, together with it, the political dimensions of the *logos*.

III

The path to the moist eye was, as Szondi notes, a path that "should not have been taken";[44] it led to a consideration of the fissioning im/partment of language and its poisoned silencing. Celan, having repudiated this path, turns instead toward the stone:

Ja.
Orkane, Par-
tikelgestöber, es blieb
Zeit, blieb

es beim Stein zu versuchen — er
war gastlich, er
fiel nicht ins Wort. Wie
gut wir es hatten:

Körnig,
Körnig und faserig. Stengelig,
dicht;
traubig und strahlig, nierig,
plattig und
klumpig; locker, ver-
ästelt — : er, es
fiel nicht ins Wort, es
sprach,
sprach gerne au trockenen Augen, eh es sie schloss.[45]

Poetic diction that tries it out with the stone is a concrescence of what remains when the narcotic calyx is torn away — of the whirl, rush, and fissioning of particles, of temporality. The solidity, opacity, and hardness of the stone are here not indications of any abiding or inherent reality, but rather of the resistance of language to diaphanous presencing, to any effort to speak "through" or "across" its articulation, thus interrupting its im/partment. The intimate association of language (rather than Being or existence) with temporality or temporization is not only prepared for, in Celan's poetry as a whole, by the figure of "sand," but in "Engführung," also by the single stanza of the third section. This stanza, the only one to speak in the first person singular, reads:

Ich bins, ich,
ich lag zwischen euch, ich war
offen, war
hörbar, ich tickte euch zu, euer Atem
gehorchte, ich
bin es noch immer, ihr
schlaft ja.[46]

Szondi notes that *ticken* carries both the archaic sense of "to touch with one's fingertips" (as in English, "to tickle") and the familiar sense of the ticking of clock-time. Both these senses come together also in Celan's poem "Und mit dem Buch aus Tarussa" where the poet speaks of an insistent "ticking and ticking," as that of "heart-stones" with their "indestructible clockwork" that have been spit "out/ into non-land and non-time" (*PC* 1: 287–91). The poet speaks both as the witness, in the first person, and with the impersonality of the "ticking" of temporalization as language. A Mallarméan pure poetry that turns from the moist, vegetative verdure of feeling to the mineral realm of hardness and structural precision can nevertheless not abjure the heart's involvement.

Gadamer, discussing pure poetry as a consummation of the idealizing tendency of art, a tendency also to artistic self-sufficiency, emphasizes that the form of the poem depends on "the constantly shifting balance between sound and sense," and that ". . . it is precisely the force of the semantic field, the tension between the tonal and significative forces of language as they encounter and change place with one another, that constitutes the whole."[47]

Thus, Gadamer notes, pure poetry is not divorced from everyday speech but restores the ordinary word to its power of naming.[48] This uncircumventable investment of form with "sense" in all the registers of feeling and signification is then what pure poetry brings to the fore.

In "Engführung," the colon that concludes the fifth stanza of section six opens, in the sixth stanza, upon the speaking of the stone, a speaking addressed "to dry eyes." This impersonal speaking consists of dyadic and triadic strings of adjectives that evoke the forms of both organic and inorganic nature and that are marked either by a high degree of contrast ("grainy and fibrous") or by almost imperceptible differentiation ("kidneyish, disk-like and / cloddish"). The singularized "dicht" can be read both as an adjective ("dense") and as the apostrophic form of the imperative *dichte* (compose poetry), in which case the massed adjectives can be read adverbially.

The stone-speaking is not only devoid of the metaphysical subject-predicate structure; its renunciation of subjectivity is emphatically indicated by the (untranslatable) shift from the masculine to the neuter pronoun ("er, es / sprach"). The distancing, neutralizing, indeed, idealizing stance of art with respect to life is discussed, in Celan's "Der Meridian," with reference to Georg Büchner's notion of art as a medusa's head that turns living beings to stone so as to allow for a grasp "of the natural as natural" (*PC* 3: 192). The artist is then, like Büchner's Lenz at the dinner table, no longer quite himself: "He who has art before his eyes and in mind is — I continue here with the story of Lenz — he is self-forgetful. Art brings about distance from self. Art demands here, in a determinate direction, a determinate distance, a determinate way" (*PC* 3: 193).

The last two stanzas of "Engführung," part six, speak of acceding to these demands and achieving a consummate poetic structure:

> Wir
> liessen nicht locker, standen
> inmitten, ein
> Porenbau, und
> es kam.
>
> Kam auf uns zu, kam
> hindurch, flickte
> unsichtbar, flickte
> an der letzten Membran,
> und
> die Welt, ein Tausendkristall,
> schoss an, schoss an.[49]

What "came" is now not a word eager to shine and make manifest, but a formal structure of crystalline perfection, precision, and brilliance. The world is here not, as it is for the late Heidegger, the mutually entrusting mirror-play of the Fourfold perdured and brought close by the things of daily life,[50] but a highly complex, perhaps undecidable, structural articulation and play. Poetry that allows such a world to take form would indeed come close to achieving the status of "a standard and a limiting case" that allows it, according to Gadamer, to claim a correspondence with philosophy as consummated in the Hegelian dialectic: "Self-bestowal and self-withdrawal — such a dialectic of uncovering and withdrawal seems to hold sway in the mystery of language, both for poets and for philosophers, from Plato to Heidegger."[51]

Celan, nevertheless, voices dissatisfaction with the crystalline purity and accomplished formal play of such a Mallarméan poetics in the seventh part of "Engführung":

Schoss an, schoss an.

Dann-

Nächte, entmischt. Kreise,
grün oder blau, rote
Quadrate: die
Welt setzt ihr Innerstes ein
im Spiel mit den neuen
Stunden. — Kreise,
rot oder schwarz, helle
Quadrate, kein
Flugschatten,
kein Messtisch, keine
Rauchseele steigt und spielt mit.[52]

Szondi notes that, in the absence of textual indications, one must renounce an interpretation of the "flight's shadow," the "plane-table," and the "smoke-soul" that are excluded from the self-repeating play to which the world commits "its inmost" and that has separated out the nights' darkness into a prism of colors.[53] Some associations can nevertheless be indicated. The flight's shadow recalls, in an oblique way, the Rilkean figure of the angel; but it also points backward and forward to the shadow-writing and trace-writing prominent in the textual landscape of the poem. The plane-table, most important perhaps, allows for the charting of the meridians, whereas the smoke-soul, apart from its obvious reference to the crematoria, recalls also certain Heraclitean fragments, notably B 7, which also are important to Heidegger's reclamation of the Heraclitean *logos*.[54]

In "Der Meridian," Celan speaks of continuing in the determinate direction indicated by art to the enigmatic place where poetry, in a surpassing of art (very different from the Heideggerian founding), can perhaps set itself free:

> Perhaps one succeeds here—since the strange, namely the abyss *and* and medusa's head, the abyss *and* the automata, seem to lie in one direction—perhaps one succeeds in discriminating between strange and strange, perhaps precisely here the medusa's head shrivels, perhaps precisely here the automata fail—for this one short instant? Perhaps here—together with the I—with the I set free and estranged *in this manner*—perhaps here something Other is also set free? (*PC* 3: 195f.).

198

What mandates the quest for this liberation — along the difficult path of art and pure poetry — is precisely the fixation on self-sameness that governs the traditional mimetic and formal interpretions of art no less than what Lacoue-Labarthe calls Heidegger's suppressed mimetology.[55] This tradition, unbroken indeed from Plato to Heidegger, has cultivated self-bestowal and self-withdrawal in such a way as to suppress and enchain the Other.

IV

In "Edgar Jené und der Traum vom Traume" (*PC* 3: 155-61), a text dating from 1948, the time of Celan's involvement with surrealist poetics, the poet raises questions concerning the interpretive resources still available to poetic language in the face of history. The facile answer, that of "the petty merchant of identities," is that "the wall which separates today from tomorrow" needs to be torn down so that "tomorrow could again be yesterday" in unbroken continuity. Regardless of the upheavals of history, things would then once again be called by their simple and proper names.

Celan acknowledges the enticement of such a rectification of names which, despite its naivete, would try to achieve "an original vision cleansed of the centuries-old residue of lies about this world" (*PC* 3: 156). For all (or precisely because of) its purgative fervor, however, this temptation must be resisted; for ". . . what had happened was more than an addition to the pre-given, more than a more or less inalienable attribute of the proper, but rather something which altered the proper in its essence, a powerful facilitation of incessant change" (*PC* 3: 156).

Celan's instauration of a new poetics takes instead the form of "marrying the strange to the strangest" by breaking down the received sedimentations of meaning and the semantic integrity of the word and by recompoundings that, in the words of Amy D. Colin, have "no replication in our memory."[56] They bring to bear a counterlight on the linguistic basis of memory and myth from which, as Alan Udoff points out, the self of atrocity was formed.[57] The offspring of such a marriage is, according to Celan, a textuality "whose light is not the light of day" and which is inhabited "by figures which I do not *recognize* but *cognize* in an initial vision" (*PC* 3: 158).

Such a poetics outstrips mimetology in that the same becomes unrecognizable and cannot be brought to a standstill or kept in memory. This erosion of stable and timeless identites together with the opening of the differential and abyssal dimensions of linguistic im/partment resist totalitarian formation and bring about an ellipsis of mastery.

Celan's insights pose a profound challenge not only to Heidegger's poetics but also to his understanding of mortal dwelling upon the earth as enabled by the poetic word, and of the (metaphysically) ungrounded poetic and artistic grounding of the historical destiny of a people—mediated, as it is, by Hölderlin's poetry.

The linguistic strategies of "marrying the strange to the strangest" continue their encrypting work in Celan's later poetry; yet the poet insists emphatically (and seemingly against all appearances) on the nonhermetic character of his poetry and on its "direct relation to reality"[58]—a reality, to be sure, which is indissociable from language. Celan's poetics is not ultimately one of rupture and disintegration, but one that insists on keeping itself "in the mystery of encounter" (*PC* 3: 198), one that seeks what Celan calls in "Anabasis" (*PC* 1: 256f.):

> Dieses
> schmal zwischen Mauern geschriebne
> unwegsam-wahre
> Hinauf und Zurück
> in die herzhelle Zukunft.[59]

The hope of this future is unlike what Derrida calls "Heideggerian hope"[60] in that it orients itself not toward the Differing but toward the figure of the Other who (unlike the Levinasian Other) is not only the other person but "every thing" as well as "every human being." The dialogue with the Other must give voice to "what is most proper to the Other: the time thereof" (*PC* 3: 199), which cannot be fully assimilated into historical temporalization. Similarly, the effort to locate the Other, the question as to its "whence" and "whereto" leads into "the open and empty," the *topos* of an encounter that neither effaces alterity in the interest of appropriation nor renounces community by a fixation on rupture.

This quest of a relation to the Other, marked in Celan's writings by the figures of the meridian, the "connected pipes," the "free- / growing tentword," which is "Together,"[61] a quest for a poetics that can reinstate the possibility of human dwelling and community through an articulation of the temporality and topology of the Other, is the most important challenge which Celan poses not only to Heidegger's poetics but to our time.

Notes

1. Otto Pöggeler, *Philosophie und Politik bei Heidegger* (Freiburg, Munich: Alber, 1972), 62ff.

2. Martin Heidegger, "Only a God can save us: The *Spiegel* Interview (1966)," trans. William J. Richardson, S. J., in *Heidegger: The Man and the Thinker*, ed. Thomas Sheehan (Chicago: Precedent, 1981), 53-54.

3. See Werner Hamacher, "The Second of Inversion: Movements of a Figure through Celan's Poetry," in *Yale French Studies* 69 (1985): 276-311; and Evelyn Hünneke, "Hoffnung auf ein menschliches Heute und Morgen: Zur Wirklichkeit in der Dichtung Paul Celans," in *Celan-Jahrbuch* 1 (1987): 141-71. Unless otherwise noted, all translations from the German here and elsewhere are my own.

4. Gerhart Baumann, *Erinnerungen an Paul Celan*, (Frankfurt: Suhrkamp, 1986), 65. Otto Pöggeler, *Spur des Worts* (Freiburg, Munich: Alber, 1986), 12-13, 145-53.

5. Baumann, *Erinnerungen*, 70.

6. Martin Heidegger, "Die Sprache im Gedicht," in vol. 12 of *Gesamtausgabe* (Frankfurt: Klostermann, 1975), 33-35. Heidegger's *Gesamtausgabe* will be abbreviated hereafter as *GA* followed by volume number and page.

7. Heidegger, "Die Sprache," *GA* 12: 11.

8. Heidegger, "Der Weg zur Sprache," *GA* 12: 254-57.

9. Heidegger, "Aus einem Gespräch von der Sprache," *GA* 12: 115-16.

10. See Friedrich Hölderlin, "Anmerkungen zum Ödipus," in vol. 5 of *Sämtliche Werke*, ed. Norbert von Hellingrath (Munich, Leipzig: Müller, 1913), 177.

11. Sieghild Bogumil, "Celans Hölderlinlektüre im Gegenlicht des schlichten Wortes," *Celan-Jahrbuch* 1 (1987): 81–125. Bernhard Böschenstein, "Celan als Leser Hölderlins und Jean Pauls," in *Argumentum e Silentio: International Paul Celan Symposium*, ed. Amy D. Colin (Berlin, New York: de Gruyter, 1987), 183–98.

12. Heidegger, "Die Sprache," *GA* 12: 27.

13. Hans-Georg Gadamer, *Wer bin Ich und wer bist Du?* (Frankfurt: Suhrkamp, 1973).

14. See Pöggeler, *Spur des Worts*, 300–34.

15.

The ores are laid bare, the crystals,
the geodes.
Things unwritten,
hardened into language, lay
bare a sky.

(Cast out upwards, exposed,
crosswise, thus
we also lie.

Door, you, before this once, tablet
with the killed
chalk-star upon it:
that one
now belongs to a — reading? — eye.)

Ways thither.
Forest-hour along
the blubbering wheel-track.
Col–
lected
small, gaping
beechnuts: blackish
opening, by
finger-thoughts queried
about —
about what?
About
the unrepeatable, about

it, about
all.

Blubbering ways thither.

Something, which can go, ungreeting
like what has turned into heart,
comes.

This poem is part of a collection *Die Niemandsrose* and is found in vol. 1 of *Paul Celan: Gesammelte Werke*, eds. Beda Allemann and Stephan Reichert, 5 vols. (Frankfurt: Suhrkamp, 1983), 251. All further references to *Paul Celan: Gesammelte Werke*, abbreviated *PC*, will be included in the text with volume and page number. In translating Celan's poetry, I have consulted Michael Hamburger's translations, notably those in *Paul Celan: Poems* (Manchester: Carcanet New Press, 1980). Despite the high quality of his translations, however, I have found it necessary to depart from them.

16. Hans-Georg Gadamer, "Celans Schlussgedicht," in *Argumentum e Silentio*, 158-71. Gadamer also makes this point in the postscript to his *Wer bin Ich und wer bist Du?*, 111.

17. Martin Heidegger, "Logos," in vol. 3 of *Vorträge und Aufsätze*, 3 vols. (Pfullingen: Neske, 1967), 6, 16.

18. Bogumil, "Celans Hölderlinlektüre," 90.

19. Edith Silbermann points out that in Celan's native city, Czernowitz, the ghetto was not a permanent institution but was established in the fall of 1941 for purposes of deportation; see her "Erinnerungen an Paul (Celan-Antschel)," in *Argumentum e Silentio*, 427-43.

20. Martin Heidegger, "Wozu Dichter?", in vol. 5 of *GA* (Frankfurt: Klostermann, 1978), 269-320.

21. Tony Brinkley and Steven Youra discuss this quotation from Claude Lanzmann's film *Shoah*, together with the whole question of witness and erasure of traces, in their unpublished paper "The Alarming Nature of Darkness: Witnessing *Shoah*," presented at the 1988 meeting of the International Association for Philosophy and Literature.

22. Heidegger, "Logos," 16.

23. Heidegger, "Logos," 16. On the unitive character of *logos*, see also Martin Heidegger, *Heraklit*, vol. 55 of *GA* (Frankfurt: Klostermann, 1979), 261–95; and Martin Heidegger and Eugen Fink, *Heraklit* (Frankfurt: Klostermann, 1970), 28–46.

24. Martin Heidegger, "Andenken," in *Erläuterungen zu Hölderlins Dichtung* (Frankfurt: Klostermann, 1981), 95ff.

25. On the thematic of a circumcision of words, see Jacques Derrida, *Shibboleth: Pour Paul Celan* (Paris: Galilée, 1986); see also Philippe Forget, "Neuere Daten über Paul Celan," *Celan-Jahrbuch* 1 (1987): 217–22.

26. Peter Szondi, "Durch die Enge geführt," in *Celan-Studien* (Frankfurt: Suhrkamp, 1972), 47–111; in English, "Reading *Engführung*: An Essay on the Poetry of Paul Celan," *Boundary 2* 11 (Spring 1983): 231–64.

27.
                          Covered it up
                              up—who?
        Came, came.
        Came a word, came,
        came through the night,
        wanted to shine, wanted to shine.

28. "Engführung," pt. 2: (None woke,/ sleep/ overcame them).

29.
        Ashes.
        Ashes, ashes.
        Night.
        Night-and-night.   —Go
        to the eye, to the moist one.

30. See Emil Fackenheim, "The Holocaust: A Summing Up after two Decades of Reflection," in *Argumentum e Silentio*, 285–95.

31. As Szondi came to realize; see his "Durch die Enge geführt," 74n.

32.
                    To the
                        eye go,
                            to the moist one—
        Whirlwinds,
        Whirlwinds, since ever,
        Storms of particles, the other,
        you

know, of course, we
read it in the book, was
opinion.

33. Hamacher, "The Second of Inversion," 292.

34. Heidegger, "Der Weg zur Sprache," *GA* 12: 241.

35. Heidegger, "Das Wesen der Sprache," *GA* 12: 155; also "Der Weg zur Sprache," GA 12: 250.

36. Gadamer, "Celans Schlussgedicht," 71.

37. Forget, "Neuere Daten," 218. the discussion focusses on the rethinking of historicity (beyond hermeneutics or phenomenology) mandated by the structure of the date.

38. Forget, "Neuere Daten," 219.

39.   It also stood written that.
             Where? We
             put a silence over it,
             poison-stilled, great,
             a
             green
             silence, a
             sepal, there
             hung on it a thought of the plant-like—
             green, yes,
             hung, yes,
             under a sneering
             sky.

40. Heidegger, "Die Sprache," *GA* 12: 27–28.

41. Heidegger, "Wozu Dichter?", *GA* 5: 312. See also Heidegger's discussion of Rainer Maria Rilke in *Parmenides*, vol. 54 of *GA* (Frankfurt: Klostermann, 1982), 195–245.

42. Heidegger, "Die Sprache," *GA* 12: 27.

43. Heidegger, "Wozu Dichter?" *GA* 5: 301.

44. Szondi, "Durch die Enge geführt," 79.

45.   Yes.
             whirlwinds, par–

205

ticle-storm, there remained
time, remained
trying it out with the stone—he
was hospitable, he
did not interrupt. How
good we had it:

grainy,
grainy and fibrous. Stalkish,
dense;
grapish and ray-like, kidneyish,
disk-like and
cloddish; loose,
branching—: he, it
did not interrupt, it
spoke,
spoke gladly to dry eyes, ere it closed them.

Note that in order to render Celan's shift from the masculine to the neuter pronoun in line seven of the second stanza, I have used the masculine pronoun *he* in referring to the stone. In English, of course, this calls unwanted attention to itself.

46.　　　　It is I, I,
I lay between you, I was
open, was
to be heard, I ticked at you, your breath
obeyed, it
is I still, but you
are sleeping.

47. Hans-Georg Gadamer, "Philosophy and poetry," in *The Relevance of the Beautiful and Other Essays*, trans. Nicholas Walker, ed. Robert Bernasconi (Cambridge: Cambridge University Press, 1986), 136.

48. Gadamer, "Philosophy and poetry," 135.

49.　　　　We
would not desist, stood
in its midst, one
pore-structure, and
it came.

> Came toward us, came
> through, mended
> invisibly, mended
> on the last membrane,
> and
> the world, a thousand-crystal,
> took form, took form.

50. Martin Heidegger, "Das Ding," in vol. 2 of *Vorträge und Aufsätze*, 37–55.

51. Gadamer, "Philosophy and poetry," 139.

52.
>   Took form, took form.
>   Then—
> Nights, demingled. Circles,
> green or blue, red
> squares: the
> world commits its inmost
> in play with the new
> hours. —Circles,
> red or black, light
> squares, no
> flight's shadow,
> no plane-table, no
> smoke-soul mounts and joins in.

53. Szondi, "Durch die Enge geführt," 91.

54. Heraclitus frag. B 7 Diels-Kranz may be translated as follows: "If all things were smoke, the nostrils would discriminate them." Heidegger discusses this fragment with Eugen Fink in their *Heraklit*, 33–35. While many of the Heraclitean fragments on *psyche* are relevant here, compare, in particular, B 98: "The breath-souls sniff in accordance with the Invisible (*Hades*)."

55. Philippe Lacoue-Labarthe, "Poétique et politique," in *L'imitation des modernes* (Paris: Galilée, 1986), 175–200.

56. Amy D. Colin, "Paul Celan's Poetics of Destruction," in *Argumentum e Silentio*, 157–82; also 171.

57. Alan Udoff, "On Poetic Dwelling: Situating Celan and the Holocaust," in *Argumentum e Silentio*, 320–51.

58. This fragment from Paul Celan's conversation is cited (indirectly) by Hünneke, "Hoffnung auf ein menschliches Heute," 143. See also Celan's *Letter to Hans Bender, PC* 3: 177–78.

59.   This
        narrowly between walls written
        unwaylike — true
        upward and back
        into the heart-bright future.

60. Jacques Derrida, "Différance," *Margins of Philosophy*, trans. Alan Bass (Chicago: University of Chicago Press, 1982), 3–27.

61. Concerning the connected pipes, see correspondence cited by Hünneke, "Hoffnung auf menschliches Heute," 167. The "tentword" is in "Anabasis." I have discussed the figure of the meridian more fully in my "Inversion and the (Dis)place of the Other in the Poetics of Paul Celan," in *Ethics/Aesthetics: Postmodern Positions*, ed. Robert D. Merrill (Washington, D. C.: Maisonneuve Press, 1988), 95–118.

9

Poetry and the Political: Gadamer, Plato, and Heidegger on the Politics of Language

Dennis J. Schmidt

> *In* itself the sphere of influence ìs larger than the poetic spirit, yet not *of* itself. Insofar as it is considered in relation to the world, it is larger; insofar as it is held fast and appropriated by the poet, it is subordinated.
>
> — Hölderlin

*A*mong Hans-Georg Gadamer's first publications is the 1934 essay that deals with the topic of "Plato and the Poets," written during the first months of the Nazification of Germany. The essay wears its own opposition to that movement not only in the special treatment of its political topic, but also in its epigram taken from Goethe: "One who philosophizes is at odds with the style of thinking of his world, and that is why the Platonic dialogues are often not only directed *toward* something, but also *against* something." Gadamer's purpose in that essay is to ask about the real standard animating Plato's critique of poetry. His answer, the most general form of which is announced when he says that "the sense of this critique of poetry is determined solely by its context: that it is found in the text on the 'state,' "[1] opens on themes that eventually show themselves to be the leading themes of Gadamer's career: tradition and culture, theory and *praxis*, language and limits. These themes are in part spun in novel ways off of Martin Heidegger's destruction of the subject and rethinking of the question of language, always demonstrating the aptness of Jürgen Habermas's characterization of Gadamer's thought as "the urbanization of the Heideggerian province."[2] That characterization rings so true because Gadamer's trademark in this and other essays is to develop that which always only remains a lacuna in Heidegger's own work; namely, the real and effective power of language at work in culture and political practice. When he asks about Plato and poetry, Gadamer does so in order to deepen his own concerns with the relation between language and political practice in a culture. And that is a concern that has moved more clearly into the current center of reflections that follow in the wake of Heidegger, Jacques Derrida, and Gadamer himself.

My proposal then is to renew Gadamer's question in light of subsequent reflections that he and others have made on the questions of language and poetry. To ask what we can say now about the mandates and possibilities of political practice as they come to be effective in a political world that is not taken to be a world constituted according to the bourgeois illusion of free and equal judiciary subjects born with rights that are innate rather than won. That, I believe, is a question worth posing because speaking about the *polis* and *praxis* is far more frustrating, less amenable to stabilization and solidity, than a world constituted according to such assumptions connected to notions of the subject can ever fully acknowledge. My intention herein is to avoid taking what might legitimately count as the ultimate poles and outcomes of action and speech as the starting points for political questioning, and, following Gadamer's reading of Plato, to start rather with action and speech themselves as the basic uncertainty of all political matters, as the real and phenomenal stuff of any *polis*. So I begin with the assumption that we live in a world that, in the words of Hannah Arendt, is "overgrown with an . . . in-between which consists of deeds and words and owes its origin exclusively to our acting and speaking directly *to* one another."[3] The task then is to speak of this "in-between," this prior community of our permeability out of which we may emerge for a while as subjects, within which we want to walk according to what Ernst Bloch describes as "the orthopedia of the upright carriage."[4]

While asking this question does not mean that one must engage in postmortems of what has been congealed in the notion of the

210

political subject—whether that notion leads to a sense of the subject as the Hobbesian aggressor "wolf" in the "war of one against everyone" or to the empathizing "needs of the heart" from which the Fichtean subject springs and to which it responds with its own repetition and affirmation—it is important that the seductions of such congealed pillars of the *polis* not pull one away from this in-between. One only resists those seductions once one realizes that the notion of the subject is more powerful and ultimately more tenable than we often realize today. But, as reflections on the relation between poetry and the political make clear, it is neither tenable, nor powerful as a *starting point* for reflections on political practice.

I have already mentioned that I want rather to begin in a way that affirms the full extent of our permeability, of the way in which we find ourselves first in this in-between, of what Heidegger spoke of as the "with-world" and Gadamer described as the site of communication. There is, of course, some sense in which we live in an isolation both arid and rich, in which we begin and end with our skin and bodies—pain is a sharp reminder of that, bodiliness, into which no doctor can see, names the limits of our permeability—but there is an equally powerful sense that "within" these limits, within our skin, even thanks to the sexuality of flesh, we find not the contours of our autonomy, but the enigma of others and the place of our still uncongealed senses of self in the world of others whom we know to be equally nondomesticated. This intertwining of flesh and the world revolves around several (and sometimes incommensurate) umbilici: some, such as sight, hearing, speech—those that take us out of the flat world of our skin—radiate from the center that we take ourselves to be; some, such as love, come at and over us rather than from us, others such as what one finds in Hegel's analysis of work in the doubling that is the dialectic of recognition are found happening in the place of our plurality. However, as Gadamer has long argued, the line of thinking especially fruitful for a thinking about *praxis* that does not adapt itself to the measure of the subject is one that asks about language as the axis along which this in-between spins.

The suggestion that it is time we turned to speaking about language as the starting point for political reflections is rather new. And it is a suggestion that accords well with the other recent suggestion that resists the language of "subjectivity" and "intersubjectivity" as unproblematic for such reflections. Michel Foucault put it clearly when he said:

> "I speak" runs counter to "I think." "I think" led to the indubitable certainty of the "I" and its existence; "I speak," on the other hand, distances, disperses, effaces that existence and lets only its empty emplacement appear. Thought about thought . . . has taught us that thought leads us to the deepest interiority. Speech about speech leads us, by way of literature as well as perhaps by other paths, to the outside in which the speaking subject disappears. No doubt that is why Western thought took so long to think the being of language: as if it had a premonition of the danger that the naked experience of language poses for the self-evidence of the "I think."[5]

The point is that language — multiple in its grammars, spontaneous in its outreach, poor at articulating itself — refuses to be repatriated to any sense of the interiority of the subject. It is, Foucault says, "the repetition of what continually murmurs outside."[6] When we reflect on language we find that it is not subject to the subject we take ourselves to be, but that we are subject to it. We sit within the folds of our grammars.[7] That, of course, is what Heidegger means when he says that we "speak only insofar as we respond to language" and that "language speaks" out of the torn middle of our possibility.[8] It is also Gadamer's point, when, with a slightly different emphasis, he says that "being that can be understood is language."[9]

Heidegger's remarks on language go as far as possible toward regarding language as a matter of this in-between that constitutes the *polis* and the possibilities of *praxis* in that *polis*. But while he speaks quite directly about the ontological possibilities of this mid-world of language, he avoids—persistently and at great effort—discussing its political and practical possibilities. Gadamer's contribution and advance over Heidegger is a response to that challenge.

Of course, if we follow Heidegger, it is to language in its preeminent sense, language that listens and speaks to itself at the moment of its greatest density and concentration, that is language in the poem, to which we must turn, and that returns us to the rather peculiar and disturbing topic of Gadamer's article on Plato: poetry and the political. Not political poetry, not poetry about politics, nor the politics of poetry, certainly not what Walter Benjamin and Bertolt Brecht described as the "aesthetization of the political," but *the meaning of political life that is found at the site of poetry's own possibility.*

It must be acknowledged that to ask about poetry and the political—as for instance Hélène Cixous does when she opens an essay of that name with the question: "What about poems in these times of repression?"[10]—always seems to feel forced. It feels odd when one reads the claim of René Char that in the future "poetry will no longer punctuate action, but move ahead of action and show it the motile path." It strikes one as somewhat absurd when one hears the poet Canetti reading from the 1939 diary of an unknown poet that "It is all over now. If I were really a poet, I could have prevented the war."[11] And it seems the height of philosophical arrogance that during the war, and the period of his withdrawal from active political life, Heidegger was not preoccupied with matters of law and resistance, justice and the state, or with the responsibilities of intellectuals in times of brutality, but with poetry, especially the poetry of Hölderlin—the "poet of poetry."

The difficulty in coping with such remarks comes in trying to determine from what point such seemingly eccentric decisions might spring.

All of those remarks spring from a sense of the relation between language, thinking and action quite different from the traditional conception of that relation. As long as we think within the framework of such a conception of the place of language and thinking in the question of *praxis*—as long as, for instance, we work with a metaphysical conception of a disjunctive relation between theory and *praxis*, discourse and deeds, a disjunction that language itself displaces—we will not be able to make sense of those apparently eccentric and irresponsible remarks that grant poetry real political power. Furthermore, as long as we think within such a framework we will never quite understand why that same framework has generated the otherwise unintelligible event that happens so frequently in times of repression; namely, the jailing of poets and literary figures as enemies of the state. Making, as Jorge Luis Borges said, censorship the mother of metaphor.

But Heidegger's purpose is to think outside of that metaphysical tradition. And that is why, in the essay that speaks against the humanistic tradition, against a metaphysics of the subject, a letter that begins with the comment, "We have not yet thought the essence of action decisively enough,"[12] Heidegger, who claims to be "thinking differently," insists on shifting the discussion from the question of action to language and poetry.

The historically decisive text—and the one that Heidegger turns on its head without directly addressing it on the relation of poetry and the political—is Plato's *Republic*. In that meditation on the essence of political life, Plato not only remarks on, but seems—even if with some hesitation—to take sides in what he describes as the "ancient quarrel between philosophy and poetry."[13] He is, as he indicates, simply inserting himself into a by then already "ancient" and well-defined quarrel, because one already finds Heraclitus, for instance, suggesting that "Homer deserves to be expelled from the competition and beaten with a staff . . . ," and that "In taking poets as testimony for things unknown, they are citing authorities that cannot be trusted."[14]

It is a peculiar quarrel, one that revolves largely around the paradigms of ethical discourse and the preservation of tradition. It is also a dispute that takes place before the entry of the force of disciplinariness into thinking about such matters, transferring the issue into one fought among disciplines carved by the academy. In short, the quarrel that Plato inherits is largely a matter of temperament, not of disciplines, but perhaps a matter of language itself. But Plato does shift the locus of this ancient quarrel for the decisive Platonic addition is to focus that feud on the relation between the possibilities of language and political action. He makes most of his significant remarks about this quarrel after having escorted some, but not all, poets to the city limits (where Socrates's story in the *Republic* begins). Lest this seem an extreme found only in the irony of the *Republic*, one should recall that in the *Laws* he establishes rigorous standards for censorship and the punishment of those poets who remain in the *polis* yet do not adequately follow the lead of the state. The problem with the poets, says Plato, is that from the vantage point of truth (*aletheia*) and morality (*dike*) they are politically irresponsible frauds.[15] Ultimately, this tension between the poet and the *polis* is said to revolve around the poet's puerile relation to language. More precisely: the poet taps into and plays with the dimension of language that relates to the irrational side of the soul (one should note the telling choice of words at this point: Plato refers here to the *alagon*—the "unspeakable"—indicating that the *logos* is never fully problematized here). To put Plato in the language of Freud: the poets, working with the merely possible, cripple our capacity to face the actual and its real principles, and they distort the economy of the human psyche. As we grow more responsible, we outgrow the need for such playing with possibilities, and we realize that if such stories (*mythoi*) are held onto too long or taken too seriously, they can breed an unhealthy mind and soul.

Plato describes that dimension of language with which the poet plays as its mimetic dimension, and while he notes that language is not alone in permitting such mimetic activity — painting, music, and dance are also discussed — the mimetic dimension of language is most threatening because its employment, more than the other mimetic arts, veils and doubles itself, dividing what should be harmonized. As Gadamer notes: "One who only really imitates an other, 'mimes' it, is no longer self-contained; he impresses himself with an alien form. But at the same time one only imitates the other, that is, one is no longer oneself and is also not the other. *Mimesis* thus refers to a self-diremption."[16] But this mimetic power of language is also dangerous because it, simply because it is language, will be picked up by all and weave its way into every place in the community defined by that language. Plato wants to guarantee that the deceptive power of language is never underestimated and so even when Plato seems to overturn his earlier judgment by allowing some poets to return[17] they are never without fetters — thus they are forbidden to make what is rightly private public because that is the sort of gesture that injects contradiction between the city and the soul. We soon discover that the real language of truth, philosophy, is not only not mimetic, it is explicitly *antimimetic*. Important for the tradition that follows, this is said with an eye to political stability, to control and to the security of power.[18] The expulsion of the poets, the practitioners of *mimesis*, is thus a matter of *dike* and *aletheia*, a matter of affirming the imperative of keeping things in their place: the imperative of placing — the imperative of finding a universal imperative that can serve as the agent of an ordering subsumption.

There is much that should be said about the irony in all of this — that in the spartan nightmare of the republic a book such as the *Republic* that disclosed the dialectical character of dialogue through its own mimetic power would not be tolerated. There is also something noteworthy in the fact that nowhere in the *Republic* is the proper mode of philosophic discourse, the *mimesis* of ideas, explicitly addressed. One might even say that the whole of the Platonic corpus is haunted by this question: the question of *diegesis* and

216

mimesis, of writing and speech. We know that the question of writing is problematic for Plato, that his teacher and hero of the dialogues never wrote, indeed refused to write lest his words betray him, and that Plato never appears in the dialogues and never speaks in his own voice, but we tend to ignore the way in which this problematic of speaking and writing links to his other—especially political—concerns. For Plato, writing, any style of writing, the very *act* of writing, is mimetic of speech. Writing, like every mode of *mimesis*, hides a certain fraudulence and concealment in its essential nature. Most problematic is that written language is not alive, that in its rigidity and inflexibility it effaces the speech that is its own origin. It hides its own truth and the truth of which it speaks. Or, put in Heidegger's more graphic prose, "in script, the scream is easily smothered."[19]

But the essential political point concerns control and the security, stability, and perfection of the *polis*, all of which, according to Plato, are undermined by the relation to language that animates certain forms of poetry. The claim is not simply that poetry can be put to dangerous use, that poets can manipulate culture, but that its very possibility is hostile to the ideals and security of any state. The stable *polis* must guard against the conditions that breed and are bred by such mimetic activity. While the philosopher-king is the expert, the one with the know-how (the *techne*) for securing the real moorage points for knowing and acting, the poet, on the other hand, has the capacity to rob those moorage points of their stability. It is an odd claim that says that the soul and the city cannot be consolidated in the presence of such speech. Aristotle, himself no poet to match Plato, felt that such a claim was simply unwarranted. For him, and this is why Western liberal thought finds Aristotle so consoling, society not only can tolerate, but positively benefits from the practitioners of *mimesis*. But Aristotle can only say this to the extent that—despite his high regard for poetry—he downplays the political originality and efficacy of poetic speech. For him one "is a poet by virtue of the mimetic element in one's work, and it is action that one imitates."[20] The speech of the poet is reactive, not culturally formative, active and potent as Plato takes it to be. Furthermore, the veiling and duplicity of the poet that Plato took as housing the pernicious possibilities of poetry, are for Aristotle simply evidence of the immaturity of poetry, not of its mature threat. The duplicity of the poet is similar to that of the child who innocently "plays at" being a fireman or philosopher. The poet is simply being playful and thereby exhibiting the underdeveloped stage of his speech. Poetry, like all forms of play, is part of the process of education, part of the fabric of culture. There is nothing hostile to philosophy or culture in poetry, it contains no intrinsic threat, but, like Hegel, Aristotle regards poetry simply as "something surpassed."[21]

Now the issue over which Plato and Aristotle divide in this case is not whether poetry has an impact upon culture. Both knew quite well that long before philosophical reflections upon courage found their focus, Homer had taught the Greeks that courage was like Achilles, that poetry is, as Heidegger argued "the original voice of a people."[22] Both Plato and Aristotle knew what Hegel—still in the spirit of the Greeks—said so well when he confessed that "The owl of Minerva flies only with the setting of the sun"[23] and the history it founds takes place in "the temple of Mnemosyne"[24]—at the limits not of the *polis*, but the day and every age; namely, that philosophic reflection always has the character of an afterthought, whereas poetic speech tends to project itself. Neither is wholly of its time, nor is there such a sharp dichotomy between afterthought and projection, and clearly philosophy and poetry both seem to be responses to a moral obligation to live in one's own time, and to have a just and appropriate attitude toward one's world. Both Plato and Aristotle knew that poetry would always have its impact upon every time, but they split over the necessity, and even possibility of, controlling and stabilizing that impact. Both more or less believed that language could and should be directed to affirming or completing contents that preexisted it; but, unlike Aristotle, Plato also believed that the mimetic dimension of speech harbored the nonreactive possibility of both creating and transforming that which it named, of stepping outside of the stable and domesticating world of ideas.[25] In short, Plato knew, or at least sensed and reacted against, the strange and un-Greek insight, that *language could unfold in the presence of nothing.* That is why he says that the poet speaks to the side of the soul that is *alogon*; that is, the poet does not respect the margins of the *logos* that define the boundaries of the thinkable and the

218

governable margins of the *polis*. Exiling the poets, sending them over the line of the *polis*, is Plato's way of putting them in their proper place. And that is its threat to metaphysics, the love and proprietor of the thinkable, the mother tongue of philosophy, and the language of its substance and stability, the governing language of the perfected *polis*. What seems to be a violent gesture that displaces the poets from the *polis* is the move that yields to their true place. When they are allowed to return, to cross the line again, it is under the suspicion that they are always capable of double crossing the polis.

Nietzsche knew that too, but—despite his claim to being the counterforce to Plato—only in attenuated form, only in the mitigated form of Aristotle's presentation. That is what he means when he says that "the metaphysical intention of art is to transfigure the real,"[26] and that is why he must invert the Aristotelian-Hegelian hierarchy obtaining between poetry and philosophy: "[W]e possess *art* lest we *perish of the truth.*"[27] Philosophy now plays a weak and second, decadent, fiddle to all the mimetic arts. The playfulness of the mimetic arts are evidence for their power, not immaturity.[28]

But two factors work to restrain Nietzsche's conception of the poetic urge interpreted as the will to power. First, for Nietzsche, language in all of its modes is derivative: "Words dilute and brutalize; words depersonalize; words make the uncommon common."[29] Language does not directly touch upon the fundamentally original, but traces itself back to music, to tones and gestures, rhythm, and glances. Mimetic activity is a relation to the fundamental audibility, not possible legibility, of the world. That is why Nietzsche can say that "even today one still hears with one's muscles, one even reads with one's muscles."[30] The body, ultimately taken as impenetrable and individuating, is the source of language, and as such language, sprung from such a desexualized conception of the body, loses its fundamentally political character. The second factor restraining Nietzsche's conception of the relation between poetry and the political is that for Nietzsche this mimetic element that refuses to be tamed in the *agon* of Dionysus and Apollo remains the production of the ultimate metaphysical subject: the pure will to power. It is the pure unfolding of the will in the presence of nothing, pure self-assertion and triumph of the will within the horizon of the subject's control. Such unfettered self-overcoming is beyond being fundamentally concerned with that issue of overcoming one's neighbor: "Whatever makes [a people] rule and triumph and shine, to its neighbor's awe and envy; that is to it the high, the first, the measure and the meaning of all things."[31] That, I believe, is the political liability of the apoliticism of Nietzsche's thought — a danger to which Heidegger succumbed when he gave the address on the "Self-Assertion of the German University" and the danger that he acknowledged later in life when, in the context of talking about his own political error, he repeatedly remarked that "Nietzsche hat mich kaputt gemacht" (Nietzsche did me in.)[32]

Heidegger first learned about the mimetic possibilities of art from Nietzsche, not Plato, but — and this is the discovery of the error of his own political engagement and the war years — in the end he learned the liability of Nietzsche from Hölderlin for whom art is not the transformation of the real under the power of the will, but the simple "advance of the unthinkable."[33] This advance is that which Plato tried to ward off, and which could find no place in the *polis*. Pressing this point in Hölderlin, Heidegger eventually outstripped both Plato and Nietzsche in the extent to which he understood what it means to say that language — now a "house of being" that no longer represents or refers to a higher world of preexisting contents — always unfolds in the presence of nothing, in what Foucault called "the pureness of the wait,"[34] and what Heidegger described as "the peal of stillness."[35]

Heidegger's claim is that all language fights the empire of representation, but that such escape only becomes visible with the release of thinking from the presumptions of the subject, and that it becomes most clearly visible in the special repetition and reflexivity of poetic language both upon itself and in its reiteration in culture. Here language is not the production of a subject, but a rejoinder to something prior, in the moment in which we are still permeated by speech and action, before either has ossified outside of us, congealing us into subjects. Language, as Heidegger says, "exposes" us; it is not our communicative tool. That is why one of the first texts in which Heidegger takes the ontological meaning of poetry seriously, a text written at a time in which his own political error preoccupied him—namely, "The Origin of the Artwork"—takes as its starting themes the disintegration of the notion of the producing subject and the structure of repetition in language. In the end, the full treatment of the relation between *poiesis* and *praxis* involves the topics of production and repetition as well as the roles that language and the subject play in the constitution of the *polis*.

But my purpose is not to give full treatment to that relation, but to ask a quite specific question concerned with the meaning of political practice in a *polis* that is generated out of the in-between of speech and action found at a site that includes the possibility of poetic speech. In other words, how does this nothing, this pureness of the wait, before which language unfolds itself weave itself into this in-between? How does what Heidegger calls the "menace of being as such through non-being"—the menace of language—manifest itself in the possibilities of the *polis*? What does it mean for *praxis* that language, that by which we bear witness to our being and being-together, harbors this nondomesticable element? How do these fault lines and rough edges of language's possibilities with which poetry plays and along which the unthinkable advances and draws up behind us play into the formation of our political and practical world and life? How does the countermovement of domestication, the extension of the thinkable and the bearable, reveal the conflict and doubling of language in the *polis*?

Plato's sense was that there was a political risk in the possibilities of poetic language. The fissures it exposed, the *hexis* it cultivated, led away from the stability of the state. That risk was measured against the dominant imperatives of the stable *polis*: placing, universalizing, technologizing (the driving question in Plato is, after all, the question of a technics of knowing).[36] The poet refuses to hold language within those borders, to respect the status of the status quo and the tradition upholding it, to live within the limits of our present domesticity, to affirm the stable. Clearly Plato would agree with Hölderlin's remark that "language is the most dangerous of all goods," but, because his sense of the *polis* was of a stable and rational place, he would not agree with Hölderlin's other judgment that poetry "is the most innocent of all occupations."

The reason is quite simple and Theodor Adorno put it quite clearly when he said: "The process which every work of art represents is as deep as it is because *mimesis* and rationality are irreconcilable."[37] Adorno, and other critical theorists such as Bloch and Herbert Marcuse, can turn the Platonic judgment about poetic production around because they acknowledge the dynamic and historical character of the *polis*. Works of art, mimetic actions, as memoranda of things no longer and anticipations of what is not yet, as displaced from the discourse of the day, introduce a utopian and thus critical element in the life of the *polis*. As able to utter the unutterable, art is the medium of the negative, the social antithesis of society. Art, for Adorno, *mimesis*, goes on living only through this antithesis. In the words of Adorno again: "[Mimetic *praxis*] is like a plenipotentiary of a type of *praxis* that is better than the prevailing *praxis* of a society dominated as it is by brutal self-interest."[38] Mimetic activity is a groping after the still uncongealed and displaced potentials of an age. Acting on behalf of the still fragmentary, mimetic activity works as a reminder of the possibility of an integrated life, and of the real damages of every present life.

Heidegger's sense of the politics of language merges easily with this sense of the utopian potential active in the mimetic arts. The war between Freiburg and Frankfurt never made much sense and should be concluded. But there is something that emerges from Heidegger's conception of poetic language that is difficult to extract from any critical theorist; namely, the fundamentally *anarchic* potential of language, the capacity of language to unfold itself outside of the boundaries of the thinkable, to take leave from itself.

Language, heard and spoken well, refuses to cling to the present; it is, as Heidegger put it "ready to renounce the old gods," to move forward, but—and this is the real tension and conservative element in all such language—it does this in order "to preserve and leave untouched their divinity," to memorialize.[39] *Andenken* not *Erinnerung* becomes the mood from out of which the poet's special relation to language issues. "It is," Hölderlin writes, "especially important that . . . [the poet] takes nothing for granted, proceeds from nothing positive, that nature and art, as he has come to know them and sees them, speak not until there exists a language for him, that is, until what is now unknown and unnamed in his world becomes known and named precisely by way of having been found in congruence with his mood."[40] Readiness for renunciation and preservation are what offer the poet his language and what the language of the poet offers. Poetry speaks out of this hesitation between memory and hope, a hesitation that Heidegger called "sacred mourning,"[41] the hermeneutics of which take us out of the present place of the *polis*. Poetry, understood as a spirit that is nourished upon such hesitation and waiting, reminds us of this authentic hesitation that should accompany every relation to the *polis*.

There is, of course, much more that needs to be said. Language is clearly a primary constituent of community—it is, as Gadamer has indicated, among the very few human possibilities that grows the more it is shared and divided among us. Property, food, and material goods shrink when we share them; language, love, friendship, and learning grow.[42] The in-between of the *polis*, the site of *praxis*, is defined as the perpetual and irreducible tension of that ineluctable shrinkage and growth, as the multiple dialectics of the material and immaterial. Language, not with a capital "L," not "Language" as a sort of universalizing house, but what Mikhail Bakhtin—in reference to the novel as opposed to poetry—called the "heteroglossia" of languages, gives shape and form, it articulates and draws the lines of every *polis*. But, as both Plato and Heidegger knew, language is poorest at giving voice to itself, it hides its full potentials. When those potentials emerge, when language comes to speak, then the untenability of the philosophical discourse about the *polis* — governed by the grammar and univocal language of ideals, of security, self-preservation, of stability — comes into view. We discover the lability and mobility of the borders of the *polis*, the line to which Plato suggested we escort the poets, when language is released from the fetters of our assumptions about it and ourselves. Naming the repressive (i.e., petrified) remnants of every *polis*, calling things by their real and possible names, revealing them for what they are, discursively robbing them of their presumed constancy, is the progressive potential of all speech. The very being of language has this potential because, as part of the formative and phenomenal stuff of the in-between upon which the place and possibilities of *praxis* take place, *the being of language renders unthinkable the very notion of the* polis *as a stable place that might be the secure home of autonomous subjects.* That, I believe, is what Char meant when he claimed that "Henceforth, poetry will no longer punctuate action, but move ahead of action and show it the motile path."

But I conclude by recalling the feeling of worry that one retains in the face of that remark. Worry because poetry never did much good in the face of violence and misery or human degradation. But then unself-critical strategic action, unhesitating action uninformed and undisplaced by either memory or hope, does not do much good either.

Even if the effect of poetic production upon the formation of the *polis* and the possibility of political practice emerges from reflections that start with Plato's critique of poetry, the real meaning of poetry remains to be questioned along the lines of its own special doubling and production. It is, as Gadamer noted, "not a plastic art . . . . The poet makes himself into the tool of his own making: he makes to the extent he speaks. But what he makes, before any forming of things, is man himself, who articulates himself in his existence and as he knows himself in action and suffering."[43] Nonetheless, even if the question of poetry must be raised anew, one can say without worry that the meaning of poetry and other mimetic activities in a world where beauty is adventitious is more than that it adds to the world objects of contemplation and pleasure. Rather, such activities, especially when they happen in language, the most political of all mimetic possibilities that draw the lines of any *polis*, always remind us that all modes of discourse strain the borders of our world, that all forms of speech are potentially transformative and so risky, and that no one has sole authority on the question of our political life, and finally — again a lesson from Gadamer's insights into the risks of authority — that in the conversation about such matters no one qualifies as an expert and listening is as much an issue as is speaking.

Notes

1. Hans-Georg Gadamer, "Plato und die Dichter," in *Gesammelte Werke*, vol. 5 (Tübingen: J. C. B. Mohr, 1985), 193. Unless otherwise noted, translations of this and other works are my own.

2. Jürgen Habermas, *Das Erbe Hegels* (Frankfurt: Suhrkamp, 1979), 13.

3. Hannah Arendt, *The Human Condition* (Chicago: University of Chicago Press, 1959), 183.

4. Ernst Bloch, *Naturrecht und menschliche Würde* (Frankfurt: Suhrkamp, 1961), 314.

5. Michel Foucault, *The Thought from the Outside*, trans. Brian Massumi (Cambridge, Mass.: MIT Press, 1987), 13.

6. Foucault, *The Thought from the Outside*, 25.

7. For a discussion of the way in which translation demonstrates this point, see my "The Hermeneutic Dimension of Translation," in vol. 4 of *Translation Perspectives* (Albany: SUNY/CRIT,1988), 5–17; see also my "Hermeneutics and the Poetic Motion," in vol. 5 of *Translation Perspectives* (Albany: SUNY/CRIT, 1990).

8. Martin Heidegger, *Unterwegs zur Sprache* (Pfullingen: Neske, 1959), 33.

9. Hans-Georg Gadamer, *Wahrheit und Methode* (Tübingen: J. C. B. Mohr, 1965), 450. See Gadamer, *Truth and Method*, trans. Sheed and Ward Ltd. (New York: Seabury Press, 1975), 432.

10. Hélène Cixous, "Poetry is/and (the) Political," in *Bread and Roses* 2, no. 1 (1980): 16.

11. Elias Canetti, *Der Beruf des Dichters* (Munich: Hanser, 1976), 5.

12. Martin Heidegger, "Brief über den Humanismus," in *Wegmarken* (Frankfurt: Klostermann, 1978), 311.

13. Plato, *Republic*, trans. Paul Shorey in *The Collected Dialogues of Plato*, eds. Edith Hamilton and Huntington Cairns (Princeton, N. J.: Princeton University Press, 1961), 607a.

14. Heraclitus frags. B 42 and A 23 Diels-Kranz.

15. A complete discussion of the grounds of this exclusion would have to acknowledge the way in which these metaphysical and ethical grounds are distinct.

16. Gadamer, "Plato und die Dichter," 205.

17. The differences between books 3 and 10 are decisive in this overturning. The place of the "myth of Er" and the possibility that Plato is making a claim to be the new poet of the *polis* hinge on these differences.

18. A detailed treatment of this question of power would need to draw in the question of a possible philosophic narrative and the way in which that question is linked to the centralization of power and the division of labor.

19. Martin Heidegger, *Was heisst Denken?* (Tübingen: Niemeyer, 1954), 20. On Heidegger's account of the importance of the relation between writing and speech in the effective-history of Greek thought, see *Einführung in die Metaphysik* (Tübingen: Niemeyer, 1953), 49.

20. Aristotle, *De Poetica*, trans. Ingram Bywater, in *The Basic Works of Aristotle*, ed. Richard McKeon (New York: Random House, 1941), 1541b. For a fuller discussion of Aristotle's contributions on this point, see Robert Bernasconi, "The Fate of the Distinction between *Praxis* and *Poiesis*," in *Heidegger Studies* 2 (1987): 111-39. Bernasconi is especially helpful in uncovering the difficulties of speaking of *praxis* not as a production of the will, but as intelligible only retrospectively in the construction of a story about it, that is, "only by submitting it to the manner of revealing characteristic of *poiesis*" (117).

21. F. W. J. Schelling is particularly interesting in this regard, and much closer to Heidegger than to Hegel on this point. See, for instance, his discussions of poetry and nature in the introduction to his *System des transzendentalen Idealismus*: "The ideal world of art and the real

world of objects are therefore products of one and the same activity
. . . ." (Darmstadt: Wissenschaftliche Buchgesellschaft, 1975), 349.
For a discussion of this point, raised with reference to Hegel by
Heidegger in the afterward to "The Origin of the Work of Art," see
Jacques Taminiaux, "Attitude ésthetique et mort de l'art," in
Recoupements (Brussels: Editions Ousia, 1982), 142–74.

22. Martin Heidegger, *Hölderlins Hymnen "Germanien" und "Der
Rhein,"* vol. 39 of the *Gesamtausgabe* (Frankfurt: Klostermann,
1980), 20.

23. G. W. F. Hegel, *Grundlinien der Philosophie des Rechts* (Frankfurt:
Suhrkamp, 1970), 28.

24. G. W. F. Hegel, *Philosophie der Geschichte* (Frankfurt: Suhrkamp,
1970), 12.

25. However this instability of the "ideas" is itself called into question in
later dialogues such as the *Sophist* where the ideas are brought most
closely into contact with language.

26. Friedrich Nietzsche, *The Birth of Tragedy*, trans. Walter Kaufmann
(New York: Vintage, 1967), 140.

27. Friedrich Nietzsche, *The Will to Power*, trans. Walter Kaufmann and
R. J. Hollingdale (New York: Vintage, 1968), 435.

28. However, in *Thus Spoke Zarathustra* Nietzsche problematizes this
privilege as well. See especially the section "On Poets" in which
Zarathustra turns this privilege against himself.

29. Nietzsche, *The Will to Power*, 428.

30. Nietzsche, *The Will to Power*, 427–28.

31. Friedrich Nietzsche, *Also sprach Zarathustra* (Munich: Hanser, 1969),
322.

32. Of course the question of the subject and politics in Nietzsche is more
complex than I have presented it here. My purpose is merely to indicate briefly the political legacy of Nietzsche's thought in Heidegger's
own work. This becomes especially clear in a text that Otto Pöggeler
curiously, and I believe wrongly, has called Heidegger's masterpiece,
namely *Beiträge zur Philosophie*.

33. Friedrich Hölderlin, *Sämtliche Werke*, vol. 5 (Munich, Leipzig:
Muller, 1913), 266. For a discussion of the political significance of

Hölderlin for Heidegger between 1933 and 1944, see Fred Dallmayr, "Heidegger, Hölderlin, and Politics," in *Heidegger Studies* 2 (1987): 81–95. See also Philippe Lacoue-Labarthe, "Poétique et politique," in *Imitation des modernes* (Paris: Editions Galilée, 1986), 175–200.

34. Foucault, *The Thought from the Outside*, 56.

35. Heidegger, *Unterwegs zur Sprache*, 215.

36. This is also the question that runs through the most Platonic of Heidegger's own texts, namely, the 1933 address *Die Selbstbehauptung der deutschen Universität* (Frankfurt: Klostermann, 1983) where the question of the relation of the university to the scientization of knowledge is introduced with a quotation from Aeschylus's *Prometheus Bound*: "Knowing, however, is far weaker than necessity" (11). This line and text is translated by Karsten Harries; see "The Self-Assertion of the German University," *The Review of Metaphysics* 38 (March 1985): 472.

37. Theodor Adorno, *Aesthetische Theorie* (Frankfurt: Suhrkamp, 1970), 81.

38. Adorno, *Aesthetische Theorie*, 17.

39. Heidegger, *Hölderlins Hymnen*, 95.

40. Friedrich Hölderlin, "On the Operations of the Poetic Spirit," in *Friedrich Hölderlin: Essays and Letters on Theory*, trans. Thomas Pfau (Albany: SUNY Press, 1988), 81. My epigraph is taken from the same text (65).

41. Heidegger, *Hölderlins Hymnen*, 87.

42. Hans-Georg Gadamer, *Lob der Theorie* (Frankfurt: Suhrkamp, 1983), 45.

43. Gadamer, "Plato und die Dichter," 202.

10

Literature and Philosophy
at the Crossroads

Kathleen Wright

L *iterature as Philosophy. Philosophy as Literature*, the
title of a recently published volume, suggests by way of chias-
mus that literature and philosophy, having travelled separate and
distinct roads in the past, now for the first time cross one another's
path.[1] At the crossroads, the future course for both literature and
philosophy is unclear. Either literature and philosophy will cross
through one another to emerge on the other side of the crossroads as
once again separate and distinct. Or literature and philosophy will
not—leading to "literature as philosophy" and "philosophy as
literature," In the first case, four roads meet at the crossroads; in the
second, three.

Two concepts are crucial: text and interpretation. Nowhere was
this more striking than in the 1981 Paris colloquium, which brought
together Hans-Georg Gadamer and Jacques Derrida. Each was to
speak about text and interpretation, Gadamer on behalf of
hermeneutics and Derrida on behalf of deconstruction. Gadamer
and Derrida, however, spoke at cross purposes. They arrived and
left the colloquium, each with different concepts of text and interpretation. Left open also was the future course of literature and
philosophy at the crossroads. Would there, following Gadamer, be
continuity so that literature and philosophy would continue on their
own separate roads? Or would there, following Derrida, be *discon-
tinuity* so that literature and philosophy would merge on the third
road of "literature as philosophy" and "philosophy as literature"?

Many literary critics and philosophers have expressed an apprehension about the third road opened by Derrida's deconstruction
so deep as to call to mind that ancient encounter at that other

crossroads "where three roads meet." For them, the deconstruction of philosophy and of literature leads to disaster, to parricide, to incest, and finally, to self-mutilation. This apprehension is warranted, however, if we assume, first, that philosophy and literature have travelled separate and distinct paths until their encounter with Derrida's deconstruction, and, second, that they will with Derrida's deconstruction follow one and the same path in the future. In the following, I renew the conversation between deconstruction and hermeneutics on text and interpretation in order to question both assumptions. I will show, first, how the challenge to philosophy by deconstruction continues to maintain the very distinction between philosophy and literature which it claims to question, and second, how Gadamer's philosophical hermeneutics merges philosophy and literature in its concepts of text and interpetation.

1. Deconstruction and the Distinction between Philosophy and Literature

In response to Gadamer's 1981 talk, "Text and Interpretation," Derrida comments without explanation that there is a quite different way of thinking about texts than that of the "hermeneutical tradition [that extends] from Schleiermacher to Gadamer."[2] Let us turn first to an early work by Derrida, and then to a recent study of Derrida in order to explain this comment.

In his 1971 essay, "Qual Quelle: Valéry's Sources," Derrida writes that the poet, Paul Valéry, "reminds the philosopher that philosophy is written. And that the philosopher is a philosopher to the extent that he forgets this."[3] The philosopher Valéry has in mind is Descartes, whose method is opposed by Gadamer in *Truth and Method*. Derrida's 1981 remarks to Gadamer make clear, however, that he thinks Gadamer fits Valéry's description of a philosopher who is necessarily forgetful of the text that is philosophy. For Gadamer's concluding statement in "Text and Interpretation" — that when the text speaks, the reader or interpreter disappears — is equivalent to forgetting that philosophy, including Gadamer's own philosophical hermeneutics, takes place in and as texts.[4] Furthermore, Gadamer's characterization of "the work of hermeneutics" as a *"conversation* with the text" in *Truth and Method* is, for Derrida, forgetful of the role of writing and of the text of philosophy rather than, as Gadamer maintains, "a memory of what originally was the case."[5]

This early essay shows that Derrida understands the *text* of philosophy to be the "unthought" of philosophy, at least in that metaphysical tradition of philosophy drawn on by Gadamer that extends from Plato through to Hegel. Derrida's task and the task of deconstruction is, therefore, "to study the philosophical text . . . ." Based on Derrida's 1971 essay on Valéry, we can conclude that Derrida understands his own way of thinking about texts to differ from that of Gadamer insofar as it is the unthought text of philosophy that directs his and deconstructive thinking about text in general.

This essay also suggests how Derrida understands *interpretation* differently from Gadamer who, as we have just seen, thinks of it in terms of a conversation. Because the text of philosophy has been the unthought of philosophy, Derrida does not look to philosophy, or to Gadamer's philosophical hermeneutics, for a concept of interpretation appropriate to the text of philosophy. Let us look at what Derrida says the deconstructive interpretation of the philosophical text involves:

> A task is . . . prescribed: to study the philosophical text in its formal structure, in its rhetorical organization, in the specificity and diversity of its textual types, in its models of exposition and production — beyond what previously were called genres — and also in the space of its mises en scènes, in a syntax which would be not only the articulation of its signifieds, its references to Being or to truth, but also the handling of its proceedings, and of everything invested in them. In a word, the task is to consider philosophy also as a 'particular literary genre,' drawing upon the reserves of a language, cultivating, forcing, or making deviate a set of tropic resources . . . older than philosophy itself.[6]

This description suggests that Derrida understands deconstructive interpretation to be a form of literary criticism. However if this is the case, then Derrida continues to maintain a distinction between philosophy and literature insofar as his concept of text is drawn from philosophy while his concept of interpretation is drawn from literature.

But does Derrida claim that interpreting a philosophical text is the same as literary criticism applied to the text of philosophy? Let us look again at the last line of Derrida's statement. It says precisely that, "in a word, the task is to consider philosophy also as a quote particular literary genre unquote." The interpreter/reader of Derrida's written text remarks the presence of what is absent for the interpreter/listener of the spoken text, namely, the quotation marks around the words "particular literary genre." Derrida uses these marks to re-mark the boundary between philosophy and literature and to call the interpreter/reader's attention to the fact that when philosophical texts are interpreted as a particular literary genre, then not only are philosopical texts understood differently but so too is the genre of texts called literature. And if the genre of texts called literature is to be understood differently, then a literary criticism which still assumes the integrity of literature cannot be used to interpet philosophical texts.

This kind of technical, some have said pyrotechnical, move is typical of Derrida's writing. Derrida does not make such moves in order to privilege literary criticism, as is often thought, not even a new kind of deconstructive literary criticism that can be used to interpret both literary and philosophical texts. Instead Derrida makes such moves that play the written against the spoken in order to affect a return to the written and to the fact of the written text — as the unthought of philosophy and of interpretation understood, as in the case of Gadamer, on the model of conversation. If deconstructive interpretation is not a form of literary criticism, then we cannot yet conclude that Derrida's deconstruction continues to maintain a distinction between philosophy and literature.

Rodolphe Gasché argues, in his study of Derrida in *The Tain of the Mirror*, against the view that Derrida's deconstruction is a new kind of *literary criticism*. His claim is that Derrida's project is, instead *philosophical*, and is related to the philosophy of reflection, in other words, transcendental philosophy.[7] Gadamer, we find in *Truth and Method*, employs the concept of reflection to characterize the language of interpretation and of text. Let us turn, therefore, to Gasché's study to see how it can explain Derrida's comment that there is a quite different way to think of text than that of the "hermeneutical tradition [that extends] from Schleiermacher to

Gadamer." Based on this explanation, we shall then return to the question of whether Derrida's deconstruction continues to maintain a distinction between philosophy and literature.

Gasché understands Derrida to be concerned with the aporias that emerge when the philosophy of reflection attempts to ground itself in itself. Briefly, the philosophy of reflection rejects Descartes's grounding of discursive knowledge in the subject's intellectual intuition of itself, and attempts to recover an absolute foundation for discursive knowledge instead by means of transcendental reflection. Gasché's title, *The Tain of the Mirror*, refers to the tinfoil or plate that backs a mirror. Although it is itself a dull and unreflected surface, the tain makes reflection in and by the mirror possible. Gasché connects the idea of the tain of the mirror with Derrida's philosophical project in the following way: "Derrida's philosophy, rather than being a philosophy of reflection, is engaged in the systematic exploration of that dull surface without which no reflection and no specular and speculating activity would be possible, but which at the same time has no place and no part in reflection's scintillating play."[8] In other words, according to Gasché, Derrida's philosophical project studies the "tain" of philosophical reflection.

According to this reading of Derrida, the "tain" of philosophical reflection is "a naivety unthought by philosophy in general . . . which is a function of the logical consistency (dialectical or not) sought and achieved by philosophical discourse . . . . This naivety is that of the philosophical *discourse* . . . ."[9] According to Derrida, Gasché argues, philosophical discourse is "naive" because its discourse is in texts which neither do nor can thematize writing's role in making philosophical discourse and its logical consistency possible. Derrida's task — to study the "tain" of the texts of philosophy of reflection — is, accordingly, to thematize the role of writing by bringing out the irreducible differences, the discrepancies and the inconsistencies, "behind," in Gasché's words, "the formal, organizational, and textual production of noncontradiction in the philosophical discourse . . . ."[10] Let us look more closely at Gasché's account of Derrida's concepts of text and interpretation.

There are, Gasché claims, three concepts of *text* that Derrida works with in his interpretations of philosophical texts. *First*, a text can be thought of as "the sensibly palpable, empirically encounterable transcription of an oral discourse, as a material opacity that must efface itself before its oral reactivation and the meaning it represents." Here the text is understood "empirically" and its unity is "the unity of a corpus." *Second*, a text can be taken as "an intelligible object . . . [that] is thought to correspond to the signifying organization of diacritically or differentially determined signifiers and signifieds." In this case, a text is taken "idealistically" and its unity is the "intelligible unity of a work." *Finally*, a text can be considered to be "the dialectical sublation, either as 'form' or 'content,' of both its sensible and ideal determinations." When a text is considered "dialectically," its unity is "the dialectical totality of its formal or thematic meanings."[11] Derrida, Gasché argues, works with and against these three concepts of text by showing in each case how the unity of a text is both possible and impossible.

The first step of deconstructive *interpretation* is, for Derrida, "hermeneutical,"[12] that is, the philosophical text is interpreted as a unity; a closed totality is constructed "with a clear inside and outside . . . ." The second step of interpretation is "deconstructive" because it goes beyond this hermeneutical first step by calling the unity of the philosophical text into question. The second step explores, in Gasché's words, "the border itself, from which the assignment of insides and outsides take place, as well as where this distinction ultimately collapses."[13] The border, or "tain," consists of those inconsistencies that make the unity of the philosophical text possible and at the same time impossible. Together the two steps of deconstructive interpretation show by means of these *inconsistencies* that the philosophical text *is* and *is not* because it is and is not a *unity*. Let us look at three such inconsistencies discussed by Gasché.

The *first* inconsistency has to do with the formation of philosophical concepts. Derrida, Gasché argues, holds that since Plato all major philosophical concepts, for example, the concepts of unity, of totality, of identity, and of coherence, are "*dreams* of plenitude." They are concepts of *plenitude*, of "states of noncontradiction, in which the negative has been absorbed by the positive, states that lack, and by all rights precede, all dissension, difference, and separation, states of peace and reconciliation." They are *dreams* insofar as they represent what ought to be as opposed to what is.[14] Gasché supplies several arguments used by Derrida to

234

show how concepts characterized by plenitude are inconsistent with the way these concepts are formed so that such philosophical concepts are "in a sense paradoxical."[15] For example, in his essay "Structure, Sign and Play," Derrida argues à propos the concept of a centered structure that "The center is at the center of the totality, and yet, since the center does not belong to the totality (is not part of the totality), the totality *has its center elsewhere.* The center is not the center. The concept of a centered structure—although it represents coherence itself . . .—is contradictorily coherent."[16] This deconstructive interpretation shows that the philosophical concept of coherence is paradoxical; it is both coherent and incoherent.

A *second* inconsistency has to do with the paradox of a philosophical text that argues for the priority of speaking over writing, for example, Saussure's *Course in General Linguistics* and Rousseau's *On the Origin of Languages*, which Derrida discusses in *Of Grammatology.* Each of these texts maintains that language is originally speech, and that writing is at best a supplement of speech. Deconstructive interpretation shows, in Gasché's words, the following inconsistencies in both of these texts:

> The various arguments concerning the origin and the supplement, speech and writing, are organized by Saussure and Rousseau in a similar manner: (1) The supplement and writing are totally exterior and inferior to the origin and to speech, which are thus not affected by them and remain intact; (2) they are harmful because they are separate from the origin and thereby corrupt living speech, which otherwise would be intact; and (3) if one needs to fall back on the supplement or on writing, it is not because of their intrinsic value but because the origin was already deficient, and because living speech was already finite before it became supplemented by writing. Hence supplement and writing do not harm origin or speech at all. On the contrary, they mend the deficiencies of origin and speech.[17]

Derrida's deconstructive interpretation shows these two philosophical texts to be inconsistently consistent when they argue by writing against and for writing.

The *third* inconsistency pertains to the identity of philosophical texts as a genre of writing different from literature. Philosophy, again according to Gasché's account of Derrida, understands its concepts and its arguments to be *pure*, that is, free from any contamination by metaphor or myth. Derrida's deconstructive interpretation of philosophical texts shows, however, that philosophy "as philosophy" erases or crosses out the combination or crossing of philosophy and literature within a successful philosophical text. For example, Derrida's deconstructive interpretation of Plato's *Phaedrus* in "Plato's Pharmacy" shows not just that philosophy *fails* to "master its relation to myth or to figures . . . ,"[18] but even more importantly that the *success* of this philosophical text depends on its sustaining a relation to myth and to metaphor. In other words, the identity of philosophy "as philosophy" depends *consistently* on the difference between philosophy and literature and *inconsistently* on the combination of philosophy and literature.

These three kinds of inconsistencies are, according to Gasché, similar to the tain of a mirror. Built into "the process of philosophical conceptualization, as well as into the practice of discursive exposition and the structures of philosophical argumentation . . . ," these inconsistencies are and must remain unreflected.[19] They are the unthought because unthinkable differences "behind" the unity and totality of the text of the philosophy of reflection. They make the unity of the text of philosophy as well as the identity of philosophy "as philosophy" possible and at the same time impossible. Thus, according to this account of Derrida's concepts of interpretation and of text, deconstructive *interpretation* plays out those inconsistencies that at once construct and deconstruct the unity of a philosophical text. Accordingly, *text* is and is not a (unified) text.

Let us look at Gasché's claim that, "the combination of opposite genres [the genre of writing called *philosophy* and the genre of writing called *literature*] in the philosophical discourse" is "irreducible" and "inevitable," and that deconstructive interpretation brings out what philosophy as philosophy crosses out.[20] Does this mean that literature and philosophy merge into that third road—literature as philosophy and philosophy as literature—that is the cause of such deep apprehension? Or does this mean instead that "philosophy as philosophy" must continually cross through "literature as literature" in order for a philosophical text to emerge successfully "as philosophy" (and vice versa)? Deconstructive interpretation, we find, continually *re-marks* the distinction between philosophy and literature in order for there to be the text of "philosophy as philosophy" to construct and to deconstruct. Deconstruction leads, therefore, not to the erasing or the *crossing out* of the distinction between philosophy and literature; instead it boldly *underlines* it.

2. Hermeneutics and the Relation between Philosophy and Literature

We have said that Derrida considers Gadamer to fit Valéry's description of a philosopher who is necessarily forgetful of the text that is philosophy. Let us turn to Gadamer's two claims, that interpretation is to be thought of as a conversation, and that when the text speaks the interpretation disappears. Does Gadamer (and philosophical hermeneutics) *forget* the text of interpretation (the text of philosophy) in proposing that interpretation is a conversation with a text (the text to be interpreted)? Or does Gadamer recollect the text of philosophy and together with it the text of literature as interpretation and text merge in what Gadamer calls the "fusion of horizons"?

Let us look first at Gadamer's claim in *Truth and Method* that "it is more than a metaphor, it is a memory of what originally was the case, to describe the work of hermeneutics as a conversation with the text."[21] Gadamer's use of the term *conversation* alerts us to the fact that the relation between interpreter and text is an I-other relation, where the *I* stands for the interpreter and the *other* for the text. By "other," Gadamer does not mean the author of the text, but the text itself as the other. The text is, accordingly, more than just the *subject matter* of the interpretive conversation; it is a *subject* within the interpretive conversation. For this reason, Gadamer claims that the text "expresses itself like a 'Thou'."

Gadamer distinguishes interpretation thought of as a conversation *with* a text from two other ways to think of interpretation: (1) interpretation is speaking *about* a text; and (2) interpretation is speaking *for* a text. To clarify the distinction he is making here, it is helpful to relate these to the three concepts of text employed by Derrida in the first and hermeneutical step in deconstructive interpretation. For each of these three ways to construct the unity of text "with a clear inside and outside" *fails* to capture Gadamer's understanding of text or of interpretation as a conversation with the text.

If interpretation is speaking *about* a text, then the text is understood "empirically." The interpreter *objectifies* the text to be interpreted, and the text is treated, like the object of a science, as something that conforms to rules or to what generally is the case. The interpreter who constructs the unity of the text empirically speaks *about* the text by making general truth-claims, which can be verified by their adequacy to the text. However, the interpreter by speaking about a text fails to let the text speak for itself. In this case, interpetation is a *monologue* and not a conversation with the text.[23]

If interpretation is speaking *for* a text, then the text is understood "idealistically." The interpreter grants that the text is an other by allowing it to speak for itself and to assert its own claim to truth. At the same time, however, as the interpreter claims to understand "the other's [the text's] claim," he claims also "to understand the other better than the other understands himself."[24] The interpreter who constructs the unity of the text idealistically speaks *for* the text without allowing the text to speak *to* the interpreter. Interpretation in this case is more than a monologue. Yet it lacks reciprocity and is, accordingly, only a *one-sided conversation.* Interpretation that speaks for the text does not allow the *give-and-take* of a conversation.

In *Truth and Method*, Gadamer argues that when the interpreter relates to a text either as an *it* that is and remains objectified or as an *other* that makes a claim comprehended by the interpreter, authority ultimately resides in the interpreter. In either case, the text must answer to the questions of the interpreter, but the interpreter need not answer to the text. In the first case, the text as *subject matter* of the interpretation never becomes a *subject* within a conversation. In the second case, the text is a *subject* but one that is *mastered* by the interpreter.[25] In each of these two relations between interpreter and text, the autonomy of the interpeter is maintained at the cost of the autonomy of the text. Correspondingly, the text of interpretation, along with the interpreter, takes precedence over the text to be interpreted. Put in other terms, to think of the text to be interpreted either empirically or idealistically and to speak about or for it empowers the interpreter and his or her (text of) interpetation such that they cannot be called into question. Therefore, according to Gadamer, speaking about or for a text does not yet constitute interpretation because the moment of application in the event of understanding is in each case deferred. Because the truth claimed by the text has not yet called into question what the interpreter has previously judged (i.e., prejudged) to be true, the condition of reciprocity is not met.

The third and "dialectical" concept of text employed by Derrida is closer to, yet significantly different from, Gadamer's concept of text and of interpretation as a conversation with a text. What for Derrida distinguishes this from the other two concepts of text is that the construction of the unity of the text results in "the dialectical totality of its formal and thematic meanings," in other words, absolute closure. Gadamer requires of a text only an *anticipation of its completion*, not its closure.[26] We know that for Derrida, the closure of the text sets the stage for the second step of interpretation when the interpreter opens up the text by deconstructing it. For Gadamer, we find instead that the text must first be opened up in dialogue before there can be textual closure. A text is, therefore, not a dialectical but a "hermeneutical" concept.

What Gadamer has in mind here is that a text is neither a *pure given* and as such found nor *purely a construct* and in this sense made. It is, rather *in part* given and *in part* made. In "Text and Interpretation," Gadamer calls the text "a mere intermediate product [*Zwischenprodukt*], a phase in the event of understanding . . . ."[27] The text or, more specifically, the written language of the text, is in part given in that it is what the interpreter returns to when difficulties arise in one's anticipations of completion. The text is in part made in that the text "constitutes itself" as a text when it "resists" integration into an interpretation which is not "according to its [the text's] meaningful sense [*sinngëmass*]."[28] In "The Eminent Text and its Truth," he adds that the written text becomes in the *process* of interpretation "the authoritative datum to which all understanding and interpretation have to measure up. It is, as it were, the hermeneutic point of identity which limits all variables [i.e., possible interpretations]."[29] As a hermeneutical concept, the written text has its true being only within conversation.

In the kind of relation between an interpreter and a text that Gadamer calls a conversation, the text expresses itself as a *Thou* to the *I* of the interpreter who is a questioner open to questions. Here, the condition of reciprocity requires that the interpreter be open to the experience that his or her own original understanding of the matter of concern (*die Sache*) in the text is either false or incomplete. It requires, therefore, that the interpreter be open-minded, thus prepared to change his or her mind about what is at issue. As is the case for deconstructive interpretation, we find an opening up of inconsistencies and incoherencies that are unreflected and as such closed, but with this difference. For Gadamer or philosophical hermeneutics, it is the unity and totality, in other words, the coherency, of the interpreter's prejudgments and judgments that are opened up and questioned and not, as is the case for Derrida or deconstructive interpretation, the unity and totality, the coherency, of the text (of philosophy).

Gadamer points to the dialogues of Plato as the *model* for interpretation thought in terms of conversation.[30] By recalling these "texts of philosophy," he is proposing that in all interpretation of texts, be these philosophical, literary, judicial, sacred, or any other kind of text, the interpreter enters into a conversation with the text by assuming a role comparable to that of an interlocutor in a Platonic dialogue. By listening and responding, the interpreter as an interlocutor allows himself or herself to be cross-examined by the text. In the course of the give-and-take of a conversation with the text, the interpreter comes to understand *better* the truth claimed by the text about the matter at issue (*die Sache*). At the same time, and even more important, the interpreter comes to understand his or her own original truth-claims about the matter at issue *differently*. Gadamer calls this *event of understanding* the "fusion of horizons."[31]

Gadamer's claim that interpretation is a conversation does not forget the text of philosophy. Instead it recollects and recognizes that one kind of philosophical text, Plato's dialogues, fulfills what is meant by interpretation. Gadamer's description of the variations that the *I-other relation* can take in *Truth and Method* allows the I-Thou relation to emerge as the standard and limiting condition (*ein Grenzfall und ein Mass*) of interpretation thought in terms of conversation.[32] This description does not reduce interpretation empirically to something like our actual and oral conversations with one another. Instead it reduces interpretation *eidetically* to Plato's written dialogues.

By modelling *interpretation* on those *texts of philosophy* known as Plato's dialogues, Gadamer redirects philosophical reflection away from the philosophy of reflection's task of self-grounding. Reciprocity, according to Gadamer, leads to opening the horizons, the limits of the self, up to the other as opposed to leading the other back to its ground in the self. Furthermore, Gadamer's concept of *text* (the text to be interpreted) anticipates but does not require the "dialectical" concepts of unity, totality, and coherence, in short, closure such as is claimed for the texts of philosophy of reflection. Instead he thinks of text hermeneutically as what produces the event of understanding by disrupting and challenging the apparent coherence of the interpreter's prejudices and judgments, in other words, the interpreter's "dreams of plenitude." I would like now to focus on this hermeneutical concept of text as *productive* in order to show the way Gadamer merges the text of philosophy and the text of literature in the fusion of horizons that marks the event of understanding.

Gadamer claims that the fusion of horizons is the moment when the text speaks and the interpretation disappears. The "last word," therefore, is the word spoken by the text itself insofar as it lives on and continues to mean more than either the author or past and present readers comprehend. This claim appears to suggest that the text of interpretation modelled on Plato's texts does not remain written and that only the text that has been interpreted does. It would seem, therefore, to support once again Derrida's claim that a philosopher, in this case Gadamer, is one who necessarily forgets the text of philosophy. Against this claim, Gadamer's description of various kinds of texts in a series of recent essays leads to another conclusion, one that links the Platonic text of philosophy with the text that remains written. In these recent essays, Gadamer performs the same kind of imaginative variation leading to eidetic reduction as we have found in the case of the I-other relation. In the previous case of eidetic reduction, we found that the *eidos* or model for interpretation turned out to be the Platonic text of philosophy. We find now that the *eidos* or model for text, for both what is productive of the event of understanding and what remains written for reading even after this event, is the lyric text of poetry. Let us turn first to this description and then to the merging of the text of philosophy and the text of literature in the event of understanding.

241

Gadamer's description of various kinds of text is to be found in five essays written between 1971 and 1982.[33] In the earliest of these, "On the contribution of poetry to the search for truth," we find Gadamer concerned with the fact that some texts are *eminent*, that is, they stand out so as to be perceived to be written. Other texts, for example, the lecture notes one uses while lecturing, do not stand out in this way. Such notes lack autonomy and serve only to remind a lecturer of what is to be said. At the end of the lecture, the lecture notes do not "stand written," that is, written for reading again. Gadamer makes use of the Lutheran expression, "stands written," in order to capture what is common to all texts that are eminent because they stand out as written.[34]

Gadamer distinguishes three kinds of texts within the domain of what is eminently text: the religious, the legal, and the poetic text. To bring out what it means to say of a text that it stands written, Gadamer looks at how the religious and the legal texts vary from the poetic text in that they require another form of saying (*Sage*) beyond standing written. The religious text, for example, requires in addition to being written a pledge (*Zusage*). "[T]he texts of revealed religion," Gadamer observes, "are a form of pledge (*Zusage*) since they only acquire the character of an address (*Sagecharacter*) insofar as they are acknowledged on the part of the believer."[35] The legal text beyond being written requires also a proclamation (*Ansage*). In Gadamer's words, "[T]he legal text only becomes valid by means of declaration, and the law must be promulgated. It is the nature of this proclamation (*Ansage*), in which the word only acquires its legal existence through being stated and without which it cannot acquire it, that first constitutes its legal validity."[36] Only the poetic text is "a saying (*Sage*) that says (*aussagt*) so completely what it is that we do not need to add anything beyond what is said [that is, beyond what stands written] in order to accept it in its reality as language."[37] The poetic text is a statement (*Aussage*), he adds, that stands written "in that it bears witness to itself and does not admit anything [such as a pledge or a proclamation] that might verify it."[38] Of those kinds of texts that are *eminent* because they stand out as written, the poetic text is *above all eminent*, Gadamer concludes, because it requires nothing beyond itself in order to stand written.

In this imaginative variation and eidetic reduction of what is eminently text, it is the poetic text which turns out to be the limiting case and standard (*ein Grenzfall und ein Mass*) for it fulfills alone what is meant by a text that stands written.[39] Here, as Gadamer's example from Dostoyevski's *The Brothers Karamazov* indicates, the term *poetic* applies to all texts of literature regardless of their genre. Yet even so we find in this essay as well as in the other essays where Gadamer performs this same eidetic reduction that the text of lyric poetry enjoys a special privilege. Let us look at why Gadamer privileges the text of lyric poetry.

In "The Eminent Text and its Truth," Gadamer remarks that it is the *untranslatability* of the text of lyric poetry that makes it most "poetic": "The full equivalency of sense and sound, which turns the text into an eminent text, finds very different kinds of fulfillment in different literary genres. This is reflected in a sliding scale of translatability of poetic texts into other languages. On this scale, the lyric poem (and within this genre the lyric of symbolism and its ideal of a *poésie pure*) stands at the top."[40] What Gadamer has in mind is that although the "full equivalency of sense and sound" as well as the "constantly shifting balance of sound and sense"[41] in the lyric poem *defy* translation, they also *endlessly* produce more translations. So too even as the "syntactic indeterminancy" and the "consequent ambiguity and obscurity" of the lyric text *resist*, in the case of Mallarmé's "pure poetry," and even *refuse*, in the case of Celan's hermetic poetry, interpretation, they *inexhaustibly* produce further interpretations.[42] For Gadamer, therefore, the text of lyric poetry enjoys a special privilege because it spontaneously fulfills the *productiveness* that makes a text "poetic." As such, it captures in the extreme the productiveness that holds true for all texts that are to be interpreted.

The text of lyric poetry is, empirically, only one kind of eminent text and distinct from other genres of literature as well as from religious and legal texts. Nonetheless as the *eidos* or model for the text to be interpreted in an interpretation, the text of lyric poetry informs these other kinds of texts both as what is productive within them of the event of understanding and as what stands written for rereading in them even after they are understood. This insight into the eidetic status and function of the text of lyric poetry together with our earlier insight into the eidetic status and function of the texts of Plato's philosophy allow us now to clarify the relation between philosophy and literature in Gadamer's philosophical hermeneutics.

In "Philosophie und Literatur," Gadamer suggests that "Perhaps the intrinsic proximity (*die innere Nachbarschaft*) of philosophy and poetry consists precisely in this: that they encounter one another in the most extreme countermovement: the language of philosophy constantly surpasses itself — the language of poetry . . . is unsurpassable and unique."[43] In this essay, as before in *Truth and Method*, Gadamer explores this "extreme countermovement" in terms of what he calls in general the *speculative structure* of language.[44] Briefly, this means that the language of philosophy and the language of poetry belong together as the ends, as it were, of the medium (*Mitte*) or continuum of language. In the case of philosophy, language is surpassed in the form of speculative propositions that "mirror the *Aufhebung* or sublation of their own immanent positings."[45] In the case of poetry, language is concentrated in the form of poetic statements (*Aussage*) that "gain in presence and illuminating power."[46] At these two extremes of the continuum of language, however, language never comes to an end. For according to Gadamer, the speculative proposition turns evermore toward the "totality of thought [that] remains a task that can never be completed"[47] and the poetic statement continues to "renew" itself because the "idea of 'pure poetry' itself remains a never-to-be completed task for poetic composition."[48] The language of philosophy and the language of poetry *belong together* even as they *diverge* from one another because of this *emergence* of language at the extremes of the medium (*Mitte*) or continuum of language.

Gadamer argues in *Truth and Method* that the speculative structure of language emerges *in a concentrated way* in the interpetation of a text. The language of philosophy and the language of poetry, these extremes of language, converge, or rather merge, in the center (*Mitte*) of language that binds together the *I* of the interpreter and the *Thou* of the text to be interpreted. This claim that philosophy and poetry encounter each other in their "intrinsic proximity" in the process of interpretation and the event of understanding the interpreted text does not mean that interpretation can only be philosophical and the text to be interpreted can only be poetic. It means, instead, that in the interpretation of the text the language of the Platonic text and the language of the lyric text merge in an extraordinary way because of their eidetic status and function.

The fusion of horizons, the event that transforms the interpreter's understanding of the matter at issue in the interpreted text, depends on the merging of the interpretation and the text. From the perspective of Derrida and deconstruction, it seems that the text of interpretation disappears and only the interpreted text remains. We have found, however, that there is another way to look at the fusion of horizons. In the event of understanding, the text of the interpretation most closely realizes its Platonic model by "sublating" its "own immanent positings" and the interpreted text most closely realizes its lyric model by gaining in "presence and illuminating power."

Gadamer's philosophical hermeneutics, we have found, does not insist on the difference between philosophy and literature while at the same time inconsistently combining philosophy and literature in the texts of philosophy as Derrida and deconstruction claim. Instead, Gadamer *insists* on the merging of philosophy and literature by modelling interpretation on Plato's dialogues and text on the lyric poem. For Gadamer, we can conclude, literature and philosophy do not meet now for the first time "at the crossroads," but instead *cross* each other constantly—for he knows that, ever since Plato, theirs is a "lovers' quarrel."

Notes

1. Donald G. Marshall (ed.), *Literature as Philosophy. Philosophy as Literature.* (Iowa City, Iowa: University of Iowa Press, 1987). I would like to thank Helge Høibraaten and Tore Lindholm for the opportunity to present an earlier draft of this essay at the Universities of Trondheim and Oslo in 1987. I would like also to thank Haverford College for enabling me to present these ideas at a symposium on Gadamer's *Truth and Method* held in Heidelberg, West Germany in 1989. Research for this essay was made possible by a National Endowment for the Humanities College Teacher Fellowship for which I am especially grateful.

2. Philippe Forget (ed.), *Text und Interpretation* (Munich: Fink, 1984), 57–58; my translation. In English, in *The Gadamer-Derrida Encounter*, eds. Diane Michelfelder and Richard Palmer (Albany: SUNY Press, 1989).

3. Jacques Derrida, "Qual Quelle: Valéry's Sources," in *Margins of Philosophy*, trans. Alan Bass (Chicago: University of Chicago Press 1982), 291.

4. Hans-Georg Gadamer, "Text und Interpretation," in *Text und Interpretation*, 55; in English, "Text and Interpretation," trans. Dennis J. Schmidt, in *Hermeneutics and Modern Philosophy*, ed. Brice R. Wachterhauser (Albany: SUNY Press, 1986), 396. All further references to Gadamer's talk refer to this (abbreviated) English text.

5. Hans-Georg Gadamer, *Wahrheit und Methode* (Tübingen: J. C. B. Mohr, 1965), 350; in English, *Truth and Method*, trans. Sheed and Ward Ltd. (New York: Seabury Press, 1975), 331; emphasis added. *Wahrheit und Methode* and *Truth and Method* will be abbreviated hereafter as *WM* and *TM* respectively.

6. Derrida, "Qual Quelle," 293.

7. Rodolphe Gasché, *The Tain of the Mirror* (Cambridge, Mass.: Harvard University Press, 1989).

8. Gasché, *Tain of the Mirror*, 6.

9. Gasché, *Tain of the Mirror*, 125.

10. Gasché, *Tain of the Mirror*, 127.

11. Gasché, *Tain of the Mirror*, 278–80.

12. Jacques Derrida, "Cogito and the History of Madness," in *Writing and Difference*, trans. Alan Bass (Chicago: University of Chicago Press, 1978), 32: "This comprehension of the sign in and of itself, in its immediate materiality as a sign, if I may so call it, is *only the first moment but also the indispensable condition of all hermeneutics* and of any claim to transition from the sign to signified"; emphasis added.

13. Gasché, *Tain of the Mirror*, 280. See Jacques Derrida, "The Double Session," in *Dissemination*, trans. Barbara Johnson (Chicago: University of Chicago Press, 1981), 270; "If the text does not, to the letter, exist, *there is* [*il y a*] perhaps a text"; cited in Gasché, *Tain of the Mirror*, 284.

14. Gasché, *Tain of the Mirror*, 127.

15. Gasché, *Tain of the Mirror*, 129.

16. Jacques Derrida, "Structure, Sign and Play in the Discourse of the Human Sciences," in *Writing and Difference*, 279; cited in Gasché, *Tain of the Mirror*, 129.

17. Gasché, *Tain of the Mirror*, 132; see Derrida, "Double Session," 111.

18. Gasché, *Tain of the Mirror*, 134.

19. Gasché, *Tain of the Mirror*, 127.

20. Gasché, *Tain of the Mirror*, 134.

21. Gadamer, *WM*, 350; *TM*, 331.

22. Gadamer, *WM*, 340; *TM*, 321.

23. Gadamer, *WM*, 340-60; *TM*, 322-41. For a more detailed discussion of the I-Thou relation, see my "Gadamer: The Speculative Structure of Language," in *Hermeneutics and Modern Philosophy*, 195-204.

24. Gadamer, *WM*, 341; *TM*, 322.

25. Gadamer, *WM*, 342; *TM*, 323. Here Gadamer draws a parallel between this mastery and Hegel's discussion of lordship and bondage.

26. Gadamer, *WM*, 278; *TM*, 261.

27. Gadamer, "Text and Interpretation," 389.

28. Gadamer, "Text and Interpretation," 389.

29. Hans-Georg Gadamer, "The Eminent Text and its Truth," in *The Bulletin of the Midwestern Modern Language Association* 13 (Spring 1980): 6.

30. Gadamer, *WM*, 344-51; *TM*, 325-33.

31. Gadamer, *WM*, 289-90, 356-60; *TM*, 273-74, 337-41.

32. Hans-Georg Gadamer, "Philosophie und Poesie," in vol. 4 of his *Kleine Schriften* (Tübingen: J. C. B. Mohr, 1977), 247; in English, "Philosophy and poetry," in *The Relevance of the Beautiful and Other Essays*, trans. Nicholas Walker, ed. Robert Bernasconi (Cambridge: Cambridge University Press, 1986), 138. All further references to this text will be to the English text.

33. These are: "The Eminent Text and its Truth"; "Philosophy and poetry"; "Text and Interpretation"; "Philosophie und Literatur," in *Phänomenologische Forschung* 11 (1981); and "Über den Beitrag der Dichtkunst bei der Suche nach der Wahrheit," in vol. 4 of *Kleine Schriften* (in English, "On the contribution of poetry to the search for truth," in *Relevance of the Beautiful*). All further references to the last text will be to the English text.

34. Gadamer, "Contribution of poetry," 108.

35. Gadamer, "Contribution of poetry," 109.

36. Gadamer, "Contribution of poetry," 109-10.

37. Gadamer, "Contribution of poetry," 110.

38. Gadamer, "Contribution of poetry," 110.

39. Gadamer, "Philosophy and poetry," 138.

40. Gadamer, "Eminent Text," 8.

41. Gadamer, "Philosophy and poetry," 134.

42. Gadamer, "Philosophy and poetry," 135.

43. Gadamer, "Philosophie und Literatur," 43; my translation.

44. On the speculative structure of language and language as both medium and center (*Mitte*), see my "Gadamer: The Speculative Structure of Language," 204-14.

45. Gadamer, "Philosophy and poetry," 138.

46. Gadamer, "Philosophy and poetry," 135.

47. Gadamer, "Philosophy and poetry," 138.

48. Gadamer, "Philosophy and poetry," 138-39.

Index